ACTIVIST FAITH

Carol Ann Drogus   Hannah Stewart-Gambino

ACTIVIST FAI✝H

Grassroots Women
in Democratic Brazil and Chile

The Pennsylvania State University Press
University Park, Pennsylvania

Library of Congress Cataloging-in-Publication Data

Drogus, Carol Ann.
    Activist faith : grassroots women in democratic Brazil and
    Chile / Carol Ann Drogus, Hannah Stewart-Gambino.
        p.   cm.
Includes bibliographical references and index.
ISBN 0-271-02549-2 (alk. paper)
1. Catholic women—Brazil—Political activity—History—
    20th century.
2. Basic Christian communities—Political aspects—
    Brazil—History—20th century.
3. Christianity and politics—Brazil—History—20th century.
4. Catholic women—Chile—Political activity—History—
    20th century.
5. Basic Christian communities—Political aspects—Chile—
    History—20th century.
6. Christianity and politics—Chile—History—20th
    century.
I. Stewart-Gambino, Hannah W.
II. Title.

BX1466.3.D76 2005
261.8'082'0981—dc22
2004023769

First paperback printing, 2006

The Pennsylvania State University Press is a member of the
Association of American University Presses.

It is the policy of The Pennsylvania State University Press
to use acid-free paper. This book meets the minimum
requirements of American National Standard for Information
Sciences—Permanence of Paper for Printed Library Material,
ANSI Z39.48–1992.

CONTENTS

ACKNOWLEDGMENTS

This book grew out of a specific question: what happened to the generation of working-class women whose grassroots activism in Catholic base communities fired the Brazilian and Chilean pro-democracy movements? After the democratic transitions and the consequent shift in scholarly attention back to traditional political actors, these women disappeared from official view. One of our goals was certainly to reclaim their stories; our purpose, however, was not simply nostalgic. The conventional wisdom that this generation of women simply "went home" after the transitions did not ring true for either of us. We were also convinced that the new forms of grassroots organization forged in Catholic base communities did not simply vanish after the democratic transitions, leaving no discernible legacy in the women's lives or—more important for the future "deepening of democracy"—in the social and political fabric of popular neighborhoods. What kind of legacies did these women and their organizations leave? In order to explore the impact of the democratic transitions on grassroots organizations that grew up in and around base Christian communities during the dictatorships, we rely heavily on extensive interviews with women who were active in their base communities during the height of the Brazilian and Chilean social movements.

First and foremost, we are deeply grateful to the Brazilian and Chilean women who shared their stories with us for this book. Carol Drogus wishes to thank particularly the women in Brazil who participated in her earlier study in 1986 and who were willing to be reinterviewed and to share their experiences of the intervening years. The willingness of all the interviewees to patiently answer questions in a long and detailed survey, occasionally provoking painful (and sometimes joyful) memories, gives this book a richness and depth that simply could not have been possible without their generosity. We have tried to keep these women's voices in the forefront throughout this book, recognizing that their experiences, lived through extraordinary and difficult historical moments in their countries, form the core of our research question.

The research in Brazil would not have been possible were it not for the efforts of Cecilia Loreto Mariz and Maria das Dores Campos Machado. They helped to plan and translate the interview schedule, provided names of women activists in the Rio area, and organized and coordinated the team who carried out the interviews. That team consisted of two graduate students, Wania Amélia Belchior Mesquita and Sílvia Regina Alves Fernandes, who traveled to the interview sites in Rio and São Paulo and conducted the tape-recorded interviews. We thank them for their intrepid and careful interviewing.

Cecilia Loreto Mariz and Maria das Dores Campos Machado also played an important role in bringing key parts of the book to completion. In fact, their analysis of the Brazilian women's attitudes toward their Pentecostal neighbors forms the basis for Chapter 6, of which they were the primary authors of the Brazilian portions. Their analysis first took the form of a paper presented at the Latin American Studies Association meetings in 2000. In addition, they analyzed the women's attitudes toward charismatic Catholics. Originally, this analysis was intended for a separate chapter on intra-Catholic cooperation. That chapter never materialized, because there are no comparable Catholic groups in Chile. Their insightful analysis of attitudes toward Charismatics, however, enters into the analysis of women's reactions to changes in the church that is set out in Chapter 4. A more complete version of their analysis was published as "Progressistas e Catolicas Carismaticas: Uma Analise de Discurso de Mulheres de Comunidades de Base na Atualidade Brasileira," *Praia Vermelha* 2, no. 3 (2000): 8–29. Because of their crucial role in formulating the analysis of the women's attitudes toward competing religious groups, we wish to recognize them as full co-authors of these two chapters. We thank them for their participation in the preparation of these chapters and for their insights into Brazilian religious attitudes, as well as for their work in organizing the interviews themselves.

We thank Maxine Lowy for her exceptional energy, devotion, and professionalism in conducting the Chilean interviews. This project obviously became a labor of love for her, and the extraordinary quality of the interviews is a result of her skill and passion. We also thank her for her willingness to read and comment on various drafts throughout the process. Since the completion of the interviews for this book, Maxine Lowy continues to meet with a number of the women, with whom she is working on a popular history of women' activism in Santiago's *poblaciones*.

The Chilean interviews also could not have been conducted without supporting funding from the Martindale Center for the Study of Private Enterprise at Lehigh University, as well as from the Lehigh University Faculty

Development Fund. Previous interviews and background research was funded by the North-South Center at the University of Miami. In addition, the Levitt Center for Public Affairs at Hamilton College provided funds to enable us to hire the interviewers in Brazil. Hamilton College also provided field research funds for Carol Ann Drogus.

We also wish to thank Philip Williams and Daniel Levine for their helpful comments on the entire manuscript. We are grateful to have had such careful and conscientious readers.

Last, but not least, we wish to thank Dawn Woodward of Hamilton College for her very thorough and painstaking preparation of the manuscript. Dawn solved the many seemingly insoluble word processing problems that occur in manuscripts that have gone back and forth as attachments too many times. She paid close attention to every detail of the final preparation of the manuscript and bibliography. She also carefully checked and rechecked our bibliographic references for completeness. Moreover, she did all this in a cheerful and timely fashion. It is not mere rhetoric for us to say, "We couldn't have done it without her!"

Hannah Stewart-Gambino offers the stories in this book to her daughters, Elena and Madeline, in the hopes that they will always know that courageous women really do make a difference. And she thanks her husband, Giacomo Gambino, whose loving support took many forms—not the least of which was his willingness to relinquish what was supposed to be a joint home office and computer. Carol Ann Drogus thanks her husband, Steve Orvis, and sons, Nick and Will, for their support and patience and for their participation in a 1997 research trip to Brazil, where the basis for this book was laid. The Brazilian portions of this book are dedicated to them, in recognition of the way that families can inspire tenacious political activism and the possibility for a better future.

LIST OF ACRONYMS

ACH   Academy of Christian Humanism (Chile)
Academía de Humanismo Cristiano

AEVB   Brazilian Evangelical Alliance
Aliança Evangélica Brasíleira

AMZOL   Association of Women of the Zona Leste (Brazil)
Associaçâo de Mulheres da Zona Leste

CCP   popular Christian communities
Comunidades Cristianos Populares

CDD   Catholic Women for Free Choice (Brazil)
Católicas pelo Direito de Decidir

CEB   base ecclesial communities
Comunidades Eclesiales de Base

CEBI   Center for Biblical Studies (Brazil)
Centro de Estudos Bíblicos

CECH   Chilean Bishops' Conference
Conferencia Episcopal de Chile

CEDAC   Center for Community Action (Brazil)
Centro de Açâo Comunitária

CELAM   Latin American Episcopal Conference
Conferencia Episcopal Latinoamericana

CNBB   Brazilian Bishops' Conference
Conferência Nacional dos Bispos do Brasil

CODEM   Women's Rights Defense Committee (Chile)
Comité de Defensa de los Derechos de la Mujer

FASE   Federation of Organs for Social and Educational Assistance (Brazil)
Federaçâo de Orgâos para Assistência Social e Educacional

FASIC	Social Service Foundation of Christian Churches (Chile) Fundación de Ayuda Social de las Iglesias Cristianas
FLACSO	Latin American Faculty of Social Sciences Facultad Latinoamericano de las Ciencias Sociales
IBASE	Brazilian Institute for Social and Economic Analysis Instituto Brasíleiro de Análises Sociais e Econômicas
IBOPE	Brazilian Institute of Public Opinion and Statistics Instituto Brasíleiro de Opiniâo Pública e Estatística
ILET	Latin American Institute of Transnational Studies Instituto Latinoamericano de los Estudios Transnacionales
ISER	Institute for Religious Studies (Brazil) Instituto de Estudos da Religiâo
IURD	Universal Church of the Kingdom of God (Brazil) Igreja Universal do Reino de Deus
MIR	Revolutionary Independent Movement (Chile) Movimiento Independiente Revolucionaria
MOMUPO	Popular Women's Movement (Chile) Movimiento de Mujeres Populares
MST	landless movement (Brazil) Movimento dos Sem Terra
MUDECHI	Women of Chile Mujeres de Chile
NGO	nongovernmental organization
PEO	Popular Economic Organization Organizaciones Populares Económicas
PMM	Pastoral for Marginalized Women (Brazil) Pastoral da Mulher Marginalizada
PPD	Party for Democracy (Chile) Partido por la Democrácia
PRODEMU	Program for Women and Development (Chile) Promoción y Desarrollo de la Mujer

PT   Workers' Party (Brazil)
            Partido dos Trabalhadores

RCC   Charismatic Catholic Renewal

SEPADE   Evangelical Development Service (Chile)
            Servicio Evangélico para el Desarrollo

SERNAM   National Women's Service (Chile)
            Servicio Nacional de la Mujer

SERPAJ   Peace and Justice Service (Chile)
            Servicio de la Páz y Justicia

SOF   Feminist Movement Sempreviva (Brazil)
            Sempreviva Organização Femenista

O N E

Activism and Its Aftermath

Women were active during the dictatorship because of the political problem that existed in those years . . . and the need to denounce and organize—for example, the soup kitchens. Our involvement was motivated by our needs. We did not get involved just for the sake of doing it, but because of the dire need. If we organized human rights committees, it was because someone had their rights trampled. Women became leaders then.

— MARITZA SANDOVAL, SANTA CRUZ DE MAYO BASE COMMUNITY,
VILLA O'HIGGINS

Maritza Sandoval's story is that of many poor Brazilian and Chilean women.[1] The Brazilian (1964–85) and Chilean (1973–90) military regimes that set out to control and depoliticize civil society ended up creating new and unexpected sources of opposition from people such as Maritza. Although many had never previously joined any kind of organized group outside the home, poor women heroically rose to meet the challenges facing their families and communities during military rule. Mobilized by the Catholic Church through its base communities, women activists represented all that was new and promising in the "new" social movements. *religion transitioning to a social mvt.*

More recently, however, the kinds of social movements that characterized the democratic transitions—church-based movements, poor women's movements—have been nearly invisible in the new democracies of both countries.[2] As a result, the question of the long-term impact of base communities and military-era social movements needs to be revisited. Authors of previous studies have explained the reasons for the declining salience of social movement organizing through the church and by poor women in the new democracies. In this book, by contrast, a different question will be addressed. We begin from the assumption that a decline in social movement activism is to be expected and ask instead what becomes of activists and whether and how they seek to maintain their movements in changed political and social contexts.

---

1. To accord with the wishes of our interviewees, we identify the Brazilian respondents by their first names and the Chilean respondents by their full names.

2. Other kinds of social movements have remained or have grown visible in Brazil, however. These include the environmental and street children's movements, as well as two movements with historically close and now attenuated, but continuing, ties with the church: the landless movement and the indigenous movement.

social muts
on a neighborhood
level

We place the base community movement and its women activists in the contexts of social movements and of theories examining movement cycles. Doing so allows us to recognize the absence of protest without assuming that it means "failure" for the movement. We focus, instead, on what may be taking the place of earlier kinds of activism. By looking at the experiences of the women from the base communities from this theoretical perspective, we can specify ways in which their organizing may have had a less visible, but a long-term, impact on civil society. The theory of movement cycles leads us to look for personal change and empowerment, but also for the creation of new organizations dedicated to both action and movement maintenance and possibly the creation of activist networks as well. To the extent that we can demonstrate that former activists such as Maritza Sandoval are actively maintaining their movements and creating new networks, we can offer powerful evidence that base communities and their associated social movements have indeed made a lasting contribution to strengthening civil society.[3] Although the current context may inhibit activism of the sort these women engaged in earlier, they may nonetheless today be building new organizational venues and networks that could become sites for future activism.

may not have been huge but successes paved ... ? they have roots which are future activists

The Personal Impact of Activism:
Confirming and Extending Our Knowledge

We listened to the voices of women base community activists in Brazil and Chile nearly twenty years after the peak of their movements' activism. Their stories convinced us that earlier studies of individual cases and countries, such as Carol Drogus's 1997 study in Brazil, were correct in their conclusion that one of the most important by-products of the base communities was the personal empowerment of poor women. Maria Socorro says of her Brazilian community, "Women began to have their rights to participate in things outside the home, because before I didn't even know these existed. Then I began to see that I could do more than clean house, sew. *We became real people* [*a gente passava a ser mais gente*]." Poor Chilean women shared this experience.

---

3. We adopt a mainstream definition of *civil society,* based on Philippe Schmitter's (1997) concept. He defines it as composed of intermediary groups that are independent of the state, market, and family; capable of deliberating and taking action based on interests or concerns; interested in influencing but not replacing state authorities; and committed to acting in a mutually respectful way (204).

"The Christian community was a place of growth for women, not only because of their personal involvement, but especially because it opened their eyes to all the things women are capable of doing," says María Espina. Angelica Molina, another Chilean, adds: "The Christian community . . . was an awakening. I learned that my life did not have to be limited to washing, ironing, or raising children. I woke up as a person. . . . My own husband did not want me near the church . . . but I went just the same . . . I learned that I can speak out. I was afraid to speak in a group but now I can do it."

Women also proved themselves able to make use of their ascribed gender roles in publicly transformative ways. By socializing these roles to meet immediate needs, the women gained the confidence to expand into new public roles. Like many other Chilean base communities, Carmen Lopez's group first responded to the widespread misery that followed the coup by starting a "lunchroom" run by women for mothers and their children and, later, by teaching skills that could help women earn money. This basic help in meeting private-sphere obligations blossomed into political activism:

> We asked ourselves why some mothers did not participate and what we could do to avoid paternalism. That's how the handicrafts and other types of workshops got started, making products that people needed, such as sheets, and generating a small income. We also made sweaters, school aprons, and whatever else was needed. Parallel to the workshops, we held sessions in which we reflected on how the dictatorship affected us, creating consciousness. The human rights committee, one of the first in Chile, grew out of these sessions. Because of the participation of great numbers of women, we also began leadership training courses. . . . They learned to value themselves as creative persons.

Similarly, Brazilian activist Cida Lima recalls:

> At that time [1978] women started from nothing. The mothers' club was a way to get women out of the house. They started making dishclothes and embroidery. And then they started to talk about their lives, their situation as women. Except at that time it wasn't possible to raise women's consciousness through struggles and all, but we started talking about local problems, for example, the lack of asphalt, sewage, day care, difficulties with school and the health

post. Then, women became conscious that to improve the neighborhood it was necessary to be making demands and to make things happen in the neighborhood. So, that step was to go to the church and participate in the community.

Out of the blurring of the lines between private and public grew strengthened self-esteem, political awareness, and citizenship, which, in turn, led to new goals and activities for many—though far from all—of their women members.[4]

Those women who became activists view their participation in the base communities as empowering in ways that contribute to their potential as citizens: individuals with legitimate rights and with the authority to voice their demands and concerns (Lievesley 1999; Craske 1999). Carmen López remembers that participation in base communities "changed women's lives. 'Now I understand that I have rights,' women would tell me." Brazilian María José says, "It was a necessary process to get where we are. I say it was of vital importance to the workers, to get where they are. All of our class consciousness I attribute to participation in the church, in the Pastorals." Sofia, also from Brazil, adds, "CEBs helped the population examine things, see what was going on, engage themselves to make demands."

These stories leave no doubt of the remarkable repercussions that base communities had in many women's lives. As Brazilian activist Edna says, "What strikes me is that we women changed radically in our way of being, of thinking." By generating a sense of citizenship and empowerment in one of the most marginalized populations in Latin America—poor women—base communities certainly contributed to the long-term building of democracy and civil society.

Our research gives greater depth to the findings that activism was "empowering" by describing the ways in which women's lives and activities concretely changed in the aftermath of their activism. We learned about the activities they engage in today, including both their volunteer and paid work, as well as their relationship with the institution in which their activism

4. As many authors, including Drogus (1997), Burdick (1993), and Levine (1992), report, not all women in the base communities shared a politicized interpretation of liberation theology or became committed political activists. In fact, many remained quite traditionally religious and viewed their base community work as "charity." We do not claim that base communities turned all their members into activists, but we looked to those women who did become more politicized activists for our interview sample, because they are the ones on whom the hopes for a more organized and resistant civil society rest.

began: the Catholic Church. We learned from the women themselves how they believe that their experience as activists changed their life circumstances. Our interviews not only confirm that activism in the base communities was personally empowering for poor women, but also enable us to be more specific about its real-life consequences for them.

The Social Impact of Activism: A New Debate

Given their prominence in the politics of democratic transitions, base communities were expected to do much more than empower individuals. By changing the political culture and beliefs of marginal groups, the new movements might become a catalyst for larger social and political change. If poor, religious women, long considered the most politically passive and conservative of social groups, could confront the military state, then, many observers thought, perhaps a new, combative civil society was being born, and the world might truly be turned upside down. Did these social movements form the basis for stronger civil societies, or was their influence limited to the personal empowerment of their women members? This is the primary question that we sought to address by learning the fate of women base community leaders from Chile and Brazil.

The popular movements these women led contributed to a significant change: redemocratization. The restoration of democratic institutions marked an important turning point, but it did not produce the inclusive politics that activists had hoped for. Civilian and military elites orchestrated democratic transitions; the Catholic Church resumed a more compliant role in both countries; and the poor remained largely marginalized from the political process. The women who led vibrant and combative political movements have little visibility today. Indeed, few social movements of any kind seem to remain from the earlier period to stir up the mix of electoral politics. As social movement activism peaked and declined in the late 1980s, there was an erosion of optimism about the cultural, political, and structural changes such movements could produce. Since the 1990s, pessimism has reigned as observers seek to understand the disappearance of those muscular social movements at a time when greater political openness would seem to be providing them with more opportunities for effective action.

The decline of movement activism, including in church-based and popular women's groups, is indisputable in both countries. On this point, there is general agreement, though different explanations are offered. Authors of studies rooted in a religion-and-politics perspective suggest the lack of visible social movements as prima facie evidence that the church betrayed its progressive members, that liberation theology failed. For feminist scholars, the lack of movement visibility may signal that "malestream" electoral politics delegitimized social movements and women's activism. Talk of the "broken promises" of liberation theology, the "myth" of the progressive Catholic Church, and the remarginalization of women's movements predominates (Nagle 1997; Serbin 1992, 405; Waylen 1994).[5] One journalist asserts that the decline in movement activism among Brazilian Catholics results from their improved economic prospects (Junqueira 1997, 62–63). Others, including some activists themselves, cite the profound challenges neoliberalism produces for social movements (Vásquez 1998).

Each of these perspectives offers an important insight into the development and decline of women's activism in and through the base communities. Each, however, is only a partial perspective on what were truly multifaceted—religious, political, women's, local, national—movements. Moreover, though each helps us explain movement decline, none addresses the question of what remains of the activism of these empowered women and what forms and venues it may occupy today. As Tracy Fitzsimmons (2000b) points out, "Given the many unsatisfied needs of women following transitions to democracy, it seems reasonable to expect a continued organizing presence of women in Latin America. The literature is only beginning to establish the complexities of what really happens in the arenas and levels of women's participation after democratization" (221–22).

Finally, each of these explanations starts from the assumption that a lack of current, visible activism is somehow proof of movement failure. The debate at the moment is over the cause of that failure. As Fitzsimmons suggests, however, we know extremely little, in fact, about the complex ways in which women activists have adapted to changing social and political conditions. Our research illuminates this issue by focusing on what women activists from the base communities are doing today. We thus shift the terms of the debate to whether these movements had lasting effects on civil society despite the current lower levels of visible activism.

---

5. Both Rowan Ireland (1999, 111) and Sarah Brooks (1999, 67–68) similarly note the widespread disparagement of progressive Catholic activism in the 1990s.

Specifically, we look at the activism of women from the base communities in the context of social movement theory, particularly examining the extended literature on movement cycles. This perspective offers us several advantages over previous approaches. First, by placing the movements in their broadest context, we avoid a pitfall of earlier studies: viewing either church change or gender issues as the sole explanation for the movements' trajectories. Such an outlook is partial and is dissonant with the women's own lived experiences of their movements as at once Catholic, women's, and popular. A broader social movement perspective allows us to tie these diverse threads together, as the women themselves do. Second, our perspective gives us concrete insights into what we can and cannot expect the long-term impact of social movements to be. It stresses that it would be unrealistic for us to expect the same kind and level of activism under changing historical circumstances, yet it also allows us to perceive that the absence of "old" kinds of activism is not synonymous with a lack of activist activity or movement. On the contrary, it suggests that we look for specific kinds of changing venues, forms, and net-works for activism—the work of "movement maintenance" that activists carry out in the context of movement decline.

Finally, the broader social movement perspective allows us to address the base communities' influence on civil society in a very specific and concrete way. It suggests that in addition to looking at long-term personal effects on attitudes and empowerment, we look for specific signs of movement mainte-nance. Many of these, especially the creation of new venues, community orga-nizations, networks, and cultural activities related to movement maintenance, correspond to the kinds of things that have been described as hallmarks of a healthy civil society. Old movements and movement activists may be laying the basis for a stronger civil society and for future activism, despite their current "invisibility." We cannot know unless we know what women are doing today.

Here and there are signs that pessimism may be unwarranted: studies of more recent movements or the few that retain visibility, for example, often seem to come upon women activists who were forged in the popular move-ments of the 1980s (see, for example, Stephen 1997). Indeed, it sometimes seems that wherever there are little pockets of activism, there are women from the base communities (Ireland 1999). But how typical are these examples? Since the democratic transitions, little attention has been paid to grassroots activists, and no one has traced the consequences of their earlier activism by looking at a broad cross-section of activists. As Fitzsimmons (2000b) points

out, "The existing literature contains much work on women's political organizing under authoritarianism and the period of transition, but little examining
women and women's groups under democracy" (220). To assess the larger
legacy of these movements, we need to know what impact activism had on the
politics of a wider group of women who shared the experience, what activities
they currently engage in, what obstacles and opportunities for political
activism they perceive, and what institutions and networks have emerged
from earlier protests. These are the questions that we seek to answer in this
book in order to understand more fully the broader legacy of protest.

We believe that listening to the stories of those unexpected grassroots
activists is the only way to answer fully the question of the long-term consequences of protest for civil society. In doing so, we conclude that the consequences of base community activism in both countries were significantly
greater and longer term than the current lack of visibility suggests. In fact, as
movement-cycle theories would predict, we found that women from the base
communities are adapting their activism to new contexts, needs, and issues.

Catholic Women's Activism: Change and Continuity

Contexts and Issues, New and Old

During the 1970s and 1980s, women from the base communities in Brazil
and Chile faced similar political contexts in which to organize. Both countries suffered under repressive military regimes. The repression was certainly
greater in Chile, where all collective efforts and meetings were banned by an
aggressively repressive state; in contrast, Brazilian women often took to the
streets to campaign for neighborhood improvements, many of which they
successfully brought about. In both cases, however, the military context
arguably provided a clear and unified target for opposition. Issues, too,
seemed clear to activists, at least in retrospect. Chilean women organized
largely around issues of human rights abuses, but also to meet pressing
material needs in their communities. For Brazilian women, community
organizing to meet needs predominated, but some were also active in human
rights work. In both cases, women from the base communities participated
in the process of redemocratization.

Today, women activists from the base communities in both Brazil and
Chile face political contexts—representative democracies—that are far less

repressive and more open to protest politics. Women from both countries, however, perceive the new politics as still marginalizing them and their issues. Although less abusive of human rights than the old regimes, the new civilian democracies are not particularly responsive to or concerned about the poor, who feel the consequences of neoliberal economics and globalization as a betrayal of democracy. As Chilean Marta Alvarez says, "We are living the consequences of what the dictatorship left in place: the neoliberal system. Before the military regime took power, Chile had a more humanitarian system. . . . The dictatorship did not end. A veiled dictatorship has been left in place. The [democratic] government . . . gave in to the military on many issues, as did the Catholic Church as well." Similarly, Edaldiva says of Brazil, "Things haven't changed much . . . unfortunately it's still necessary to fight a great deal. . . . We don't see a democracy. I think things are still very closed. It's difficult to change this picture."

The presidencies of a Socialist, Ricardo Lagos, in Chile and of the Worker's Party's Luiz Inácio da Silva (Lula) in Brazil may change these women's perception and increase opportunities for protest politics. At the time of the interviews in 1999, however, the women faced a particular political context that seemed to render the tactics of popular organizing that they used under the military surprisingly and unexpectedly obsolete. Their concerns continued to be marginalized despite democracy and a decrease in repression—and at the same time, the possibility of electoral opportunities seemed to delegitimize protest politics.

Similarly, although poverty and community deprivation persist in both countries, the new economic and political structure of neoliberalism appears to make them less susceptible to community pressures. Brazilian women overwhelmingly cited unemployment as the number-one problem facing them and their communities, but many felt they could not systematically address this situation. Elza succinctly describes the problems she sees in her neighborhood: "Unemployment, violence, and, I think, low salaries, because we [distribute charity food]—we've done so for a long time—we give this little help, but we know it's just a palliative." Chilean women concur that poverty is still an issue, but in some ways a less visible and therefore less tractable one. Mercedes Montoya argues that superficial improvements have masked increased levels of debt since the transition to democracy. "Unemployment is widespread, possibly more so than during the dictatorship. There is veiled poverty. People are in debt. They all have television, telephones, even mobile phones, but they live precariously in debt." Neoliberalism's insistence on individual solutions to poverty, free markets, and lower levels of state intervention in the economy make it difficult for activists to see how the demands of social movements on the state might result in reducing the burdens of poverty (Vásquez 1998).

Other problems that plague the women's communities are new or have intensified during the democratic eras. María Ortega Soto describes the situation in her Chilean community: "Drug addiction is strong and drugs are sold here. Medical attention is poor. The new clinic building is lovely on the outside, but inside it lacks equipment and doctors. Education is fairly inferior in municipally run schools. Children can barely read and hardly know multiplication." Chilean women listed drugs, poverty-related issues, and delinquency or other youth-related difficulties as the top three problems facing their communities today. Neide perceives the similar dilemmas in Brazil: "The financial situation itself. The question of drugs, too. Violence. Another thing that the financial situation provokes, the question of domestic violence." After unemployment, Brazilian women consider health, education, sanitation, and crime to be the biggest challenges to their communities.

In short, these women face many old problems as well as substantial new or newly salient ones, such as drugs and rising crime. For the former activists, the question is how to continue to fight for their communities in a new political context of representative democracy and neoliberal hegemony that make their older forms of activism appear obsolete. It is a vexing question, but one of the most remarkable legacies of the earlier era of activism is a group of women fighters who will not give up.

New Ways to Struggle . . . and Old

As Tracy Fitzsimmons (2000b) notes, "Under democracy, oppression now looks different, as do the oppressors and the circumstances in which women might win or lose. Similarly, the reasons why women mobilize, how various women's groups interrelate, and how women and the state interact have also changed" (217). These women continue to believe strongly in the efficacy of collective action, but so many things seem now to inhibit the old forms: a changed political culture characterized by passivity and individualism, the loss of support from the church, unresponsive elected officials, and a lack of clarity. The old organizations—the base communities in particular—may no longer be so vital and effective, but the activists have not surrendered. Formed by their particular experience of the intersection of biography and history, women continue to be active individually in a variety of ways. They seek new venues and new organizations to meet the challenges that the transitional democracies present for civil society.

Nearly all the Chilean women interviewed remain active in some form of local or national activist organization, although many have left their Catholic parish base community. Some are active in political parties and neighborhood councils and others in women's groups, while others have joined groups organized around health, social service, or environmental concerns. Even women who remain active in producing "women's work" in their base communities continue to find their activities empowering in ways that reinforce their sense of worth as individuals and their belief in their potential as citizens. According to Clotilde Silva Henríquez, "Women from the base communities of the seventies and eighties are everywhere. I am always running into people from those days who are doing things. Some work in the area of health, others with women, young people or children. [Even] those women who left their homes to reproduce traditional women's roles—sewing, knitting, cooking—do so in a social context."

Although both groups remain highly active, the Brazilian women are slightly less engaged than the Chileans. About three-quarters continue to be involved in neighborhood organizations, while more than half participate in activism outside their immediate communities. Their activities are varied. Those who remain largely rooted in the church still work on social improvements; Maria das Graças, for example, works on health, and Ilda Cipriano coordinates the social-issues area of the diocesan mothers' clubs. Some have gone considerably beyond the church to political parties, neighborhood associations, and so on. Melania, a former neighborhood association president, now works with a citizen education group. Nine women from São Paulo participate in a grassroots feminist organization. Madalena describes one of their projects: "We created a legal center called the Maria Miguel Center. We have three lawyers and nowadays we are working on violence against women. We've had this work going on for three years come August, and so there have already been over four thousand women who have gone through this work of ours." Another colleague, Emerencianá, works with women's mental health through the same organization. As Edna says, "Most of the women who went far beyond the church—theology, sociology, who advanced in this—passed through this process of militancy in the CEBs during the period of dictatorship, and I think that is one of most marked things the CEBs contributed."

Like activists elsewhere facing conditions less hospitable to organized collective action, these women have found new ways to adapt their activism to changing times. Although their current activities in base communities or new venues cannot be described as elements of social movements, the women continue to create and work in organizations that strengthen the fabric of civil society, despite their lower levels of visibility. Like others who have been strongly marked by the experience of political activism, however, they also hope to recapture the level of militancy and organization they experienced before (McAdam 1988). They continue to believe in the potential, if not actual, efficacy of movement organization and seek to make new connections and revitalize movement politics. Our research illuminates what these new connections and strategies may be.

Methodology: Making the Invisible Visible

To explore the effect of religious women's grassroots activism during the Brazilian and Chilean military regimes in light of its social movement implications, we needed to focus on the experiences, perceptions, and trajectories of the women themselves since the apex of the social movement cycle in which they participated. Close examination of the women's own stories allows us to link their interrelated identities (gender, religion, class, partisanship) to the larger structural questions inherent in social movement maintenance. How has individual activism changed, what strategies do grassroots activists employ to adapt to new political realities, and with whom do they choose to ally? In pursuit of answers to these questions, we interviewed women we could positively identify as activists in grassroots Catholic base Christian communities (CEBs) during the period of military rule.

The consequence of social movement activism is a relatively neglected field of social movement inquiry, in part, perhaps, because of the methodological difficulty of establishing a movement's impact (for long-term social and personal change), much less a movement's unintended consequences (Giugni 1999 xiv–xv, xxii). Our study in Latin America suffers from some of the same methodological limitations that have plagued similar research in the United States—small sample size and the inability to establish an appropriate control group—and, as a result, we make limited claims for the generalizability of our results (McAdam 1999, 121). At the same time, however, our research has successfully overcome a variety of methodological problems associated with similar studies of movement consequences elsewhere. For example, Doug McAdam (1999) criticizes such studies for geographic restrictions, for the research being conducted at the peak of a cycle, and for a failure to establish control groups or "before and after data" (121). In contrast, we interviewed our activists in multiple locations in each country in an effort to represent different movement contexts, though we have not represented rural activists. Moreover, by looking at activists well after the period of peak movement mobilization, we can separate out the extent to which their political involvement is a consequence of earlier experiences rather than just of the times. And though we lack "before and after" data, we do have the activists' own reflections on their evolution to draw on, and we have biographical statements that now trace a trajectory of considerable length. We thus can explore the dynamics of change for individuals and groups (Giugni 1999, xxiv).

Most important, perhaps, our research is comparative. By contrasting similar movements in different contexts, we can effectively explore the ways that movements in the same institutions, mobilizing similar people around similar issues, had different long-term consequences. We chose to compare Brazil and Chile not because we thought that individuals' experiences would differ sharply, but rather because we believed that differences in the two countries might produce differences in the women's long-term ability to maintain and broaden networks and activism. In many ways, the two countries present a common picture. For example, pacted transitions sent the military back to the barracks, leaving in place political systems that serve to exclude other actors from negotiation and remove many political and economic issues from the political agenda. Further, the church in both countries withdrew support from grassroots organizational networks. At the same time, however, there are significant differences: the form of church sponsorship of the base communities, the nature and timing of the church's withdrawal, characteristics of the feminist movements and their connections with grassroots women's groups, and the levels and implications of partisanship. These all suggest that within this common trajectory there might be substantial differences in Brazilian and Chilean women's ability to maintain and forge mobilizational alliances as a result of structural differences in the opportunities and constraints available in the two countries' political (as well as religious and social) contexts.

In Chile, although popular women mobilized in parishes led by progressive priests and religious or lay personnel throughout the country, we chose to confine our interviews to Santiago. This was in part because of the capital's size, which allows a great deal of variety and comparison across parishes and ecclesiastical leadership, and in part because of Chile's highly centralized political system, which makes Santiago the hub of national politics. The forty-eight Chilean interviewees were chosen across thirty-five different parishes that were known for their active participation in the prodemocracy mobilization and that are located in *poblaciones* that also were well-known to be organized and combative during the dictatorship. The selection of individuals was based largely on their reputation in their communities for being active participants in both the religious life of the base Christian communities and the organizational work of the antimilitary social movements. The broad range of Chilean parishes represented by the women we interviewed allows us to clarify the way in which differences such as religious leadership, access to resources, and networking opportunities shaped grassroots strategies for survival and protest during the dictatorship as well as the legacies of these strategies in posttransition democratic politics.

In Brazil, the assistance of Cecilia Mariz and Maria das Dores Campos Machado permitted us to reliably locate and reinterview many Brazilian women who had been interviewed for earlier studies by Brazilian researchers as well as for Drogus's earlier (1997) book. This added a valuable dimension to our ability to explore the interviewees' current perceptions as well as changes in their attitudes and their relationships to the church, state, and other actors in civil society. Our twenty-five Brazilian interviewees were located in Rio de Janeiro and São Paulo, two important sites of base community organizing. Indeed, São Paulo and the periphery of Rio de Janeiro were home to some of the church's most progressive bishops and were the sites for organizing some of the most widely known challenges to the military regime. Our activists were all chosen for their prominent and established roles in some of the most engaged and activist communities in Brazil. Thus, the interviewees in both cities share a common history of urban base community activism. However, by broadening our study beyond São Paulo and the parish studied by Drogus, we include a range of communities and experiences that is representative of urban women's base community participation and ensures that all interviewees have a similar experience of high levels of activism, while mirroring the Chilean sample's distribution across many parishes.

The interviews themselves covered six major areas of inquiry: the nature of the base communities during the military years; the level and type of support each community received from various levels of the church at that time; current levels and types of church support; the base community's current potential for forging ties with other groups in civil society, specifically, secular women's organizations or Protestant groups; the respondents' perceptions of the problems and possible solutions in their neighborhoods today; and the respondents' attitudes toward feminism and so-called women's issues.

These women's individual stories are, in themselves, valuable as an important addition to the "official story" of the Brazilian and Chilean transitions. The individual stories also allow us to shed light on the larger questions of social movement dynamics and impact. We do not claim to be able to speak for the experience of all women activists, all poor activists, or all Brazilian or Chilean activists. Future studies based on larger and more rigorously representative sampling will be required to fill in the gaps of our understanding of the ways in which grassroots activism during peak periods of social movement mobilization affects civil society over long periods. The value of this study lies in using the more targeted interviews to trace out the connections between individual legacies of empowerment and longer-term sociopolitical change missed by studies focusing on single identities (gender, religion, class, partisanship). Our conclusions are based on neither an exhaustive survey nor a representative sample; rather, we explore in detail one group of popular women—those active in the Catholic base Christian communities—whose protagonism during the pro-democracy movements was seen at the time as the proof of far-reaching political, gender, and social change. We identify the complex legacy of their empowerment, which, to date, remains beyond the notice of mainstream scholars. While we cannot generalize to all popular activists, we believe that the research has implications for understanding both base communities and popular women's organizing more generally, as well as their long-term effects.

Objectives and Structure of the Book

This book contributes to our understanding of the personal and social impact of social movement cycles through an examination of one key sector among the groups that pressed for redemocratization. While centrally concerned with the fate of these activists and the meaning of the current period of movement decline for civil society, we also address debates in related areas. The base communities operated at a crossroads of religion, class, and gender. As a result, we are able to address questions about the role of religious institutions in mobilizing protest, the impact of gender on political protest and mobilization, the effects of participation on women's identification with feminism, and the possibilities of cross-class feminist alliances. While we do not devote specific chapters to each of these themes, we have tried throughout the book to remain cognizant of the fact that individuals we interviewed are poor, female, and Catholic. This awareness compels us to take each facet of their identities seriously; we refer to scholarly research on class, gender, and religion as necessary. In doing so we attempt to remain faithful to the women's own words and perceptions.

The book is divided into two parts. In the first, after placing the communities and activists in a theoretical context, we discuss the history of the base communities. We show how the women activists perceived this history, and in Chapter 3 we contrast the relationship between the base communities and the Catholic Church in the two countries. In Chapter 4, we compare the periods of movement decline and loss of church support, emphasizing the women's perceptions of this process and concluding with a discussion of their efforts to maintain their activism. In these chapters, we show the profound and enduring impact that participation had on the women who became activists, as well as their sense of loss and disillusionment at the church's subsequent "abandonment" of the base communities and their project. We also illustrate some institutional differences in the churches in the two countries, which we believe have consequences for the activists' subsequent attempts to maintain and build movement networks.

In Chapters 5–7, we turn to the possibilities for renewing organizations and building new alliances that could empower new activism. In Chapter 5, we provide an overview of the paths that women in each country have taken since redemocratization, examining their membership in various organizations, including political parties, community groups, and newer entities such as community forums. In Chapters 6 and 7, we turn to the question of whether new alliances can be and are being built to empower new activism. We describe the links that already exist between the women and various other groups and we discuss their views on how such linkages could be created or strengthened to serve their communities. We examine, in Chapter 6, whether alliances across denominations are possible. In the context of growing Protestant conversions among the poor in both countries, we wanted to know whether these Catholic activists were making connections with their poor, Protestant neighbors—or even believed it was possible to do so. Finally, in Chapter 7, we turn to the question of relations with mainstream feminist groups. In Latin America, grassroots women's groups, including those organized by the church, are often grouped together with more traditional feminist movements under the rubric of the "women's movement." Moreover, second-wave feminists in both Chile and Brazil have been very determined in their attempts to reach out across class lines and have had some significant successes in this effort (Stephen 1997, 12, 20). Marysa Navarro and Susan Bourque (1998), among others, speculate positively about the future of grassroots feminism and the possibility of cross-class women's alliances. They note that "besides creating collectives, magazines, radio programs, health and research centers, and casas de la mujer (women's centers), [national women's organizations] also founded groups (usually NGOs) whose activities were directed toward women in poor neighborhoods or shantytowns" (187). We ask, in Chapter 7, whether these women activists have, in fact, made connections with cross-class feminist organizations, and we examine their perceptions of feminism, of feminists, and of the possibility of their allying with them.

TWO

Understanding Invisibility:
Perspectives on Social Movement Decline

The more you get close to a God of history the more you confront reality and must assume a real commitment to life. That's the radical challenge of Jesus. Then you can't escape the cross, you can't avoid a commitment. Then you change from a Christian who gives alms to a new practice—to one who's in the streets. . . . It's much more [than alms], it's discovering a more political and social discourse.

—EDNA, BRAZIL

People started questioning more things. They reread the Bible through different eyes. The base communities started to reflect on the Bible, and then . . . people started to discover evangelizing action was not giving someone a fish, but you have to teach how to fish. And there were broader issues that had to do with more fundamental changes. . . . We started to make the connection between our personal, family lives and the life of the wider community, and from the wider community to social activism, and from there to the country that has a structure that makes some people poor and others rich, some that are prisoners and others who imprison them, etc.

—VERONICA PARDO, CHILE

In Brazilian and Chilean base Christian communities—in which small consciousness-raising and reflection groups inspired by liberation theology were formed—poor people, and especially poor women, experienced both individual and collective empowerment. Veronica Pardo's testimony above captures this transformation in women's lives in her Chilean community. Women's expanded awareness produced an impressive range of new grassroots entities: community-survival efforts such as soup kitchens and handicraft workshops; specific community-needs facilities such as health clinics; protest movements to demand urban services; and groups promoting solidarity and consciousness-raising activities regarding human rights, the plight of prisoners, and domestic violence. The extent of grassroots organizing—in the breadth of the population affected and the range of needs met—was astounding, especially given that the participants and leaders were primarily poor women organized largely through the Catholic Church.

Our task is to understand the fate of these women activists and their organizations, the base communities. As described in the previous chapter, they have lost visibility since the 1980s, leading many observers to conclude that they were ineffective or had little enduring value. We believe that this assumption is premature; it is a product of the paucity of research on the specific trajectories of the most activist and committed women from the base communities. Women's and Catholic groups were particularly vital, and they were ongoing players in the process of redemocratization. Thus, their fate deserves special attention. As Jane Jaquette (1995) points out: "The new wave of women's political mobilization in Latin America has drawn women into social movements, not into parties or interest groups; there is no institutionalized way of linking women's political concerns to the political system and no established means by which parties and governments can be held accountable. The study of what happens to social movements after the transitions are over is thus a critical area for research" (126). Similarly, writing of the progressive Catholic groups whose presence was so ubiquitous in the process of redemocratization, Sarah Cline (2000) declares that "[t]he fate of members of grassroots communities as the Catholic hierarchy has adopted increasingly conservative positions [since redemocratization] certainly warrants research" (251). To date, however, there has been no study following up on a range of these activists and no attempts to discern how redemocratization has affected the women and their movements. Women's and Catholic groups were particularly vibrant in the transitions, and our research focuses on the base communities, where these overlapped.

Further, viewing base communities and their women activists in the context of social movement theory equips us to better assess their long-term impact on civil society than has been possible in many previous studies. We make three arguments. First, base communities can be understood as social movements with special characteristics, which we describe below. Second, placing them in this context allows us to see them as more multifaceted and complex than would a focus on their either religious or gendered components alone; the insights of social movement theory deepen our understanding of base communities in the context of research on movement cycles. Third, once we have placed the communities and activists in this theoretical context, we can move beyond analyzing movement decline to look closely at what can be expected in its aftermath. Social movement theory leads us to look not only for individual empowerment, but also for movement building and maintenance that may contribute to the long-term health of civil society. The fate of earlier movements and activists is important because their structural and organizational legacies can strengthen civil society by providing an organizational basis for protest, "a vehicle that is available to even the most powerless segments of society" (Minkoff 1997).

Both Brazil and Chile face situations in which encouraging civic participation, expanding popular access to policy making, and enhancing social
equity are crucial to a democratic future. Individual empowerment and the
creation and maintenance of civic associations and networks are vital to this
process, because they undergird a civil society able to call politicians to
account (Minkoff 1997). Such empowerment and networks may be especially
important to poor women. Since women have yet to attain significant incor-
poration into democratic politics, the kinds of social movements associated
with earlier activism will remain vital as a way to "acquire visibility in the
public space" (Marques-Pereira 1998, 222). As Daniel Levine and David
Stoll (1997) write: "Without such networks and the heritage of social capital
that makes them possible, political systems neither 'hear' nor respond to the
demands of citizens: their demands remain inarticulate and invisible" (65).
Rather than assuming that the absence of visible protest means the absence
of such organizational and network building, we use social movement theory
to argue for and assess the possibility that such construction is taking place
through the daily activities of women from the base communities.

Base Communities and Social Movements

Our analysis rests on the belief that, for purposes of interpreting their impact
on civil society, base communities can be understood as examples of social
movements. This assumption does not deny the fundamentally religious
nature of the base communities. Indeed, the pastoral agents who started the
communities viewed them as primarily religious organizations; they carried
out many spiritual and ritual tasks; and, particularly in Brazil, individuals
joined the communities primarily out of a religious commitment. Nonetheless, base communities, like many religious movements and venues, became
a prime source for movement mobilization around issues not directly related
to religion itself (C. Smith 1996a, 8). At the least, base communities are
connected with social movements in the function of important organizational venues, or as "'midwives'" of social movements per se (17).

Many authors have gone further than this, looking at base communities
as *themselves* examples of social movements (C. Smith 1991; 1996a; Burdick
1993; Vásquez 1998). They commonly appear in lists of movements associated with redemocratization (Escobar and Alvarez 1992; Hellman 1997).
Unfortunately, the definition of *social movement* remains contentious and is

often only implicit. We can assert, however, that base communities share characteristics found in the two primary schools defining social movements in the current literature, one that emphasizes collective political action, and one that stresses culture and values.[1]

For the first school, social movements are characterized by political engagement and especially "'collective challenges, based on common purposes and social solidarities, in sustained interaction with elites, opponents, and authorities'" (Tarrow 1998, 4–5; see also Giugni 1999, xxi–xxii). More succinctly, Doug McAdam and David A. Snow define "the pursuit or resistance of social change through engagement in noninstitutional tactical action" as the key feature of a social movement (xxi). In contrast, theorists of the new social movements, that is, members of the second school, tend to focus on cultural aspects of challenge: building social solidarities, cultural resistance, and new values in sometimes diffuse and less organized structures (Johnston, Larana, and Gusfield 1994; Escobar and Alvarez 1992). Ultimately, members of both schools of thought have begun to conclude that the distinction between the political struggle for access and the cultural struggle for identity/solidarity are interrelated and are both central to social movements (Escobar and Alvarez 1992, 5; Giugni 1999). Moreover, both schools of thought have tended to emphasize social movements as the particular political vehicle available to less powerful segments of society (Johnston, Larana, and Gusfield 1994, 7; Tarrow 1998, 3).

Thus, we can see a kind of convergence around a definition of social movements as collective action on the part of less powerful groups that involves both political action and cultural change. On this basis, we can agree with Christian Smith's (1991) contention that the base communities themselves can properly be considered "social movements" (53). The actions of the base communities encompassed political action, solidarity, and efforts at cultural change. They involved a commitment to change people's ideas of what it means to be a Christian as part of a project of facilitating engagement in social change. Moreover, these mobilizing efforts took place among some of the most disenfranchised groups in society, and often sought to

---

1. The former is sometimes called the American school and is associated with the writers Sidney Tarrow, Doug McAdam, and Charles Tilly. The latter, sometimes called the European or "new social movement" school, is represented by Alain Touraine and Jürgen Habermas, among others. Melucci (1996) provides a summary of these positions and an argument for synthesis in chapter 1. Similarly, see Giugni 1999 for an argument for synthesis.

engage them in the kind of extrainstitutional politics that all students of social movements define as important.

While we would argue that it is therefore appropriate to consider base communities in the context of social movement theory, we must also recognize that they were movements of an unusual and particular type. First, as described earlier, they drew on many identities simultaneously—primarily religious affiliation, socioeconomic status, and gender—to define and mobilize their activists. As we have seen, this is a source of some scholarly disagreement, since groups that some see as acting on religious identity are perceived by others as acting on gender identity. In fact, for the activists themselves, both were often salient. Seeing them as simultaneously Catholic, women's, and class-based movements allows us to understand them in their full complexity.

Second, the base communities were unusual in espousing an umbrella goal (the realization of the kingdom of God on earth) that allowed them to host a large variety of submovements. Many movements create more specific spinoff movements; indeed, this process can enhance a movement's viability (Moyer 2001). Few define an overarching goal as broad as achieving "social justice," but this may not be out of line with the new social movements' emphasis on broad, pragmatic, pluralistic, and often somewhat vague goals (Johnston, Larana, and Gusfield 1994, 7).

Third, base communities were unusual in their strong institutionalization within the Catholic Church. Although religious institutions have often provided strong bases for social mobilization, this has been rarer in highly structured, hierarchical ones such as the Catholic Church (Zald and McCarthy 1987). Moreover, as Christian Smith (1991) points out, in this case it was elites within the church rather than the powerless per se who initiated the movement (67–68).

Finally, Brazilian and Chilean base communities must be understood as social movements associated with processes of redemocratization (Escobar and Alvarez 1992; Hellman 1997). These movements constitute a subset of social movements about which we are less theoretically informed. Many authors have argued, however, that movements associated with redemocratization processes will be subject to decay and decline in the aftermath of democratic elections (Fitzsimmon 2000a, 14–20).

Because of their peculiarities, base communities are critical to understanding the impact of social movements in Brazil and Chile. Their nature as religious/class/gendered organizations, their formative role in spinoff movements, their institutionalization within the strongest institution in

Latin American civil society, and their association with redemocratization render them critical cases for understanding civil society today. Moreover, it was precisely the activists we interviewed—poor women making a first foray into critical politics through the church communities—who, as symbols and as individuals, were the focal point of all the hopes and aspirations for stronger democracies in postmilitary Latin America. We would therefore argue that base communities and the women who ran them are *the* critical social movement and subset of activists to follow in order to understand the long-term impact of movements on postmilitary civil society.

Our understanding of the base communities as social movements, particularly as movements associated with redemocratization, leads us to argue that a framework based on social movement research on movement cycles and maintenance will best enhance our understanding of their long-term impact. Our understanding of the complex and unusual nature of base communities as social movements, however, also leads us to argue that we must look at them in a particular way. We could, as Christian Smith (1991) suggests, look only at maintenance within the institution of the church—the work of church elites. The base communities were fundamentally sites that mobilized poor laywomen, however. Thus, we must know what these activists are doing to maintain the movements' bases, as well as what changes have occurred within the Brazilian and Chilean churches, to assess the long-term consequences of mobilization for civil society. In other words, we must understand not only what caused the decline of base communities, but also what has happened to them in the democratic aftermath. And we must understand this in terms of what has occurred not only within the institutional church, but also in the lives of individual activists.

Viewing the base communities broadly in the context of social movement theory facilitates this by allowing us to view them as part of a movement cycle related to redemocratization. By doing so, we gain specific insights into what to look for in the activists' lives and their organizations for signs that their activism has had a lasting effect on them and on society. In the following section, we look at the base communities as part of a movement cycle.

Base Communities: The Advantages of a Movement Cycle Model

Despite their different (religion or gender) lenses, the authors of most earlier studies of our activists' movements argued that changing external (social, economic, and political) conditions led to their decline. They identify many obstacles and inhibiting factors, but different observers stress different factors depending on whether they viewed the movements as "church movements" or primarily as "women's movements." The religion lens led Manuel Vásquez and W. E. Hewitt to conclude that economic neoliberalism, globalization, party politics, changes in the Vatican, and the general loss of church support have all made organized action by such activists as Edna and Veronica Pardo increasingly difficult (Drogus 1999, 36; Ireland 1999, 111). Those who identify popular women's organizations as the cycle's backbone are more optimistic, but also consider the reversion to party politics, neoliberalism, and tensions created by the transitions within the larger women's movement as sources of strain (Alvarez 1998, Lebon 1998, Valdes 1998). Fatigue, disillusionment, or heightened individualism and stimulated consumerism also figure in some analyses, and these probably do also account for the falling away of many people who participated in earlier movements (Levine and Stoll 1997, Ireland 1999, Hellman 1997). The women we interviewed, in fact, often cite such factors in explaining the current lack of activism.

Despite differing lenses, the overall consensus holds that the reemergence of partisan politics, the growing strength of neoliberal ideology, and economic hardship combined with such specific factors as a loss of church support or the existence of class divisions within the women's movements to undermine popular activism. These explanations are indeed valid, and we discuss some of their details in the following chapters. We do not dispute that political and economic contexts for movements have changed, or that the current context is one in which grassroots mobilization via the church is simply not feasible.

Focusing on changing contexts helps us explain decline, but it does not contribute much to our understanding of what happens to activism in the aftermath. It simply seems to "disappear" when political opportunities and facilitating contexts make active protest less feasible or effective. This may account for the generally pessimistic interpretation of the long-term impact of base communities and women's organizing.[2] Rowan Ireland (1999) describes the trend as follows:

> Critical studies of the [Christian base] communities in the 1990s depict them variously as only shallowly, temporarily, and never

---

2. This is particularly true among studies of religion and politics. Feminist scholars are also cautious but remain somewhat more optimistic, citing examples of continued popular women's activism.

extensively established among the politically marginalized popular classes; as signally failing to fulfill those civic functions, more usually working as specifically religious communities not too different from traditional parishes; as having been all but destroyed by the application of Vatican policies restoring hierarchical clerical control and requiring a retreat from politics; as having failed in competition with other religious movements inside and outside the church; and as having faltered before the destabilizing effects of economic globalization. (111)

Increasingly, he suggests, such observations lead to the rejection of the Tocquevillean argument.[3] Scholars tend to assert either that base communities "failed" or that their success was partial at best. Daniel Levine and David Stoll (1997), for example, argue that base communities did empower individuals psychologically, enabling them to perceive themselves as citizens with legitimate rights. They failed, however, in the crucial area of creating enduring civil associations and networks, thus creating what the authors refer to as the "gap between empowerment and power."[4] Similarly, Nikki Craske (1999) concludes that women's movements failed to achieve organizational empowerment, "although personal empowerment might be more resilient to changing political conditions" (136).

Rather than seeing the current juncture as de facto evidence of the failure of earlier social movements to establish a well-rooted civil society, we argue that such developments may—or may not—be taking place now. Specifically, rather than the 1990s being seen as marking a definitive end to the social movement activism that accompanied the democratic transitions, the aftermath of the activist peak must be understood as part of a movement cycle, and indeed a critical part. Only by examining the content of that decline—what happens to the activists, how they try to maintain and expand movement networks, and whether they are able to do so—can we comprehend the full implications of the liberationist church and its related social movements for civil society. If we do so, we may, as Rowan Ireland suggests, be able to save the Tocquevillean parallel.

3. See also Brooks 1999, 67–68.
4. In another article, Levine (1995) argues that the liberationist church failed to focus on the "middle ground" of organization and coalition building (128).

Studies of the "low phase" in movement cycles suggest that social movement activism can have enduring social effects even in decline. Indeed, it is
in the down phase that much of the hard work of building and maintaining
civil society occurs, as activists reassess their goals and strategies and—if
they are successful—perhaps find new ways to maintain networks and solidarity. What Levine and Stoll (1997) call the daily "challenge of renewing
organizations and making them work effectively for the community" is
precisely the work of maintaining social movements through the "doldrums"
(65).[5] That is why we argue that looking at the activists and their current
practices—whether and how they are performing this work of maintenance—
is the key to evaluating the success or failure of their earlier wave of activism.
To elucidate this argument, we first must suggest briefly that the activism
accompanying redemocratization in both countries was part of a protest
cycle. In fact, we would argue that the base communities and their activists
provide a central piece of evidence that defines the redemocratization mobilizations as the peak of a movement cycle.

The Redemocratization Cycle and Base Communities

As Patricia Hipsher (1998) notes, "In Latin America, cycles of democratization have generated cycles of protest" (154). We agree with her and Salvador
Sandoval (1998) that Chile (1983–87) and Brazil (1977–89) constitute recognizable cycles of peak protest, while the current period is one of decline.[6]
These cycles are characterized by early mobilization in response to limited
political openings by the regime, the emergence of new actors, the generation
of widespread mobilization and protest, and a subsequent decline with the
reemergence of party politics. Protest cycles typically begin with the "usual
suspects," such as students and labor unions, but a true cycle is characterized
by its pervasiveness, as a wide spectrum of unexpected social actors take the
opportunity to organize, mobilize, and join in the protest. New actors and
new innovations in organization typify the upward phase of a movement
protest cycle (Tarrow 1998, 142).

---

5. One of the earliest sources of this idea, and in particular the source of the term "doldrums," is Rupp
and Taylor 1987.

6. We use Sandoval's periodization for Brazil, because his longer time frame includes both union and
social-movement activism and is thus more relevant to our study. Hipsher (1998) concentrates on labor
union protest. See Sandoval 1998.

The emergence of the very groups we are studying suggests, in part, that both the Brazilian and Chilean redemocratization processes fit this description. In both countries, as expected, many of the initial protests against military rule came from the normal sources of political protest. Brazilian trade unions (as early as 1968) and students were among the first to protest, for example, even before the initiation of what eventually came to be known as the *abertura,* or "opening" (Skidmore and Smith 2001, 170). Union activism and the creation of the "new sindicalism" typified the protests of the late 1970s in Brazil. Protest in Chile gathered momentum in 1983 after the copper workers' union called for a national day of protest (Hipsher 1998, 158). However, the most remarkable thing about the height of the protest cycles in both countries was the presence of "unusual" suspects, especially church-based groups and women's groups (sometimes the same thing).

The church's vital role in both protecting and organizing opposition to military rule marked a significant and surprising departure from its previous mode of elite accommodation and institutional politics. The church appeared to have fundamentally and irrevocably changed its relationship with the state and society. Hierarchies throughout Latin America declared themselves to be "the voice of the voiceless" living under authoritarian conditions. Given the church's declared "preferential option for the poor," the Latin American Catholic episcopates seemed prepared to serve as bastions of democratic civil society for those still remaining outside formally democratic institutions. National bishops' councils such as those in Brazil and Chile that publicly supported democratic transitions legitimated widespread popular mobilization against military rule by making individuals' private religious identity consistent with their political and economic interests. Even more important, the church's *organizational* contributions to the opposition movement (from protection of grassroots groups to the creation of national networks for channeling international aid, training, and material support to opposition groups) were critical to the creation of opposition social movements.

In Brazil, outspoken leaders such as Cardinal Arns of São Paulo led civil society's challenge of the military's human rights abuses. The São Paulo church also provided vital resources for the development of the independent trade union movement, and eventually, its activists played a key role in creating the Workers' Party (PT). Chileans commonly credited the church's prophetic role with helping to transform historical partisan rigidity, leading to the ability of opposition parties from the left and center to ally and subsequently oust the military from power.

> What happened in 1973? . . . In the first place, it produced a much
> more real and less prejudiced rapprochement . . . between many
> church people and all levels and people of the left, of whatever
> party, Christians or not—with flesh-and-bones people [who were]
> suffering, persecuted, and repressed. . . . People on the left who
> before had little knowledge of the church have been drawn to it and
> have moved toward it. . . . On the other hand, a very important
> nucleus of people within the church came to understand that there
> is a wide range of thoughts and perspectives on the left, that things
> are not so monolithic and that, therefore, there is a strong possibility
> of being a good Catholic and a leftist. (Llona 1988, 199)

The emergence of the church and church-based lay activists was one sign
that protest was developing toward the peak of a cycle, spilling over from
the usual suspects to encompass new groups.

Church activism also overlapped with the mobilization of other unexpected
groups in the protest cycle: the poor and women. The church's grassroots
organizations were surprisingly effective in mobilizing poor women, whom
many would have considered unlikely at best to participate in social struggles.
According to one Chilean study, women constituted approximately 80 percent
of the leadership in the new, grassroots self-help and community survival
organizations born under the dictatorship (Hardy 1987, 162). They made
up anywhere from 55 to 90 percent of the membership of Brazil's small
Christian communities (Drogus 1997, 2). Women filled the groups' ranks
and leadership positions in part because their function was consistent with
traditional spheres of women's responsibilities: family survival and community work. According to Chilean Rebecca Rebolledo:

> In general, women always have been active in this country. What
> happens is that in certain historical periods they gain notoriety. The
> whole issue of human rights during the dictatorship was organized
> by women; they are the ones who made the denunciations, they are
> the ones who mobilized. The majority of the executed and detained-
> disappeared were men. So, it was their surviving women who raised
> the issue of human rights. It is not an accident that women were
> leaders in that. . . . We women always take on the identity of ser-
> vant . . . but during that time, there was a general identity and the
> women's struggle started to have some advances.

Similarly, women activists from the base communities turn out to be the backbone of many of the "revindication" movements for health care, education, and so on that are often analyzed as "grassroots women's movements" (Alvarez 1990, Machado 1993). The same female base community members could be understood simultaneously as part of "church movements" and part of the broader "feminist movement"—both unexpected actors mobilized at the crest of movement activism.

Further, the base communities exemplify a second characteristic of protest cycles: organizational innovation. As explained in more detail in Chapter 3, the communities were innovative within the church. Lay-led and emphasizing consciousness-raising based on teachings in the Bible, they departed substantially from traditional, sacramental practices. The idea of organizing the poor in solidarity networks within neighborhoods and of establishing these as autonomously of parties and patrons as possible was also substantially new in the larger societies, characterized as they were by tight partisan affiliations (Chile) or patron-client politics (Brazil) (Gay 1994). The many organizational spinoffs of the base communities—from soup kitchens to collective purchasing, from human rights groups to petition drives and demonstrations for day care—were also innovations, particularly for the newly mobilized women actors who led them.

The level and amount of protest typically intensify and then gradually decline during a protest cycle. Again, this characterizes the Brazilian and Chilean experiences. Hipsher (1998) demonstrates that the number and size of protest events in Chile follow a clear cyclical pattern between 1983 and 1987 (162–63). Similarly, Sandoval (1998) suggests four phases in Brazil's redemocratization, with social movement protest gradually increasing, waning, then gathering strength and waning again. Ana Maria Doimo (1995) broadens this argument considerably by showing that multiple movements in Brazil that were centered on disparate demands followed a common cycle of intensification and decline from the late 1970s to the mid-1980s.

Thus, the very existence and activism of the base communities lends credence to the view that Chilean and Brazilian redemocratization can be considered as cycles of protest in two important ways. First, they themselves exemplify the idea of "conflict across the social system" and "diffusion of collective action from more mobilized to less mobilized sectors" (Tarrow 1998, 142). Second, their solidarity networks and participation in movements with multiple demands (especially in Brazil) contributed to the intensification of protest in terms of numbers and events at the apex of the cycle, as well as constituting some of the characteristic new forms of organization. Base communities and their attendant movements were integral to and characteristic of the protests of the redemocratization cycle. Indeed, Judith Adler Hellman (1997) lists them along with urban popular movements and local self-help organizations (with which they often overlapped) as hallmarks of social movement activism in this period (14).

Cycles, Invisibility, and Movement Maintenance

Understanding our respondents' activism as part of a movement cycle leads us to ask whether the current period might be interpreted differently, and perhaps less pessimistically. Since movement cycles necessarily wane, the current invisibility of social movements does not necessarily mean either the failure of earlier movements or the absence of a significant, independent civil society. Instead, it indicates an expected and predictable downturn, a period in which earlier political openings have closed for various reasons (neoliberalism, fatigue, partisan politics, loss of church support), and one in which the work of maintaining movement links and building new networks may be moving forward. Responding to these changed political opportunities, activists and their movements may desist—but it is also possible that they find new ways and means with which to maintain an activist presence and build on earlier activism. Although less visible than street demonstrations, such effects nonetheless form the basis for potential future activism—the infrastructure of civil society (Tarrow 1998, 165).[7]

Some of the effects of activism are biographical, as Doug McAdam (1999) argues.[8] Like McAdam, we are interested in understanding how movement participation affects participants' future lives, potentially moving them in directions that would not otherwise have been predicted, had they not engaged in activism. We also share McAdam's interest in understanding how activism changes in the wake of movement decline. Thus, we ask not only whether these women continue to be active, but also what form that

7. Similarly, we could conceptualize this period in terms of what Melucci (1996) calls "latency." He argues that while much social movement theory has concentrated on visible protest, movements are also present in the decentralized networks of everyday life, particularly as these contribute to building solidarity and identity.

8. Other examples of research on the aftermath of activism in the United States include Fendrich 1993, McAdam 1989, and Rogers 1993.

activism takes, how they and their movements have responded to changing political contexts and opportunities. As Sarah Brooks (1999) argues, an absence of specifically social movement activism does not imply an absence of activism altogether. Rather, as times—and activists—change, activists must adjust their desire for political change to fit new forms and venues of activism (79).[9] Of course, as Bert Klandermans (1994) demonstrates with regard to the Dutch peace movement, some activists stay, some desist, and others move on to other political issues, often for different personal reasons. We examine who stays and who leaves in Brazil and Chile and we compare the trends across the two countries. To the extent that we find pockets of individual empowerment and persistence, as well as activism in new venues, we can conclude that earlier activism has had an important effect on marginalized groups in civil society. Building on McAdam's (1999) study of American activists, we also look for new forms of political engagement (local party politics, for example) and professional work that is consistent with the activist experience (121).

We are also concerned with activists' ability to move beyond personal commitment to maintain their movements' base in some way in a period of diminished political opportunity. Most studies of movement maintenance have focused on the United States, but they can provide some clues on where to look to discover if and how base communities and activists are adapting to movement decline. First, we can, as Christian Smith (1996a) suggests, look at the institutional church itself. Suzanne Staggenborg (1998) argues that movements must be rooted in an institution to survive a movement cycle (187). In Chapters 3 and 4, we look at the history of the church in Chile and Brazil, and its relationship with the base communities from the activists' perspective. Unfortunately, in neither country has the church proved a reliable institutional base for activists or their movements, although the Brazilian church seems to be more successful in fostering and maintaining some institutional space for base communities and their activists.

In the absence of a strong institutional home or the professionalization of the movement, however, entities that Aldon Morris (1984) calls "movement halfway houses"—organizations without a mass base—may still exist. In the U.S. civil rights movement, these halfway houses were not movement orga-

9. Brooks (1999) argues specifically that changes in political context mean that activists must adopt new methods. We do not investigate or validate that conclusion, but we do share the concern with looking at how activists persist and act on their commitments in new ways.

nizations like the National Organization for the Advancement of Colored People (NAACP) or Southern Christian Leadership Conference per se. Instead, they were the Highlander Folk School and other "citizenship" schools that were started specifically to train activists and organized separately from the old institutional movement hosts (Morris 1984). As Zald and McCarthy (1984) point out, halfway houses may preserve movement ideas, practices, and traditions and may be more capable than movements of surviving the fluctuations of movement cycles (74). Thus, the church itself may not be the only keeper of the base community flame. We should determine whether and what kind of alternative organizations the activists participate in and may even have started because these may serve as movement halfway houses.

Similarly, Verta Taylor (1997) has argued that the U.S. women's movement persisted in the 1950s through "abeyance structures." Abeyance structures, like halfway houses, have small memberships and do little overt protesting. Nonetheless, they prove important to maintaining activist networks, collective identities, and repertoires of strategies and tactics. To the extent that grassroots activists from the base communities now participate in other organizations that share or build on their earlier activist identity, they may be building such abeyance structures in their respective countries.

Other studies suggest that we should also be looking for adaptation within the base communities and among the activists themselves. For example, Staggenborg (1998) found that women's organizations maintained themselves in part by taking on more cultural or identity-building activities and by decentralizing (187). Fitzsimmons also suggests that movement leaders may reorient a movement's focus toward more local issues, and even toward more personal, educational approaches (Fitzsimmons 2000a, 22–23). Educational groups, support groups, and organizations that provide services in health clinics or offer legal aid—though less politically satisfying to activists—can all be vehicles enabling movements to survive through the downturn in a movement cycle. Thus, we need to know what kinds of activities our activists are engaging in along these lines and whether they perceive them as a means to maintain and build their movements.

Finally, movement maintenance may involve building and expanding networks and potential bases of support. This may involve defining new, broader goals to attract followers from a population larger than that on which the earlier movement was based (23). It may also require the creation and maintenance of horizontal networks among such groups. McAdam (1988) argues that "by sustaining political organizations and maintaining links to others, the [activists] are preserving the social contexts out of which movements have typically emerged" (237). Similarly, a number of authors follow Alberto Melucci (1996) in believing that submerged or invisible networks play a key role in developing identity and solidarity during periods of movement latency (Mueller 1994, 237–38; Johnston, Larana, and Gusfield 1994, 24–25).

For Melucci (1996), networks are particularly important because movements are now often decentralized, highly fragmented, and segmented. They may join groups with quite distinct day-to-day identities and concerns. These often largely autonomous groups need the structure of networks in order to maintain contact and share information. In a "hidden or latent" structure, networks of groups maintain solidarity and contact that preserves a movement, even in the absence of a visible, more traditional organizational structure (113–15). This networking structure allows each group to maintain internal cohesion in a way a larger organization could not, yet it also facilitates the continued contact that may allow the relatively autonomous groups to engage collectively in visible protest again (116).

The emphasis many researchers now place on networking as part of movement maintenance seems particularly apt for our case. Increasingly, observers of Latin American civil society are sounding a call for the creation and maintenance of networks. Hellman (1997) quotes a grassroots movement leader who believes such linkages are necessary to avoid competitiveness and parochialism among local groups. She concludes that movements can only realize their potential "when they manage to ally with others in a wider political organization—or even, a political party" (18; see also Calderon et al. 1992, 23, 26). Similarly, writing of women's movements, Craske (1999) notes, "The success of the social movements indicates the potential of grassroots organizations, but their weaknesses highlight the need for the continued engagement in negotiations to form alliances" (136). Levine and Stoll (1997) contemplate the lengthy process and difficulty of creating deeply rooted civil societies: "Constructing power in civil society is also an immense project, and time alone will not do the job. Success requires sustained effort, with attention not only to the building of networks but also to the whole process of putting together and maintaining linkages among levels" (78). Our interviews focused on this process of network and alliance building, arguably the most difficult and complex task in a period of movement decline. While we expected to see individual women maintaining their activism in various forms, we were less certain what kinds of movement maintenance and network building we would find. Yet such network building and maintenance would be crucial to any claim that the activists are building civil society in this period of movement "doldrums."

We were particularly interested in looking at whether the activists were finding and making contact with potential allies in the church, in their neighborhoods (with Pentecostal neighbors), and in feminist organizations that have a history of working with grassroots women's groups. In addition to seeking evidence of such network building, we explored the women's attitudes toward such work and its feasibility. We were interested in knowing with what other groups they believed they might find common cause and whether they believed it was feasible to overcome the dense but segregated networks of groups divided by religion and class to form a broader, united front. Such connections would be a sign of the kind of segmented networks that Melucci emphasizes, and would be consistent with the multifaceted nature of the base communities themselves.

Armed with these insights from social movement theory, we argue that assessing the impact of base communities requires going to the grass roots rather than simply looking at the role of the church. The church has not proved a hospitable movement host in either Brazil or Chile in the long run, but this is not surprising. Its declining political commitment—and perhaps even relevance—is part and parcel of the decline in the structure of political opportunity for all social movements, and base communities in particular, that followed redemocratization. Changed political opportunities and cyclical decline, however, do not necessarily spell the end of social movements. They have certainly left a legacy in terms of individual empowerment. Social movement theory leads us to look to individual activists to see whether they have found or built abeyance structures and networks outside the base communities as well.

Conclusion

Many of the day-to-day concerns facing Brazilian and Chilean women are not substantially different from the challenges they confronted during the dictatorships. However, the conditions under which women meet adversity, and, therefore, their strategies, are different. During the dictatorships, both Brazilian and Chilean women worked in visible, contentious popular movements based in the church. Now, for reasons we explain in subsequent chapters, such visible movement activism seems less viable. These activists' stories make clear, however, that they did not simply "go home," leaving the dramatic participatory experiences of the 1980s with no lasting effect. On the contrary, the base communities and popular movements of the 1980s have had lasting—if currently less evident—effects on individuals and societies that may be important in the longer term.

First, activism had a profound impact on the individuals involved. These women still feel empowered by their earlier activism and have a clear sense of the community problems they want to address. Second, the earlier cycle of movement activism created a base of people and, in some cases, organizations in civil society that can potentially reconnect in a new resurgence of movement activism should a political opening appear. Finally, although they are eloquent about new obstacles to mobilization, many of the women continue to weave the basis for a strengthened civil society through a variety of new organizing activities concerned now with problems of drugs, poverty, street children, or other issues. New conditions, however, require new strategies. As Cida Lima says: "We're living in a phase of technology, of much unemployment . . . it's globalization and that whole situation out there. So we have to think in a different way, not do things as we did them in the past. The times are different and today is a different moment." We address what those strategies might be in the final chapters of the book, where we focus on both actual and potential networks.

The women we interviewed convinced us that the optimistic story of the base communities was, in many respects, accurately told. Along with the women we interviewed, we see the current low ebb of mobilization not as a proof of failure, but as part of a downward trend in movement activism during which new goals and strategies must be mapped out to lay the basis for future activism. These women did not just go home in defeat; rather, they continue to struggle to seek those new and future directions, to keep the basis of movement solidarity alive in new ways. Their earlier experiences convinced them of the importance of activism and of collective action by the poor. We hope that this book will not only document the remarkable past and achievements of these grassroots activists, but also help to explain their strengths and weaknesses and contribute to an understanding of how the collective empowerment they continue to seek might be achieved in the future.

T H R E E

Resurrecting Civil Society:
Christian Base Communities Under Military Rule

I began really in Pernambuco, in the evangelization movement of [the 19]70s, dom Hélder's movement. During all that time of repression, the place where people mobilized, where people grouped together, was in the church.

— MARIA JOSÉ, BRAZIL

We were very afraid, but people came [to the church] out of necessity. Later, representatives of the Vicaría de Solidaridad came to conduct weekly analyses of the situation with us. That's how we began to overcome the fear.

— AURORA HERNÁNDEZ, CHILE

The Catholic Church was uniquely positioned to play a crucial role in the resurrection of civil society and the upsurge of protest that accompanied redemocratization in Brazil and Chile. Although other sources of opposition, besides the church, existed, many of these, such as independent unions, in fact depended on church support and protection. Moreover, none had the reach, legitimacy, or protected status that enabled the church to mobilize people from many walks of life. Thus, from the perspective of most ordinary citizens in poor urban areas, it could seem, as Neide says, that "the CEBs were the only movement that was really resistant, that resisted the dictatorship." The story of the grassroots women activists in this book begins in the church, though in many cases that baptism of fire in the base communities carried them well beyond the church to a political involvement that remains vibrant today. Indeed, to understand their current activities and options for keeping activism alive, we must begin with the context of the base communities in which they first organized.

The church's key role in mobilizing anti-regime protest seems surprising because of its historical position as an ally of ruling elites and source of legitimation for the state through religion. It is less surprising, however, when we recall that religion is often an important pillar of an independent, even confrontational, civil society. Religious identity as a child of God in a community of believers is an empowering self-conception; under conditions of dictatorship, such a discourse transcends personal empowerment and becomes crucial to political resistance (Alvarez 1998).[1] Liberation theology is only the most recent

---

1. Irma Parraquez remembers that "we learned that God is present even in such dire situations. The situation helped us to know God in this way, which was different from the way I was taught in the countryside.

Latin American movement to legitimize rebellious behavior through religious values and symbols.

The truly novel aspect of the military era is the degree to which the church put its extensive institutional resources at the service of this liberationist project. Once it had done so, however, it became a formidable agent of mobilization. Although slower than more decentralized organizations to engage in mobilization for social change, episcopal structures such as the Catholic Church are particularly well suited to generating social movements (McCarthy and Zald 1987, 72). Their potential impact is great because they powerfully convey values and beliefs and because they have a preexisting, far-reaching infrastructure with which to nurture nascent movements (69–70).

Popular mobilization in Brazil and Chile relied on both these factors, as Daniel Levine (1986) has argued. The church, particularly the base communities, nurtured new egalitarian, participatory values (14). It also offered institutional resources to create linkages within local communities and provide "concrete material and organizational links to other levels to form a collection of ladders reaching up and out from the group to other arenas and levels of institutional life" (1992, 334, 53). "This capacity to mediate between everyday life and big structures," as Levine (1992) asserts, "is crucial to whatever possible impact liberation theology may have, now or in the future" (53).

Our activists' recollections, as well the institutional histories that are available, allow us to paint a portrait of the ways in which each church's base communities contributed both values and resources, including network building, to the development of political protest. The women's stories suggest that the Chilean and Brazilian churches developed related, but somewhat different, models of how to foster political liberation among the poor. Both models contributed to the development of activists and to the protest cycles in their respective countries. They may have different long-term consequences, however, for the activists' ability to maintain and construct civil society in the current down phase of mobilization and protest.

Base Communities: Two Models of Facilitating Protest

Scholars will probably continue to debate the origins of the various churches' decisions to offer institutional resources to the liberationist project for a long

---

My mother was a very religious person who taught us that God was way up there and we had to honor him. Now I know that we honor him through our lives."

time to come. By now, however, many factors are well known.[2] Since we wish to explore how this change contributed to the redemocratization protest cycle rather than debate the precise origins of the change, for our purposes it is sufficient to recall the key factors that are widely recognized.

Social changes in the 1950s in both countries raised new concerns about rural poverty and urbanization among the clergy. Vatican II (1960–63) encouraged more openness to the world, to political action and analysis, and to lay participation. Inspired by this and by the worker-priest movement, Latin American progressives moved to disassociate the church from its traditional identification with elites. Particularly in Brazil and Chile, progressive priests and bishops began to publicly condemn social and economic injustice, using liberation theology as a point of departure for denouncing the "structural sins" of dependent capitalism. Liberationists argued that in Latin America, Christianity required solidarity with the poor and their legitimate aspiration for freedom from economic, political, and social oppression. The consensus of the 1968 meeting of the Latin American Episcopal Conference (CELAM) in Medellín, Colombia, committed the church to a "preferential option for the poor," giving impetus to these trends.

At Medellín, the bishops also adopted a pastoral strategy based on the existence of small groups that would combine worship, Bible study, and a commitment to serving the communities' social needs. They called these neighborhood-based religious groups "base Christian communities" or "base ecclesial communities" (CEBs). Although the bishops intended the communities to be part of the parish structure, their actual relationship with church authority varied widely across countries, dioceses, and parishes, depending in part on the diocesan bishop and local priest. Their nature and purposes— whether liberationist or not—differed significantly as well. In fact, the small-community model proved attractive to conservative church leaders as well as to liberationists.

Daniel Levine (1992) identifies three broad types of base communities, dissimilar in their attitudes toward and objectives for members' political and religious beliefs; the outcome they sought for members' behavior; and their relationship to official church structures. At one extreme, liberationists saw the base communities as the "praxis" of liberation theology, a place for the Christian poor to gain political consciousness and empowerment. This

---

2. See, for example, B. Smith 1982; Mainwaring 1986; Hewitt 1991; Levine 1992; Gill 1998. We will not enter into the debate over the origins of the "preferential option for the poor," but the interested reader can consult these and numerous other sources.

"radical ideal" embraced the idea of the church as the "people of God," saw popular religion as the "religion of the oppressed" (the essence of liberation theology), and sought to promote confrontational political action both locally and nationally. At the other extreme, "conservative base communities" eschewed politics, seeking instead to bring the poor to a more orthodox Catholicism and into a closer relationship with the church. Such communities' goals for members' behavior focused on sacramental rather than political action. Levine describes both radical and conservative CEBs as closely linked to official church structures. In between, the "sociocultural" model, closer to the radicals than the conservatives, embraced much of liberationist language and goals. These groups welcomed expressions of popular piety more warmly. They focused more on local politics and engaged in less confrontational political action. They aimed to promote lay leaders' autonomy and to be more independent of the church's formal structures (47–48). All three types of base communities coexisted, in some cases locally as well as nationally, often depending on specific local personnel and issues.[3] The same community might even change direction when a new bishop, bringing a new group of pastoral agents with a different orientation, replaced an earlier one.[4]

The Chilean church distinguished between types of groups by use of linguistic measures. Confusingly, however, in Chile the term *CEB* is commonly used for traditional, sacramental groups that are closely associated with the traditional, hierarchical church. For grassroots Christian communities that approximate the Medellín ideal, Chileans use the term *CCP*. Elena Berger says that "the *comunidades eclesiales de base* (CEBs) were much more developed in Brazil than in Chile. Here, what are known as CEBs often were tied closely to the parishes and were controlled by the priest. . . . Other communities . . . met in homes or met in the parish building . . . but were not controlled by the parish. They were simply called 'base communities' [or] 'comunidades cristianas populares' (CCPs) because they were located in the working class sector and depended on lay leadership. Today they are generally known as parish communities."[5] As Chile's hierarchy has become more conservative it has

3. Levine also notes that "from ground level," what people tended to see was a variety of "options" in the form of CEBs they might adopt, not a monolithic structure (48).

4. W. E. Hewitt (1991), for example, points out the weight of church structures in determining much about the CEBs and notes the importance of pastoral workers in determining their political orientation (58).

5. Sonia Bravo, executive director of the Coordinadora de Comunidades Populares from 1988 to 1991, confirms the use of the terms *parish community* or *popular Christian community* (CCP) for liberationist base communities.

increasingly favored the term "CEB," making it a politically charged label among former grassroots Catholic activists. For example, in the 1980s, archbishop of Santiago Carlos Oviedo created a new coordinating body for all parish-level groups, including CCPs, which he tellingly called "Christian ecclesial communities" (CEBs). The purpose of the new coordinating body was to subordinate all grassroots groups to the church hierarchy's authority. Not surprisingly, the new, national structure was strongly opposed by progressives in the church, including the grassroots activists interviewed for this study.

In contrast, Brazilians pervasively used the term CEB for small subparish groups, but recognized that not all self-styled "CEBs" were necessarily socially or politically engaged (Drogus 1997, 35). Ilda, for example, explained that while her CEB's preoccupation during military rule was "consciousness-raising about the political moment," "not all CEBs" shared this view. Several women held so strongly to the ideal of CEBs as socially transformative groups that they did not apply the term *CEB* to their own group because "it did not quite achieve" that standard. Or, like Emerenciana, they might see the same group as a CEB or not, depending on its political engagement at a given time. She says of her own group: "At that time [under the military], it was [a CEB]. The change two years ago changed the church a lot. [Before,] it was the work of the CEBs."[6] As in Chile, church officials in many areas in Brazil use CEBs to designate all subparish groups, including quite conservative or strictly sacramental ones. Lay activists, however, view those that come closer to the sociocultural or radical models as the "real" thing.

Because of these differences in terminology, we refer to both Brazilian and Chilean groups simply as *base communities*.[7] Both Chileans and Brazilians most likely came from a mix of sociocultural and radical communities. Unfortunately, our interviews do not allow us to distinguish individual communities, given the limited number of interviews from any particular community. The interviews clearly show, however, that none of the women came from a "conservative" community.

---

6. Some Chilean activists share the Brazilians' more exacting standard for "Christian base communities." Chilean Aurora Hernández laments that "the Christian base communities do not exist anymore. There is a certain confusion about the word. In the past, it meant a community with a social commitment. Today, Christian community just means all the people who go to mass. . . . There are not real base communities anymore. Before the communities called meetings and the priests attended like the rest of the people. Today, the priest has to approve everything."

7. We use this term in our text. Other authors may use *CEB,* as do our respondents, in places.

They further indicate that, despite variations, each country overall adhered to a distinctive base community model.[8] For Levine (1992), Chilean base communities in the 1970s followed the "radical ideal," while Brazil represented the "socio-cultural transformation" model. As the women described their base communities' membership, political activities, location, and structure, they confirmed Levine's characterization of the differences between these two models as well as their association with each country.

Brazil: Sociocultural Communities and Popular Movements

Many Brazilian pastoral workers, such as the ones described by women from São Paulo's Zona Leste, embraced the sociocultural model of base communities. Brazilians called this tendency "basismo," putting an emphasis on the inherent value and political potential of popular piety and on a rejection of "outside" intervention and manipulation by bourgeois reformers, especially in the camp of partisan political activists. Endorsed by Brazil's leading progressives, among them Leonardo Boff, this model dictated the location of many base communities in Brazil's rural areas and urban peripheries, as well as their size, membership, and activities. It also influenced the national church's strategy of encouraging "popular movements."

In the urban areas, pastoral agents organized subparish groups, which created an associational network much denser than that of the parishes. One parish typically housed numerous base communities. These groups needed first to find locations closer to the far-flung parish neighborhoods they served.[9] In many cases, Brazilian base communities initially operated out of individuals' homes, moving later to cement-block community centers or

8. We do not wish to overemphasize the homogeneity of the base communities within national churches. On the contrary, base communities varied enormously within cities, dioceses, and countries. As we note, Brazilian and Chilean women in our sample no doubt came from a variety of base community types, irrespective of nationality. Nonetheless, we believe that it is useful to conceptualize an overall climate or approach within each national church, and we argue that the ethos of the national church in Chile was closer to the radical model, while the Brazilian ethos (exemplified in, among other things, the writings of highly visible theologians such as Leonardo and Clodovis Boff and Frei Betto) was closer to a sociocultural model.

9. In São Paulo, for example, many of our interviewees come from a single parish that at one point in the 1980s boasted more than thirty base communities (Drogus 1997). At the same time, however, such density was not necessarily characteristic of the whole urban periphery in a particular metropolitan area. Depending on the orientation of the local auxiliary bishop and pastoral agents, for example, some poor regions of São Paulo had very few base communities.

"churches" built by local groups themselves. These churches held religious services led by lay ministers and occasionally by one of the parish priests. They were also the hub of other activities, from meetings of subgroups within the communities, to literacy classes, festivals and bazaars.

Liberation theologians considered a small, intimate base community the ideal setting in which to foster community and mobilization, and most Brazilian women remember their communities as close-knit groups. Two-thirds of Brazilian women recalled their communities having, at their peak, fewer than one hundred members. Half said that they had fewer than fifty members. In some communities, such as Cida Morais's in the Zona Leste of São Paulo, much larger groups might appear for Sunday services, especially if the priest officiated (Drogus 1992). To the activists, however, the true membership of the community seems to have consisted of the smaller core group that organized most activities. Cida, for example, remembers "thirty or forty" people participating.[10]

Adding to its small size, the homogeneity of the membership may have only reinforced Brazilian activists' sense of being part of an intimate community. In keeping with the sociocultural model, Brazilian pastoral agents encouraged laypeople to form the core group of communities and hoped gradually to lead them (or allow them to evolve) toward a new religious and political identity. As a result, most Brazilian base communities drew members primarily from among practicing Catholics, particularly poor Catholic women whose faith had been developed in the rural interior of Brazil (Drogus 1997, 79). Several women mentioned having been Daughters of Mary or participating in similar traditional religious groups earlier. In contrast, none came to the base communities from previous political experience, although some had engaged in the more politicized Workers' Pastoral, a church group that operated in parallel with the base communities. These women had in common not only their neighborhoods and socioeconomic status, but also their background of practicing Catholicism and their status as political novices.

Despite the wariness of Brazilian pastoral agents and local leaders toward politicization by *partisan* activists, Brazilian base communities were not apolitical.[11] In fact, base communities protected and fostered critical political

---

10. This seems consistent with Hewitt's finding of average membership of eighteen, in 1988, and twenty-two, in 1984, for São Paulo (Hewitt 1991, 41–42).

11. It is important to note that Brazilian authorities regarded base communities with suspicion. Nonetheless, only two women, both from Rio de Janeiro (Maria José and Neide do Carmo) mentioned the

discussion, especially in the 1970s prior to the political liberalization. As Neide do Carmo recalls:

> In Volta Redonda during the national security era it was very diffi-
> cult. We worked with visits in houses and as much as possible we
> oriented people. But everything was very much under surveillance.
> There were things we didn't perceive. I went with a guy and I didn't
> know he was a federal agent. So people got close to someone who
> was in the environment so they could infiltrate it . . . the preoccu-
> pation was with orienting people, but people were really afraid.
> When the police came they really beat people up, especially because
> in a National Security area things are very complicated. . . . At that
> time it was just discussion because it was before *abertura* and people
> were afraid.

Participation in these discussions, however, was on the part of mostly political neophytes, such as Neide, or trusted grassroots unions activists who
might themselves have begun political activism in the church. The few
well-known leftist activists who "went underground" in Brazilian base communities became causes célèbres, reinforcing the preoccupation of priests
and bishops with making sure that party activists did not "take over" or
"infiltrate" the base communities. Nevertheless, overall, it seems clear that
Brazilian party and non-party-political activists did not participate (or go
underground) in the base communities to a significant extent.

Brazilian women tended to see their groups' contribution as, rather than
facilitating exposure to more experienced political activists, bringing together
those who might not, in the anonymous urban peripheries, know one
another intimately or have enough trust to discuss politics (Doimo 1995).
As Maria Edwiges says, "People didn't have the right to speak, people were
repressed, and there was a place where people had a very similar identity, so
we felt stronger as a group, as people. We felt the force of knowing that we
were going to conquer something greater." These were places primarily for
learning and building, and perhaps that is why even the mothers' club or
the community bazaar could be so important. As Maria do Socorro recalls: "I
joined the group of women where the priest gave talks teaching us to under-

---

degree to which the church seemed to offer a "safe haven" and the need they felt, even there, to be on guard
against the repressive forces of the state.

stand politics, to read a paper, see what was behind the news, the political situation of the time. . . . At the time I joined, I was a person completely out of it, then he gave us books to read."

Perhaps because the women were political novices, the sociocultural base communities emphasized consciousness-raising and concrete, local solidarity work. Brazilian women recalled consciousness-raising going hand in hand with activism. As Célia recalls, "The [base communities] really fought a lot against the military regime, and principally for the consciousness-raising of the population." Maria Edwiges adds: "I think the [base communities] were focused on raising people's consciousness of their rights with a simple language, their conquest of their rights." Twenty-two women (88 percent) recalled their groups emphasizing religious and political reflection in light of liberation theology, while nineteen (71 percent) said that their communities engaged in some form of social or political mobilization.[12]

Consciousness-raising was central to other activities in which the women engaged. For example, nearly all the women mentioned craft or other production workshops as a hallmark of the communities' mothers' clubs. Sewing, knitting, painting on fabric—mothers' groups taught all these income-supplementing skills to poor women, and some tried to help them market their products. Activists, however, viewed these practices as incidental to their experience in the base communities. While these classes were desirable if they helped women meet economic needs, most of the organizers distinguished these groups from women's consciousness-raising groups. They themselves participated in the latter, which seem to have had the most influence on them. Many respondents from Rio, for example, distinguished politically oriented "women's groups" from the economically motivated "mothers' clubs." Some, such as Maria Melania, indicated that the "women's group" worked with the mothers' club to try to raise political consciousness. Where only one "mothers' club" existed, activists like Maria Antônia, Elza Valeria, Cida Lima, Célia, and Madalena second Ilda's assertion that the group engaged in "handicraft work, but the principal objective was women's formation and their social engagement." Neide do Carmo, who began her participation by teaching "cutting and sewing" to women in the 1970s,

12. Their recollections as activists may overstate the reality of base community practice. W. E. Hewitt found in 1988 that 45 percent of base communities engaged in consciousness-raising, 90 percent in reflection, and 55 percent in community action (Hewitt 1991, 45). It seems likely that our identifiable activists tended to emerge from the more politicized and politically active CEBs.

says: "And in that work I carry along the question of raising women's consciousness—of their rights, the situation they live in, to take themselves out of the 'I, me,' out of the four walls of the house and into participation." Craftwork and economic incentives were often simply a means to attract women. Only Ana Lima described contributing to women's income as the primary objective of handicraft work.

For Brazilian women, consciousness-raising led to a specific form of activism. It was neither the solidarity of local-production groups and soup kitchens, nor (except in brief flashes) the solidarity of engagement in national-level anti-regime protests. As repression diminished in the 1980s, women in the base communities began to define activism as protest to improve the situation in their neighborhoods. As Maria José recalls:

> I think at that time things were much more focused on neighborhood revindications. The strength here in São Paulo at that time of repression was the cost-of-living movement. It was very strong. [The movement] against poverty. Where the movement of the church got together, the strongest movement was cost of living. At a demonstration in the Praça da Sé there was a lot of repression, and we were all there. Where people got together a lot was through the neighborhood struggles. There were always meeting and assemblies, real reflection. . . . Public demonstrations were always a help. Here in São Paulo, the neighborhood movements always had greater reach, broader. It was never a thing of just one neighborhood. The focus was always Praça da Sé, the church in Sé.

The Brazilian interviewees recalled the locally based movements as a quintessential political feature of most of their base communities. This was the kind of participation that they hoped the focus on handicrafts in the mothers' clubs would generate, by attracting women to whom they could then pass on "information and orientation" (Maria do Socorro). In many areas, women's groups from the base communities spearheaded these neighborhood movements. Sofia Dias's community women's group fought for day care, as did many others in the Zona Leste of São Paulo. In Maria Antônia's community, a group of nine women made up the "social action" group, which was distinct from the mothers' club.

The neighborhood movements often did unite across geographic zones, and the church connections facilitated these contacts. The church also aided regional support for the strikers in the important ABC strikes in 1979, which many women from São Paulo recall (Hewitt 1991, 44). Moreover, base communities occasionally participated in larger national demonstrations, such as the protests for amnesty and for direct elections. They did not entirely eschew party politics. As we shall see, many members became active in the PT, a left party strongly linked to the popular movements. But this partisan identity grew out of the base communities. However, the series of neighborhood-based movements in which they participated—cost of living, day care, garbage, lighting, transport—defined the Brazilian women's experience, even if these were linked to movements in other areas. This focus on local-level politics and neighborhood mobilization, along with the other characteristics described above, places the Brazilian base communities as a group within the pattern of sociocultural CEBs.

These small, homogeneous groups, with their emphasis on consciousness-raising and social action, helped some of Brazil's least empowered citizens to develop a sense of political efficacy and the capacity to engage in political mobilization. As Cida Morais says: "At that time [the 1985 landless movement] I opened my eyes and saw that we had to fight for liberty. It was at that time that I began to see things differently. Before, I sat at home, the man's voice was everything. At times, what I disagreed with I cried about, but I thought I had to keep quiet and I saw that all the women acted like that. And not just women. Poor people had to keep their mouths shut." Helping people like Cida engage with political institutions and develop a sense of efficacy was one of the crucial ways in which the churches contributed to expanding the cycle of protest.

We do not wish to imply that because they succeeded in engaging women politically and even involving them in protests, the communities necessarily imbued them with any particular political outlook. The base communities were primarily religious, not political, and they brought together people of varying religious and political attitudes.[13] Moreover, members differed among themselves in their level of commitment to specific activities, and even in their interpretation of the political meaning of these activities.[14] This diversity means that we must be wary about attributing specific kinds of political motivations or consciousness to participants in base communities.

13. According to Vasquez (1997) and Drogus (1997), traditional charitable activities and traditional religious services continued alongside social mobilization and liberationist masses in most base communities.

14. Indeed, we discuss their current political affiliations and activism in Chapter 5. Other studies (Drogus 1997; Burdick 1993; Vasquez 1998) have noted that we must be cautious about interpreting the base communities' impact on individuals' political beliefs.

The social movements organized by base communities brought together conservative as well as more radical parishioners in movements that all could understand as being "for the common good" (Drogus 1997). Nonetheless, we can safely say that base communities played a critical role in generating protest activities, not by inculcating a specific political ideology or under-standing, but rather, simply by empowering individuals as citizens and fostering their political engagement and activism. Women activists most often defined this in terms of liberation from the confines of the home and traditional gender roles. Neide do Carmo, who has coordinated the mothers' clubs in her region since 1989, stresses the importance of her work for raising women's consciousness and "pulling them out of the house." The work has been important for her personally: "Now the question of growth, it was through [the work with women's groups] that the world opened up for me. The little world I lived in." By raising women's political consciousness and giving them a sense of efficacy and rights, the base communities played a key role in generating the redemocratization cycle of protest. In the women who had never before been politically active, the base communities found and created a reservoir of new activists who would swell the wave of protest.

Basismo and the sociocultural model of the base communities shaped the local emphases that created the formative personal experiences of Brazil's activists. As we shall see in the second half of this chapter, they also permeated critical sectors of the larger church and influenced church decisions that shaped the organizational context in which local activists carried out their activities.[15] Activists probably felt this context only indirectly at the time; it was perceived as the "glue" that brought neighborhood protest groups together in the Praça da Sé or at the city council. Of more importance was their daily experience of consciousness-raising and local organizing. These characteris-tically sociocultural activities differentiated their experiences from those of their Chilean counterparts.

Chile: Radical Communities, Popular Survival, and National Protest

The Chilean church also reached deeply into society during the military regime, fostering base communities and other forms of popular organizing

---

15. The church as a whole was not by any means *basista* or even liberationist. Strong pockets of conser-vatism persisted and may even have been numerically preponderant throughout the military regime. But *basismo* and liberation theology provided the dominant discourse during the protest cycle, and liberationists and their sympathizers created many of the organizational bases that supported the base communities.

among the poor. As in Brazil, the church was particularly concerned with the survival and organization of the poorer sectors of the population. As a result, there, too, base communities sprang up primarily in poor urban neighborhoods. Because they aimed to be smaller, more intimate subparish groups, the base communities in Chile also faced the task of finding new venues. They often operated out of individuals' homes or simply constructed wooden "chapels," built by the members. As in Brazil, these hosted many activities, not just religious services. In other ways, however, the Chilean base community experience at the local level differed from the Brazilian one. For poor women activists, both types of base communities provided a baptism into politics. The more radical Chilean model, however, seems to have produced differences in membership and activities at the local level, as well as a different articulation with national church structures.

Although more intimate than large, sprawling urban parishes, Chilean base communities appear to have been, on average, larger than their Brazilian counterparts. Almost three-quarters of Chilean respondents said their communities had one hundred or more members, and the remainder estimated membership at three hundred or more. In contrast, only one Brazilian claimed membership of three hundred or more people. These numbers may overstate the difference, because Chilean activists may be citing figures for attendance at religious services, while Brazilians may be counting only those who participated more intensively. Brazilian women nonetheless experienced and recalled their base communities as more intimate, and therefore closer to the liberationist ideal, than the Chileans did.

Chilean base community members also came from a wider range of religious and social backgrounds. This is partly because Chilean communities more often took in people who were already political activists. The 1973 Chilean military coup outlawed virtually all groups in civil society. As a result, many Chileans—including men and women who had never been active in the Catholic Church or were Marxists historically opposed to the church—turned to base communities as an organizational alternative. María Teresa Díaz recalls: "Prior to the coup, Villa Francia was home to a group of strong political leaders, members of the Socialist and Communist Parties. When their meeting places were closed off, the Christian community opened its doors to them. It was a safe place to meet, even though the police later raided the church building as well. At first the Christians and these political people clashed."

Similarly, Suzanne Leiser, a former nun who has lived in the Chilean municipality of Cerro Navia since 1970, describes the diversity within her local base community:

> After the coup, the church became a neutral ground where everyone who could not exist elsewhere felt sheltered. The nucleus of some organizations within the communities were people from leftist parties, who could not have an office of their own and whose homes might be raided. . . . Activities centered on health, food, and ways of expressing the need to bring the dictatorship to an end. . . . Everyone agreed on these things and there were no problems. Later when it became possible to do social-oriented work from other places, many people left.

In contrast to the Brazilian *basistas,* with their wariness of political activists, most Chilean bishops tolerated the increased autonomy and politicization of local base communities led by laypeople who espoused a variety of political and religious perspectives.[16]

Chileans recalled their communities as places that gathered the politicized and the political neophyte and that played a strong role in protecting those who might suffer political persecution. As in Brazil, many poor women in Chile first gained political consciousness through the base communities. However, the political protection and safe haven Chilean communities afforded to activists may have contributed to their apparently greater emphasis on solidarity over consciousness-raising. In contrast to women in Brazil, only 58 percent of Chilean women said their base community engaged in liberationist biblical reflection, while 88 percent cited enabling solidarity with national groups (such as political prisoners or families of the disappeared-detained) as a main function.

At the same time, the economic devastation wrought first by the military occupation and then by an unrelenting imposition of export-oriented, neoliberal

---

16. Several Chileans mentioned that they had been active prior to the coup in 1973 in either the Movimiento Obrero de Acción Católica (MOAC) or the Joventúd Obrero Catolico (JOC). Unlike most Latin American Catholic hierarchies, the progressive wing of the Chilean church had developed linkages with the working-class and union sectors since the 1950s. While not "liberationist" by today's standards, both the MOAC and JOC did provide a space within the Catholic Church in which *pobladores* could be both Catholic and political leftists. For example, the theological model "see, judge, act"—one legacy of organizations such as MOAC and JOC—may be the readiness with which the church was willing to cast its protective umbrella over grassroots partisans after the coup (Baeza Donoso 1985).

economic policies resulted in a collective search for community and personal survival. Thus, the Chilean women recall a dual emphasis on organizing local self-help groups and participating in national protests. Chilean women were much more likely than their Brazilian counterparts to mention artisan workshops (69 percent) or economic self-help efforts such as soup kitchens, food co-ops, and feeding centers (75 percent).

To meet their communities' economic and survival needs, Chilean base communities organized locally to form innumerable self-help groups to deal with specific local needs. For example, 75 percent of the women surveyed remember their base community organizing health clinics to deal with local medical needs, including emergency medical attention for inhabitants injured in military raids. Another 58 percent participated in child-care cooperatives that allowed women to work at paid employment. As we shall see, the church often supported these survival initiatives at a very high level and helped to coordinate and expand them. By the 1980s, Chilean leaders who had emerged from base communities were organizing in coalitions to share information and resources across a number of broad fronts.

Chilean women always recalled these economic activities, however, as coexistent and intertwined with broader political activities. Although they did engage in such specific local activities, they remember their solidarity work more as national mobilization in support of national goals than as the construction of broad coalitions aimed at local goals, which characterized Brazilian popular movements. They most often describe solidarity work as consciousness-raising and participation in national movements for human rights and democracy instead of efforts aimed at local policy changes. Juanita Riveros's memory of Mujeres de Chile (MUDECHI), a coalition of grassroots activists from across Santiago that grew out of the parish-level responses to community issues, confirms the more nationally focused Chilean experience: "MUDECHI was a citywide group that met in the parish or in our homes to talk about political problems and human rights. We did action to raise awareness and protested as women against the dictatorship. Most of us had husbands or children in prison and even some of us had been in jail. We informed the parish council once a week about our activities. We held a general assembly once a month in different parts of Santiago." Even local health groups became linked in participants' minds to the national anti-Pinochet struggle for democracy: "The health group is an example of how groups matured. People learned how to assist people because of poor attention in the public clinics. In the time of protests, the health groups helped people who were wounded by the military" (Ruth Saldías Monreal). Clotilde Silva Hernández recalls that although "from 1973 to 1980, the focus was survival," local activities soon "became focused on solidarity and denunciation."

Thus, Chilean women's activities and protests more closely fit the "radical" model of base communities. While both groups of women contributed to the waves of protest growing in their countries, the nature and forms of their protests—and of the protest movements that were growing—were different. Consistent with the radical model, Chilean women's protest combined with local work, but more often was exercised in national demonstrations in the capital city aimed at large questions such as human rights. In contrast, Brazilian women who were engaged in popular movements aimed their efforts toward making changes in their local contexts.

The common commitment by both Brazilian and Chilean women to link faith with action, however divergent their specific practices, gave base communities in both countries a key role in helping some of their least empowered citizens to develop a sense of political efficacy and the capacity to engage in political mobilization. Chilean Flor Gonzalez describes herself and others whom she knew at the time as "women who had no place even within their own homes" until they joined their base communities and felt empowered to speak out in the public domain. As in Brazil, however, this does not mean that all members shared a particular political perspective. In Chile's diverse base communities, tensions could be especially acute between more experienced political activists and "Christians." Mercedes Montoya Leiva, one of the early members of the Chilean Sebastian Acevedo Movement Against Torture, recollects that "there were always struggles between the social activists and the traditional laity. The lunchrooms [comedores] and charity work existed in the beginning years. Then the base community added the human rights committee and health groups, but they always lacked unity. One group came to accept a greater social commitment while the others always resisted social-political work." Similarly, Alicia Ubilla says: "The human rights committee began as a confrontational Anti-Repression Committee. When we realized that the name scared people, we changed it to a human rights committee so as to reach out to more people. We had ten to twelve people when it was called the Anti-Repression Committee. With the name change, we often had more than thirty people at our meetings." The base communities did not produce political uniformity, but they provided a venue for activists to find new allies. At least as important, they convinced some of those poorer, less-educated women for the first time that they, too, could engage in politics.

The Chilean women who joined the communities as activists looking for "cover" experienced them differently. Their change in consciousness often took a more spiritual direction. María Teresa, who described the diversity within Villa Francia's base communities, recalled: "Little by little, both groups of people [activists and Christians] experienced a transformation. The Christians became more political and the political people become more spiritual. It became one single large and complete community." While the political activists' spiritual transformation remains deeply significant for them personally, the politicization of members of the Christian community has deeper ramifications for the emergence of protest and for civil society's ability to build on that earlier experience during the down phase of a protest cycle. These were new and unexpected activists. To the extent that they carry on activism in the posttransition period, civil society is strengthened.

The local experience of base communities seems to have been quite different in Chile from what it was in Brazil. Communities were more politically and socioeconomically mixed, and even included some activists who were not, in fact, Catholic. Consciousness-raising, while important, took second place to solidarity work. That work itself combined specific local self-help projects and national-level work, particularly in defense of human rights defined as civil rights and rights of bodily integrity, rather than social rights. Despite these differences, the personal impact on poor women seems to have been similar: a new sense of political empowerment and an ability to act on behalf of their poor communities. If the radical model had similar consequences at the level of individuals as the sociocultural model in Brazil, however, the organizational context in which those newly empowered individuals were developing activism was rather different.

National Choices And Strategies: Connections to the Larger Church

Both the sociocultural and radical models of base communities emphasized grassroots solidarity and autonomy, encouraging "the people" to emerge as a force that would shape their own history. How this ideal would be realized, however, was a question that the two models answered in dissimilar ways. What kinds of connections to and support from the larger church would facilitate this historic change? What kinds of connections to other groups—political parties, other social movements, and so on—should the church foster? Were the new autonomous popular organizations that the base communities were creating meant to be a lasting form of popular democratic organization, or did the church see them more as a temporary response to repressive conditions—a response that would eventually give way to other organizations when the people's will could again be expressed through voting?

Neither country developed a single, fully articulated answer to these questions at the national level. In fact, both hierarchies included individuals with strongly conflicting opinions, and local base communities faced different conditions depending on their bishop. Overall, however, we can distinguish two national patterns. They conform roughly to Levine's (1992) distinction between a sociocultural, Brazilian model disposed toward a decentralized, coordinating role, and a radical, Chilean model disposed toward strong institutional church backing for popular groups.

Brazil: Decentralization and Popular Movements

Brazilian *basismo* espoused a distinctive idea about the appropriate relationship between popular movement groups and other entities, including the church. Brazilian clergy preferred autonomy and decentralization for their groups, and hoped that organizations beyond the local level would play only a coordinating role. Base communities were meant to stand on their own feet, to represent the popular classes without the intervention of politicians or other "outsiders" from other classes, who might bend the movements in undesirable directions. Obviously, many pastoral agents and the church as a whole could be construed as just such outsiders, however much they might express their solidarity. Moreover, Brazilian pastoral agents feared that the base communities would become overly dependent on the church, replacing the clientelism of politicians with the clientelism of bishops.

What would this perspective mean in practice for how the base communities should relate to the church as an institution? This was an especially thorny question since the communities were obviously part of the church, and the church had no desire for them to split from it doctrinally or institutionally. The compromise, at least in the case of São Paulo, seems to have been to opt for a strongly decentralized structure that let subunits of the church (dioceses, pastorals, and so on) respond to local needs while maintaining a strong local presence. As Manuel Vásquez (1998) says, the groups "thrived in close connection with the official church, receiving substantial episcopal support" (48).

These groups, in turn, were coordinated at—but their programs were not dictated by—higher levels (Hewitt 1991, 34–35).[17]

Although no document seems to have outlined the mechanics of the relationship, the grassroots membership perceived a consistent pattern of base community connection to the institution in both Rio de Janeiro and São Paulo. In practice, autonomy meant primarily "decentralization" vis-à-vis the national church. Reliance on local church resources was not ruled out. The Brazilian women, in fact, recall heavier reliance on local resources than do their Chilean counterparts. Ninety-two percent say the communities used some parish resources (rooms, telephones, and other things); 84 percent say the local priest actively participated in the community's activities; and 80 percent say the parish contributed to the base community in some way (financially or through training or other support activities). The local church played a critical role in supporting the base communities and the popular movements they helped create.[18] Many of the Brazilian respondents correlated the history of their groups with the comings and goings of local pastoral agents, some more and others less progressive and supportive of the base community's work.

In contrast, Brazilian women do not recall as much support for the communities from higher levels of the church. Only 52 percent said the diocese contributed resources or training, for example. Most responded that they "did not know" when asked about contributions from regional, national, or international levels of the church. When they could recall such contributions, they named religious orders or societies, or groups with which the local priest had a connection, rather than offices or institutions at these higher levels specifically charged with working with base communities.

Thus, "autonomy" from the church seems to have meant quite specifically independence from any centralized church control and planning. The base communities in Brazil clearly depended on local resources, and this could sometimes be to their disadvantage when newer, more conservative pastoral agents withdrew these local resources. This model of dependence on

17. Hewitt (1991) points out, for example, that Cardinal Arns created nine subarchdiocesan units, each with its "own set of pastoral programs, which were defined and oriented with an eye to resolving local problems." Similarly, eighteen pastorals on issues such as health, unemployment, and children were allowed to coordinate and plan activities independently on their own respective topics (35).

18. For example, twenty-three Brazilians mentioned support from other religious personnel, particularly nuns, but also seminarians, consecrated lay workers, and, in one case, an ex-priest. Six mentioned having received financial support or training from religious congregations or regional church organizations.

local resources, however, fits with the sociocultural model. The decentralized nature of the groups' connection to church institutions reinforces the emphasis on the church's role as coordinator, rather than as a centralized, institutional backer and planner of popular organizing. Each community might organize (or not) with its own local resources, while the larger church performed a coordinating function for the activities.

Because its coordinating role was limited, the church did not create new, national structures that intervened in an ongoing way in local communities. It did create a national office of base communities, as well as other entities that helped prepare material for popular education and consciousness-raising, worship, and organizing in the base communities. These were resources the communities could draw upon, however, not a national agenda that was imposed on them. Indeed, in some case multiple offices—for example, from different subregions of São Paulo—produced and circulated educational materials from which communities could choose (Hewitt 1991, 35). The emphasis on coordination and providing opportunities for networking among communities was thoroughgoing. This is reflected in one of the primary ways in which the higher levels of the church connected to the base communities: the organization of base community "encounters."

Several of the women we interviewed, including Geralda, Maria Melania, and Neide do Carmo were involved in preparing for and participating in the periodic national encounters of base community leaders, the first of which occurred in 1974. Such meetings were important to activists in a variety of ways. Maria Melania says, "I only got to know about what CEBs were preparing for the interecclesial meeting in [19]79/[19]80, to participate in the third inter-ecclesial encounter in [19]81, in Itaici. . . . From that moment on, my engagement began." Neide do Carmo recalls of a base community encounter, "One can get experience with other women who come to spend a week getting experience with the women there, so that is all growth, and we can bring it back. So we learn reality there, and apply it here." Through such meetings, the ideas and tactics of the otherwise diverse and fragmented popular movements coalesced and spread. The gatherings served a networking function for base community activists at all levels, from the municipality to the nation.

This decentralized networking function also typifies the church's relationship with the social movements that were associated with the base communities. Again, it reflects a very specific definition of *autonomy,* in this case one that the popular church shared with many other left social actors of the time. For the Brazilian popular church, grassroots autonomy meant autonomy from both the state and traditional political parties (Cleary 1997, 270). It meant poor people's ability to organize themselves from "the base." Brazilian progressives sought not just to ensure poor people's survival under military rule; they sought the larger objective of creating "the people as the subject of their own history" (Doimo 1995, 73). Not surprisingly, given Brazil's history of clientelism and corporatism and the absence of an institutionalized political Left, they believed that only direct popular participation and popular demands would create real autonomy and democracy. Many progressives in the Brazilian church saw the grassroots organizations as fundamentally new, lasting forms of mobilization and as popular forms of democratic action.

Although the church was not monolithic in this view, the most vocal liberationists saw the popular movements as an innovative, more democratic alternative to traditional parties. Their eventual support for the Worker's Party (PT) hinged on that party's emergence from the autonomous union movement and its close alliance with a variety of popular movements. Typically, liberationist pastoral agents exhorted the communities to support parties and candidates who had a record of working with the popular movements, and members of the communities responded in large numbers throughout the 1980s.[19] Along these lines, when the base communities entered into the discussions preceding the drafting of the new Brazilian constitution, they did so most prominently by playing a leading role in collecting signatures to introduce an amendment on popular participation (Doimo 1995, 197).

For a time, this vision of what popular autonomy and popular organizing meant coincided with the view of other groups at work in civil society. In particular, leftist intellectuals and ecumenical social-action groups shared a similar emphasis on grassroots empowerment (75). The church was able to collaborate with ecumenical groups beginning in the 1970s, and with leftist social scientists, beginning around the same time, on projects of urban community building and empowerment (85, 92–93). Although the Brazilian military regime was by no means benign, the lower levels of repression during the *distensão* (liberalization) and eventual prolonged *abertura* (opening), as well as the military's heterodox economic approach, made it possible and realistic

19. According to Doimo, about 44 percent of new PT members enrolled between 1981 and 1988 had participated in Catholic Church organizations.

for Brazilians to think about organizing themselves to make demands for popular well-being on the state. The church was able to cooperate with other groups in civil society whose members shared the vision of popular autonomy. Out of this cooperation, many of the networks that supported social movements were born.

The church's discourse on human rights, like its views of autonomy, helped to facilitate its role in promoting popular organizing.[20] The Brazilian church linked the notion of human rights to social rights and thereby to the concept of popular movements that could be linked to and supported by other groups in a nascent civil society (192). As we saw, activists recall these popular movements, rather than human rights work or local survival activities, as central to their communities' lives and activism. Most of the women described their community's social engagement as a string of popular movements, from day care to streetlights to asphalt to health.[21] The church's discourse on human rights facilitated and legitimized this activism.

In addition, the church helped institutionally to create the networks that promoted this mobilization and linked it across different communities. This institutional support was not always obvious, however. For example, when Ana Maria Doimo set out to study a variety of popular movements in the 1970s and 1980s, she quickly discovered that, in her words, she could not avoid the church (140). Yet this had not been obvious to her initially, because the church did not generally create new, institutionally sponsored "movements" or "movement headquarters," for example. In keeping with its emphasis on autonomy, it often served primarily to establish linkages through its pastorals or other offices between what would otherwise have been fragmented local movements, allowing them to coalesce into something recognizable as, for example, the Movimento de Saúde, or Health Movement (118). As Scott Mainwaring (1986) points out, church leaders tried to resist "the temptation to turn CEBs into instruments of popular movements" (167).

Base communities themselves became a network of local-movement webs (Doimo 1995, 96). Often, in fact, particular individuals themselves became the "web." As the same group of activists participated in different specific

20. The church's role in organizing around and protecting the individual human rights of those abused by the military regime should not be discounted. The well-known saga of the production of *Brasil: Nunca mais*, attests to its importance, as does the history of its clandestine lobbying of the military on these issues (Serbin 2000).

21. On this point, see Drogus 1997, Mainwaring 1986, and others.

movements, they were able to form connections between movements around different specific issues.

The church also provided more direct institutional support, and indeed this support was often crucial to a movement's success. One of the earliest popular movements to test the regime, the cost-of-living movement of 1973, depended heavily on parish-level support (Doimo 1995). Local parishes provided secure spaces for organizational meetings and offered training as well as material and sometimes financial support. The movement faltered when the church discontinued support following the involvement of clandestine parties that it saw as manipulating the people. Similarly, with church backing, a movement against unemployment reached national levels of organization in 1983–84, but equally high levels of unemployment were unable to produce a popular reaction in 1990, when the church did not proffer support (109).

After their initial "baptism" in the cost-of-living movement, many parishes went on to support other local movements and to create similar networked webs though the base communities, such as the housing and health movements. Overall, the church reached extensively into civil society by playing this articulating role among a variety of popular movements. Without its support, few movements would have succeeded.

The institutional church did not always rely on base communities alone to create the impetus and glue for popular organizing. In addition to initiating metropolitan, state, and national CEB encounters, which supported the movements indirectly, the church hierarchy created specific intermediate institutions and pastoral movements to bolster them. In most cases, and in keeping with the commitment to autonomy and decentralization, however, it gradually sought to make these institutions autonomous from the church itself, wary of mixing religious and political missions. For example, the Federation of Organs for Social and Educational Assistance (FASE), a group that developed from local church influence in Rio de Janeiro, was made autonomous in the 1970s and emerged as one of the most important supporters of the popular movements that existed in the city (Doimo 1995, 162). The church gradually made other groups autonomous from the mid-1980s onward. Some, such as components of the pastoral movements, among them the Pastoral Land Commission (1975) and the Workers' Pastoral, remained within the church but were reoriented to the needs of the popular movements in the 1980s (84, 162). Nonetheless, the church continues to see these offices as serving—through offering resources, mobilizing the faithful, and so on—movements that have their own institutional bases and homes outside the church (Mainwaring 1986, 167).

Thus, the Brazilian church brought to bear on the base communities a particular idea of "popular autonomy" and "grassroots organizing." Decentralization and networking were the hallmarks of this approach, meaning that while base communities might depend heavily on parish resources and support, the church also encouraged them to form networks with one another and with secular movements that shared their ideals, particularly those of leftist intellectuals and ecumenical groups. Nearly half the Brazilian respondents (eleven) were able to name specific groups outside the central structures of the church who supported their work. Teachers' organizations, the PT, other political parties, feminist groups, and church-linked but independent organizations such as the Institute for Religious Studies (ISER) and FASE were all named as collaborators. Women from Rio mentioned the ecumenical non-governmental organization (NGO) Center for Biblical Studies (CEBI) and the Brazilian Institute for Social and Economic Analysis (IBASE). Overall, then, one could argue that despite their somewhat closer links to a particular parish, Brazilian base communities apparently had more diversified sources of support that extended beyond those in the direct control of the church hierarchy. The supralocal church institution tended to serve primarily as the basis for a nationwide network among activists, and its various encounters and institutions brought together the activists who were formed in the base communities. It filled this role of networking as no other institution could, particularly in some key areas such as São Paulo, where this role and the popular movements generally enjoyed the support of the hierarchy. Finally, while it created quite a few intermediate groups, it generally tended to emancipate these from church control. As a result, it spawned the creation of a variety of NGOs linked in many ways with the church, but not entirely dependent upon it. This orientation, so consistent with the sociocultural ideal of base communities, contrasts significantly with the activities and characteristics of Chilean base communities.

Chile: Centralized Support for Survival

Although observers had long regarded the Chilean church as one of the more progressive in the region, the extreme conditions of the dictatorship pushed the church, including through the National Bishops' Conference, to swing its institutional weight behind support for parish-level base communities and the struggle for social justice.[22] By the mid-1970s the Catholic bishops' moral denunciation of the dictatorship served as virtually the only counterweight to the military's monopoly on the public discourse, and it was the church's tangible, institutional support that made the difference in the lives of poor. As always, however, the question was how to define the church's role and, specifically, how to create church mechanisms to channel support to grassroots communities. In contrast to circumstances in Brazil, in Chile the harshness of the political repression and the intensity of the economic crisis led the Chilean church to adopt a more centralized and interventionist strategy, tying base communities in a far more structured way to the national church. Not surprisingly, the Chilean church's strategy focused more than the Brazilian's on economic survival as well as political solidarity and human rights. The major mechanisms for this more structured and strategic church role in the lives of base communities were the vicariates, newly created intermediate entities that could channel resources both to individual communities and to groups fostering network-building activities across neighborhoods.

At first glance, it appears that the Chilean communities depended somewhat less on the church—at least at the parish level. Although roughly the same percentage of Brazilian respondents remember receiving some form of support from the parish (80 percent) as Chilean (73 percent), there are some differences in the kinds of parish-level support they identify. Twenty-five percent of Chileans recalled receiving financial support from their parishes (28 percent of Brazilians); 17 percent mentioned material support (48 percent of Brazilians); 56 percent cited training (76 percent); and 79 percent said the parish provided meeting space (88 percent). While they depended less on their parishes, the Chilean base communities did rely heavily on the newly organized national vicariates, funded through the Archbishopric of Santiago. Ninety percent of the Chileans recall their community receiving various types of support from the vicariates. While only 15 percent remember receiving financial resources from the vicariates, for example, 31 percent cite legal services, 40 percent material support, and 60 percent training.

The Chileans' descriptions of aid are consistent with both the organizational structure and the stated missions of the vicariates. The best known of the new national institutional spines of the church's famed "protective umbrella" was the Vicaría de Solidaridad, created in 1975 by then-archbishop

---

22. Ivan Vallier was the first observer of the Latin American Catholic Church to note the progressivism of the Chilean church throughout the twentieth century. See Vallier 1967.

Raul Silva Henríquez. By the late 1970s, it provided the central framework
for a national network of organizations, from small-neighborhood to national
groups organized around issues ranging from human rights and economic
survival to employment training and technical assistance.[23] The *vicaría*
housed six departments, of which four were especially important for extending
the reach of the church into the popular sectors.[24] The first, the *vicaría*'s legal
department, housed teams of attorneys and social workers who, especially in
the first years after the coup, offered virtually the only legal aid available to
human rights victims and their families. The legal department also ran training
programs throughout the country on the rights of political prisoners, the
detained-disappeared, the accused, exiles, and families of victims of repression.
The second, the publication department, produced the bimonthly *Solidaridad,*
a twenty-four-page magazine oriented toward the grassroots communities.
Pelagia Bulnes, a progressive theologian who was active in Villa Francia in
the late 1970s, remembers how vital *Solidaridad* was during the worst days of
censorship: "I remember when we began going to Villa Francia. There we could
find out what was happening. People were isolated. The media were controlled.
So you had no idea what had been going on in other places. The newsletter
printed by the vicariate was important in keeping us informed. . . . [It] was
handed out in all the chapels." According to one estimate, *Solidaridad* had a
readership of approximately 150,000 throughout the country at the height
of the dictatorship (Gonzalez 1990, 165). The *vicariate*'s third department,
education, promoted consciousness-raising and the development and preser-
vation of a sense of agency in the citizenry. In addition to offering the use of
educational equipment and materials, this department trained agents to lead
grassroots workshops in human rights, participatory methods for organizing,
and community solidarity strategies throughout the country.

Finally, and perhaps most important for our purposes, the department for
vicarías zonales, created in 1982, sought to decentralize the *vicarías'* work

23. The Vicaría de Solidaridad was created after the military government pressured Archbishop Silva
Henríquez to close down the ecumenical Comité Pro Paz, created by Catholic, Methodist, Lutheran, Pentecostal Methodist, and Jewish leaders along with support from the World Council of Churches. The
Comité Pro Paz was created on October 6, 1973, just a month after the coup, to respond to the horrors in
the aftermath of the military takeover (Vicaría de Solidaridad, 1991).

24. The other two departments were less important for our purposes, but they were vital to the func-
tioning of the *vicaría.* The first, a financial department, was not only in charge of the *vicaría*'s accounts but
also finding and soliciting outside funding for the vast range of activities. And the second, a department of
"support," provided computer and research assistance to the other departments (Archdiocese of Santiago,
"La Vicaría de Solidaridad," photocopy, 49–52).

with grassroots groups. Each new zonal vicariate fielded teams of social workers and health professionals to work with community-survival groups (involved in feeding programs, training workshops, and local cooperatives); ran a wide range of training programs for women, youth, senior citizens, pastoral agents, and grassroots leaders; coordinated national programs that were run through the Vicaría de Solidaridad; and administered health, housing, and human rights outreach programs (Vicaría de Solidaridad, photocopy). One study credits the Vicaría de Solidaridad with supporting an annual average of 1,600 grassroots organizations during the dictatorship in which an estimated 60,000 people participated per year. The same study estimates that the *vicaría* worked with 17,211 grassroots groups with a total of 712,653 participants during the entirety of the dictatorship (Gonzalez 1990, 165).[25]

This newly created strata of organizations contributed enormously to grassroots economic survival. In her study of the urban popular economic organizations (PEOs) during the dictatorship, Clarisa Hardy (1987) demonstrates just how critical the church's role was to these survival groups.[26] At the time of the study in 1986, approximately 90 percent of fourteen hundred PEOs examined received external support of some kind—the majority of which (75 percent) came from Catholic Church sources, including 59.5 percent from the *vicarías zonales* and another 14 percent from other church sources (193).[27] In fact, Catholic Church sources, especially the *vicarías*, accounted for a larger proportion of PEOs' support than any other source (196). The

25. Other church-sponsored or related organizations also formed critical spines in the church's "protective umbrella"—these organizations included the Academy for Christian Humanism (ACH), created by Cardinal Silva Henríquez in 1977, which served as a conduit for international funding for research institutes such as the Facultad Latinoamericana de Ciencias Sociales (FLACSO) and the Instituto Latino Americano de Estudios Transnacionales (ILET). The ACH housed six new academic centers for research in issues pertaining to agriculture, human rights, education, economics, and politics; courses in these and other social sciences were taught by more than three hundred Chilean academics who had lost their jobs after the military purges of higher education and were subsequently employed by ACH. Intellectuals in FLASCO, ILET, and other think tanks provided invaluable independent research on the economic, political, and human rights effects of military policy. See Lladser 1989.

26. Popular economic organizations (PEOs) include a wide range of grassroots organizational activities: *talleres laborales, amasanderias, huertos, ollas comunes, comprando juntos, comedores populares, grupos de vivienda y deudas, grupos de salud poblacional y sindicatos de trabajadores independientes o eventuales,* among others (Hardy 1987, 43).

27. According to another study, almost one-third of the PEOs founded during the 1970s and 1980s took religious names—either of saints or the Virgin Mary (approximately 21 percent) or of religious symbols or values (approximately 10 percent) (Razeto et al. 1990, 213).

church was especially critical, relative to other sources of support, in providing technical and material support.[28]

According to one study, in 1982 approximately eighty thousand people participated in PEOs of all types in the metropolitan region alone. Sixty percent of these individuals participated in and benefited from feeding organizations (Razeto et al. 1990, 193), and 93 percent of these organizations received support either from the *vicarías* or other church sources. Thus, the church sources directly touched the lives of virtually all of the approximately forty-eight thousand participant-beneficiaries of food-related PEOs. The authors also estimate that in 1989, 10 percent of all people living in Santiago *poblaciónes*, 10 percent of those classified as "poor," and 27 percent of all "indigents" were participants-beneficiaries of grassroots PEOs, the majority of which were supported by or related to the Catholic Church (195).[29]

In addition to supporting economic survival, the church provided training to enable grassroots groups to organize and build supportive networks across neighborhoods. The Vicaría de Solidaridad played a crucial role by housing teams of lawyers, social workers, pastoral agents, and others trained in grassroots facilitation. In addition, the lesser-known Vicaría de Pastoral Obrera, created by then cardinal Silva Henríquez in 1977 and headed by progressive Afonso Baeza, served as the principle protector of the heavily repressed workers' movement throughout the dictatorship. At the height of its work, this *vicaría* had a staff of more than forty. Until the mid-1980s, it coordinated support for a wide range of national and grassroots workers' organizations, from unions to grassroots training, self-help, and economic-survival groups (Afonso Baeza, interview with Hannah Stewart-Gambino, March 22, 1995). The Vicaría de Pastoral Obrera, even more than the Vicaría de Solidaridad, saw its main mission as supporting *organizational* life under the dictatorship. In the words of one internal report, "'Those without a voice' are not individual people whose interests the church knows how to reveal, but they are organizations, people committed to a search for a social change, and much of the support that they want from the church has to do with help in constituting themselves as social and political subjects (organizational support, meeting places, consciousness raising, etc.)" (Vicaría de Pastoral Obrera, photocopy, 36). The Vicaría de Pastoral Obrera provided training sessions for labor and

---

28. According to Hardy, PEOs reported receiving support from the *vicarías* in training support (58 percent), technical assistance (64 percent), and material support (80 percent) (Hardy 1987, 196).

29. Comparable data do not exist for popular economic organizations in Brazil.

other grassroots groups, intensive "summer school" programs throughout the country, and training materials, meeting places, and other (nonfinancial) support (Alberto Gonzalez, executive director of the Vicaría de Pastoral Obrera, interview with Hannah Stewart-Gambino, March 14, 1995). Many credit these two *vicarías* with playing *the* critical role in protecting party, worker, and peasant leaders who had escaped assassination or exile, thus preserving at least the skeletal remains of civil society until these critical actors could reemerge in the early 1980s.

It is important to note, however, that the Chilean Catholic Church was not equally supportive of all grassroots activities. As we have seen, the church worked closely with community survival groups, particularly those organized around feeding the hungry (for example, *ollas comunes* [soup kitchens], *comprando juntos* [food co-ops], *comedores infantiles* [preschool feeding centers]) and those dedicated to providing job training for the un- or underemployed. However, in contrast to the Brazilian church, its counterpart in Chile played a relatively minor role in supporting issue-specific movements or groups. For example, private and other nongovernmental sources contributed far more than the church to organizations concerned with either housing or health-care provision. The biggest difference between Chilean church sources and other origins of support, however, concerns contributions to groups whose main purpose was the expression or articulation of worker demands (for example, unions).

According to Hardy (1987), no revindicalist groups received financial or material support from church sources, whereas 62 percent received support from NGOs, and slightly more than half (52 percent) received support from other (primarily trade union) sources. Church structures provided a protective umbrella to political-party and labor leaders, but their activities in turn were supported by nongovernmental and international sources. Thus, in contrast to what occurred in Brazil, the Chilean church's centralized intervention on behalf of the poor and their grassroots communities were not intended to supplant or replace traditional political-party or union work. Rather than creating autonomous working-class organizations, the church's protective umbrella protected many party and union activists, which was crucial to the ability of parties and unions to reemerge as leaders of the pro-democracy movement in the 1980s.

At the heart of the Chilean church's commitment to democracy was a perpetual distinction between protecting the human rights of political players and promoting *partisan* activity. On the one hand, as many of the Chilean respondents recall, the church and the vicariates, in particular, were early on committed to the defense of human rights. The church helped found and sustain the first national organizations dedicated to studying human rights violations and defending the victims and their families. The majority of the respondents recall receiving human rights training from church sources, usually supported by the Vicaría de Solidaridad, as well as the church's organizing a range of community activities such as prison visits, its participation in national human rights demonstrations, and its solidarity with organizations for victims and their families. Several women remember personally participating in denunciations of human rights violations staged outside of known detention centers, and many participated in the annual Vía Crúcis (stations of the cross) organized initially by the Vicaría de Pastoral Obrera. The Vía Crúcis, always staged to end at a detention center or graveside of victims of the regime, became a well-known expression of popular opposition to the military regime (Puga 2000). Other activities related to human rights, such as organizing community health centers to tend to neighborhood victims of military assault, especially during the nights of the national protests, also figure prominently in the memories of the vast majority of the Chilean respondents. The national church, through the vicariates, as well as many local priests and religious personnel, actively supported these activities.

On the other hand, the official church was far more ambivalent about the role of base communities as key players in the mobilization of the mass, pro-democracy protests beginning in May 1983. The regime met the protests, which marked the first turning point in the long struggle to return to democracy, with substantial violence, especially in poorer neighborhoods.[30] While the church supported the kinds of community-based defensive and solidarity organizing mentioned above, the hierarchy began backing away from an appearance of active support for the national protests, most notably after the promotion of Juan Francisco Fresno to archbishop of Santiago in 1983. Deeply committed to drawing a sharp line between the church's pastoral mission and partisan activity, Archbishop (later Cardinal) Fresno committed the church to a mediating role in the escalating conflict by hosting talks between the opposition alliance and the military (Stewart-Gambino 1992).

30. States of siege were in force from November 1984 through mid-1985 and again in 1986–87. Throughout the years between the first explosion of protests in 1983 and the final days of the regime, the military conducted routine *allanamientos* (military occupations) in the *poblaciónes,* during which all men were rounded up temporarily while their documents could be checked and their houses searched. Casualties, particularly during the nights of protests, were higher in poor neighborhoods than anywhere else.

This role had important ramifications for poor neighborhoods and, in particular, for the base communities. First, the church included only the centrist political parties in its mediation efforts, leaving not only most of the political left but also the autonomous popular organizations, such as base communities, marginalized in the process that eventually led to redemocratization. Thus, while church officials increasingly distanced the church from active support of protest mobilization, base communities (often with support from more liberationist priests and sometimes bishops) emerged as critical hubs for neighborhood mobilization by virtue of their hard-won organizational experience and leadership gained during the first years of dictatorship.[31] That the majority of the Chilean women in our study remember participating in and helping organize some aspect of the national protests at the same time that church officials began withdrawing support from such "partisan" activity signals the beginning of the change in church strategy, discussed at length in the following chapter, which left the Chilean women feeling far more betrayed and angry than their Brazilian sisters.

The combination of the Chilean church's more institutionalized support of economic survival and human rights at the grassroots level, while distinguishing church work from the proper work of political parties and other traditional actors, contrasts sharply with the Brazilian model of fostering new, autonomous popular movements able to successfully place demands on the state. Although many progressive Chileans agreed with the precepts of the Brazilian model, the nature of the Chilean church's strategy had the effect of inhibiting the inception of such a model. The church supported network building aimed at preserving democratic spaces and actors or denouncing human rights violations, but church leaders also continued to recognize the traditional role of (particularly centrist) political parties, trade unions, and other mainstream revindicalist organizations in the Chilean political arena. During periods when these traditional mechanisms for citizen demands were underground, the church was willing to cast its protection

31. Cardinal Fresno's choice to dedicate the church to the role of mediator rather than supporter of the opposition led to the first clear, public signs of division within the hierarchy—both between liberationist and more conservative bishops and between the grassroots, popular church and the hierarchy. Bernardino Piñera, in his capacity as president of the Episcopal Conference, described these growing divisions in a statement made to John Paul II during the 1987 papal visit: "When we [the Episcopal Conference] meet twice a year, some difficulties arise. Those of the strictly pastoral order are not the most grave, but they exist. The diverse currents of thought in the universal church . . . also divide us. More difficult to reconcile are the differences in judging the reality of the country—social and cultural, but also economic and political—and the attitude that our episcopacy should adopt toward it" (Stewart-Gambino 1992, 29–30).

over individuals in danger. This strategy allowed traditional political organizations to reemerge and empowered some (to the exclusion of the more
radical left and the popular sectors) to lead the country through the difficult
negotiations leading to democratic transition; however, it also helped inhibit
the creation of a vital, autonomous network of social movements similar to
those in the Brazilian case.

Conclusion

In this chapter we have seen that the churches in Brazil and Chile played
similarly vital roles in the resurrection of civil society through the creation
of base communities and that these organizational venues helped to facilitate
the mobilization of poor women, who swelled the rising tide of protests
under the military regime in each country. Each church reached extensively
into society at a time when other organizational opportunities were not
available. Each provided previously marginalized individuals with a new
sense of citizenship and experiences of participation. There were also substantial differences between the two countries, however, in part because of
the different political contexts in which they operated.

Brazilians perceived base communities as sites where individuals could
be mobilized for autonomous popular movements, which were a good in
themselves. Although the church also spoke out on human rights, base
communities, particularly during Brazil's long *abertura*, organized primarily to demand socioeconomic rights for their communities. Indeed, the
church saw these socioeconomic demands as an extension of human rights.
Consequent to its commitment to creating the "people as a subject of their
own history" and the availability of allies in civil society, the Brazilian
church was able to provide a much more decentralized support system for
the CEBs and their popular movements. Base communities worked with a
variety of organizations, including eventually the PT (seen as a legitimate
party because of its relationship to the popular movement), and the church
often sought to transform the intermediate structures it created into
autonomous or semiautonomous NGOs in service to the popular movement.

In contrast, conditions in Chile as well as different attitudes on the part
of the hierarchy led to a somewhat different experience for base communities
there. Human rights organizing and protection was critical, and base community members recalled their involvement in national protests around this

issue in particular. It would probably have been fruitless as well as dangerous to link the issue of human rights to socioeconomic rights in Pinochet's Chile, however. Unlike in Brazil, there were few obvious allies organizing in other kinds of spaces. Moreover, base communities housed some activists with strong, prior partisan identities and whose outlook was informed by their own partisan agendas rather than having grown out of the base communities. Finally, at various points in time, economic survival may have been more truly critical in Chilean base communities. As a result of a number of factors, then, the Chilean church devoted its resources to creating intermediate structures, such as the *vicarías,* that were vital to popular protection and survival. This meant that Chilean base communities had a more concentrated base of support within the church and fewer outward links with other actors. It also meant that no lasting alternative, autonomous social movements—separate from political parties and other traditional political actors—were created.

Both of these models produced activists, particularly from among poor women. They produced rather different organizational networks and linkages, however. As we shall see in the following chapter, the results for activists when the church withdrew its support in each case was similarly devastating, but also different.

Earthquake Versus Erosion:
Church Retreat and Social Movement Decline

Hannah Stewart-Gambino, Carol Ann Drogus,
Cecilia Loreto Mariz, and Maria das Dores Campos Machado

There was a big change when the urgency of the dictatorship passed . . . the church thought that now the groups meeting in the chapels should not continue occupying the space. Now that they had the possibility of occupying other spaces without danger, they should look for other spaces and the church would return to religious things . . . in 1986, the year of the assassination attempt against Pinochet, and decidedly after 1987, the church was changing to a more conservative line. Also it was an excuse to make activist groups look for other spaces . . . because fundamentally they didn't want partisan people in the church. They only wanted religious people in the church.

— PELAGIA BULNES, CHILE

I remember well that we fought hard when the CNBB [Brazilian Bishops' Conference] said that the church had a supplemental role in activities outside the church. . . . For me it was a little bit of that, it was when the hierarchy of the church retreated from this social role, entered more into religious problems. I think that's where the change began a little in the degree of participation. In my opinion it began to change there. I don't see another key point. . . . Because when the church says, let's go, it begins to say, it's civil society's problem, it's not ours, then people also begin to withdraw and not participate in things anymore.

— LÚCIA, BRAZIL

The transition to democracy changed the church, society, and politics in both Chile and Brazil in many ways. Changes in the politics of the church that coincided with the decline in the cycle of social movement protest deeply affected women activists. Similar forces in both countries—including Vatican pressures, religious competition, the complexities of party politics, and a neoliberal economic agenda—combined to diminish the commitment of the church in both countries to politically active base communities. This retreat from a social role had strong repercussions not only for the base communities, but also for the social movements they had helped organize.

In this chapter we examine the churches' retreat and its impact. We briefly review the institutional side of this process and then proceed to the women activists' interpretations of this change. We want to know how they perceive the sources of decline of both the base communities and the social movements in which they participated. What changes led to the current period of movement "doldrums," in their view? In addition, we want to know what they believe these changes mean for the future of social activism. Thus, we also consider their views on whether Catholic base communities continue to play a role in organizing civil society and whether such a role should—and could—be expanded to facilitate a new cycle of activism.

We contend that both the specific political context in each country and the different national models of base communities influenced the women's experience. Chilean activists—more closely tied to the church through the *vicarías* and more similar to the radical base community model—experienced a more abrupt, traumatic breach in support. As a result, they have developed a more critical, radical perspective on the church and on activism in general. Brazilian women, while also critical of their church, perceived a more nuanced change and remain more hopeful that their base communities could once again be resuscitated as part of a broader popular movement.

Institutional and Social Sources of Church Withdrawal

Chile: Resurgence of Conservative Control

For base community activists, the Chilean church's withdrawal from civil society was abrupt and radical. However, the story of how this most heroic of churches, in the forefront of the struggle for human rights, came to distance itself from its commitment to base communities reveals that underlying tensions over the church's social role always existed. Like all Catholic hierarchies, the Chilean church was never monolithically progressive, and in fact the strength of conservatives who opposed the base community experiment grew throughout the military era as Pope John Paul II's new appointments swelled their ranks.[1] In retrospect, the bishops were always more ambivalent about base community activities than either the progressive parish priests or the *vicarías*. During the dictatorship, however, military harassment of

1. Papal Nuncio Angelo Sodano (1978–88) is widely credited with starting the process of conservative appointments in the early 1980s. Sodano is known for his intense loyalty and tenacious support for the pope's traditional view of the role of the church, and his hand can be seen in the consistently conservative appointments that were made throughout the 1980s, including in Chile's first two Opus Dei bishops. Sodano was rewarded for his successful management of the transformation of the Chilean episcopate with a substantial promotion to secretary of state of the Vatican.

church personnel, the *vicarías'* visibility, and the bishops' consensus about democracy contributed to the public's perception that "the church" had adopted the goal of extending its reach into civil society through support for grassroots social movements. Yet once the democratic transition began, the church no longer had to defend itself against right-wing and state-sponsored attacks, allowing the deep division between traditionalists and progressives in the hierarchy to reemerge (Stewart-Gambino 1992).

Several factors account for the shift to an apparently more conservative church. Not the least of these was the toll that years of physical and verbal attacks from the military and its supporters took on church officials. These attacks convinced many bishops that the church must retire as quickly as possible from political debate, and with the return of democracy, they welcomed the opportunity to reach out again to the upper classes.[2]

More important, Chileans—both within the church and in society at large—viewed the church's role during the dictatorship as a temporary necessity until traditional political institutions could reclaim their rightful functions. In contrast to the situation in Brazil, the Chilean political-party system had been largely stable and deeply entrenched in civil society since the 1930s; therefore, political parties historically have been widely regarded as the appropriate institutional mechanisms for aggregating and representing society's needs and demands. Because of the historical strength of the Chilean party system, a well-defined and nationally recognized political elite ranging across the political spectrum not only survived the dictatorship (in part because of the protection of the Catholic Church), but also played a crucial role in the transition to democracy. With the reemergence of the political parties and the inevitable partisan competition inherent in democracy, many Chileans believed that the need for church intervention in the political arena—particularly on behalf of any constituency or social sector—was no longer necessary. For example, writing in 1988 on the eve of the democratic transition, Humberto Vega (director of the worker studies program at the

2. According to a 1991 CISOC-Bellarmino publication titled *Businessmen and Their Vision of the Church in Economic Matters,* the Chilean business class had felt abandoned by the Chilean church since the 1960s. One respondent states: "After my generation . . . the church abandoned the education of the upper middle classes with an irresponsibility bordering on the incredible. They used to educate the type of people who were characterized as leaders of society (for example, at St. George, San Ignacio, and other Franciscan schools). . . . [But] all of a sudden they said, 'The rich have to educate themselves,' and they stopped" (Aldunate y Morandé 1991, 20). Several refer to the Chilean church's "abandonment" of the business class when the hierarchy adopted the "preferential option for the poor" (ibid.).

Academy of Christian Humanism) distinguishes between worldly partisanship and the proper role of the church, above politics. This distinction was
often heard in lay circles and from the church hierarchy itself.

> The church's mission is fundamentally eschatological and, therefore,
> the church must not be linked to historical visions of utopia. The
> kingdom of God always is going to go farther than that. . . . I think
> that the church must not get tied up with any type of utopia that
> guides political undertaking. The construction of the kingdom is
> always going to transcend, going to be richer, more dynamic than
> the construction of a society in terms of a particular utopia. . . .
> [The church] must not . . . take the part of any particular partisan
> project. (Vega 1988, 177)

Writing in the same 1988 publication, Christian Democrat Ignacio Walker
asserts explicitly that the church should withdraw to its traditional pastoral
role and allow political parties to assume their historical function:

> [W]hat the church has accomplished since 1973 as an institution
> and moral power has given it a tremendous organizational power. . . .
> The parties, in contrast . . . have had nothing to offer. . . . [Parties]
> are organs of mediation between society and the state . . . [and since
> 1973] there has been no state; therefore, they have not been able to
> satisfy society's demands and needs. . . . [H]owever, the consolida-
> tion stage is different. Obviously, in the democratic consolidation
> phase, in a stage of real normality, the political parties can resume
> the natural role . . . as mediator between society and the state, and
> they can assume their protagonist role. . . . In turn, from the church's
> point of view, a certain withdrawal is necessary. (1988, 204–8)

Adding to the changes caused by the reemergence of the traditional party
system, the more extreme leftist parties, in particular those associated with
the Movimiento de Democracia Popular (MDP), sought to mobilize the very
popular sectors that the church's "preferential option for the poor" represented in an attempt to force the military and the mainstream parties to
include them in the negotiations over the transition. Under these conditions
of escalating partisan wrangling, church leaders very much wanted the church
to retreat to its traditional position above politics.

Not only did the bishops agree that the political parties should retake the reins of pro-democracy opposition to military rule, they also wanted to refocus institutional resources toward the more traditionally pastoral work of the church. Many worried that the church had neglected its religious mission during the dictatorship, allowing both secularism and religious beliefs other than those promulgated by the church to gain ground in Chilean society. Indeed, despite the Catholic Church's vastly extended reach into popular sectors, Pentecostalism grew steadily from the 1970s on, particularly among the poor.[3] By the early 1980s, many church officials, including Cardinal Juan Fresno, attributed this growth to the Catholic Church's failure to address the poor's pastoral and sacramental needs. The church had difficulty focusing on sacramental and parish life during opposition protests and the military crackdowns. The return to democracy would offer a welcome respite and a chance to recapture a wandering flock.

Forces outside the church also pushed the bishops away from liberationist concerns and toward a defensive posture on moral issues. With the return to democratic electoral competition, women's organizations successfully pressured progressive politicians from the center and left, eager to increase their share of the vote in a crowded electoral field and thus place on the table issues concerning women's rights, the family, and sexuality. Yet progressive and conservative bishops alike currently oppose legislative proposals to legalize abortion, divorce, sex education in the schools, and access to a range of reproductive rights. All find themselves allied with the political right in opposing the "decline" of the "moral foundations" of Chilean society. For conservatives, this is nothing new. However, progressive bishops who forged ties with leftist politicians during the dictatorship now also actively lobby government politicians, "collecting the bill" for extending protection during the dictatorship. Fanny Pollarolo, Socialist deputy, describes Bishop Carlos Camus: "[H]e is very dear, [and was] very progressive in the fight against the dictatorship . . . we love him a lot, but on the issue of divorce he is the worst. And he is the one pressuring the Socialist Deputies" (Haas 1999, 60).

Since the transition, bishops' statements and pastoral letters have dealt almost exclusively with birth control, divorce, premarital sex, drugs, and other issues of personal morality. Repeated exhortations to Catholic "unity" and to "obedience" to church leaders whose authority is in grounded natural

---

3. Estimates of Pentecostal numbers differ; according to Cleary and Sepulveda, Pentecostals had grown from 5.58 percent in 1960 to 13.2 percent in 1992 (Cleary and Sepulveda, 1997, 106).

law and social doctrine give the appearance of agreement among the bishops. Hierarchical division, particularly in the Chilean National Bishops' Conference, which has a strong tradition of operating consensually, drastically reduces the range of issues—particularly of a social and political nature—that bishops are willing to address. The Chilean bishops are loath to publicly address issues that highlight doctrinal, philosophical, or political disagreement or tension, and this preference for consensus limits the ability of progressive bishops to continue promoting "politicized" ministries such as the base communities.

The 1989 Chilean Episcopal Conference publication "Certainty, Coherence, and Confidence: Message to Chilean Catholics in an Hour of Transition" (Conferencia Episcopal de Chile 1989) foreshadowed this new consensus in the 1990s. The bishops briefly reaffirm their concern with economic justice, human rights, and other issues generally associated with a progressive understanding of Catholic social doctrine. The bulk of the statement, however, concerns the danger that democracy might facilitate the growth of secularism, modernity, moral decay, declining traditional family life, and liberalization of women's roles. On issues of personal morality and gender roles, the bishops take a uniformly conservative view. They depict women exclusively as wives and mothers, whose most important job is the "support of [their] husband[s] and education of [their] children" (31). Legalization of divorce is unacceptable, and the only explicit reference to the dictatorship is an expression of gratitude to the regime for its prohibition of abortion in all cases that was passed into law in 1989 (18).

Since the transition, the hierarchy's statements also have shifted the discourse on social and economic justice in a more theologically traditionalist direction. The 1991–94 pastoral orientations, readopted by the bishops in 1995, for example, redefined the church's "preferential option for the poor" to mean the emotionally and spiritually deprived as well as the materially poor. The list of the "poor" now includes "the incurably ill, including alcoholics and drug addicts; [the] socially marginalized, especially AIDS victims, prostitutes, [and] prisoners; the homeless; seasonal agricultural workers; indigenous peoples; and those most unattended, including by our pastoral, such as the hospitalized, children, workers, and single or abandoned mothers" (Conferencia Episcopal de Chile 1990, 84–85). This definition contrasts sharply with the almost exclusively material definition ("lack of the most elemental material benefits in contrast to the accumulation of riches in the hands of the minority") first used by the Latin American Bishops' Conference at Puebla in 1979 and adopted by the Chilean Bishops' Conference in their 1982–85 pastoral orientations.[4]

The bishops have also redefined "poverty" from being a social condition resulting from the structural sin embodied in dependent capitalism, it became an individual condition to be ameliorated by traditional charity. The bishops now reemphasize charitable giving among wealthy Chileans, and the organization Hogar de Cristo has mushroomed into Chile's largest charity with a large staff of paid personnel.[5] Soliciting money from wealthy donors for distribution to the poor is a far cry from the the aspiration to enact social and economic justice, as expressed in the church's liberationist statements of the 1970s and 1980s, in which "charity" was viewed pejoratively. Finally, the Chilean episcopate's pastoral orientations no longer include support for base Christian communities—a significant absence, after highlighting them as a pastoral priority since 1968.

At times, politically progressive bishops such as Carlos Camus (Linares) and Carlos Gonzalez (Talca), both of whom played critical roles in constructing the church's "protective umbrella" during the dictatorship, continue to issue strongly worded statements on sociopolitical issues of national concern.[6] While like-minded bishops welcome such statements, however, those of opposing viewpoints easily ignore them as the opinion of only one bishop. More commonly, the bishops try to present a single voice by moving toward a more conservative posttransition consensus (Haas 1999).

In addition to changes in the hierarchy's public statements, substantial *structural* changes in church organizations signal the progressives' marginalization. The church's most dramatic step to relinquish their involvement in civil society came in 1992, when Archbishop Oviedo closed the Vicaría de

4. In 1991, Cardinal Oviedo published *The Poor Can't Wait*, a work whose title seems in keeping with principles of liberation theology. However, the text is addressed primarily to employers, and the message is a traditional exhortation to do their Christian duty toward the poor. The appropriation of liberationist language for traditional messages is the dominant device in most bishops' statements throughout the 1990s (Cristián Parker, prominent sociologist of religion, interview, May 11, 1995).

5. Father Alberto Hurtado founded Hogar de Cristo in the 1940s. His canonization as one of Chile's only saints in 1994 gave the bishops a platform from which to launch a national campaign for contributions. Progressive bishops remain critical of charity as a substitute for solidarity with the materially poor. Bishop Gonzalez (1994), for example, writes: "Works such as the Hogar de Cristo [the largest Catholic charity in Chile] exist, thank God. They are necessary and they do great work . . . but their help is transitory and not permanent"(26).

6. For example, Bishop Gonzalez published two extremely outspoken pastoral letters in the early 1990s, *Camino para Crecer en Confraternidad Cristiana* (1991) and *La Pobreza se Supera en la Solidarid* (1994), criticizing neoliberalism for creating an unacceptable gap between the rich and the poor.

Solidaridad. He argued that because the return to democracy allowed "properly political" entities to return to their legitimate roles without censorship, the church no longer needed to house human rights legal teams, church publications, or groups of professionals dedicated to preserving space for grassroots or national organizing. The closing meant that prominent national organizations such as the Association of the Families of the Disappeared (as well as related human rights organizations) were left without a national home.[7] Most important for hundreds of thousands of poor Chileans, the *vicaría's* abrupt closing left a vast array of grassroots organizations, including the base Christian communities, without any national coordinating structure or access to training and professional support, much less a channel for external funding or resources.

In another move to reassert the hierarchical control of the official church, in the 1990s the bishops created a new ecclesial office, the Pastoral for Base Christian Communities, under the jurisdiction of the archbishop of Santiago. The new pastoral was not intended to replace the Vicaría de Solidaridad, however. Rather, it replaced the Coordinadora Nacional de Comunidades de Base, the body that had grown out of the base communities in the 1970s. Because grassroots leaders themselves created and led the *coordinadora,* its closing (at the behest of Cardinal Oviedo) and replacement by the new pastoral meant a loss of autonomy for the grassroots groups. Similarly, in a move to rein in what church leaders consider "political" manipulation of Catholic offices or symbols, in 1990 Cardinal Oviedo asked the organizers of the annual popular ritual Vía Crúcis to disband. The Vía Crúcis, as mentioned earlier, is a celebration of the stations of the cross that became widely associated with opposition to the military regime's use of torture and assassination of dissidents. The celebration was one of the largest annual popular mobilizations during the dictatorship, and although nominally convoked by the Vicarios Zonales, it was organized largely by lay leaders who were active in the Coordinadora Nacional de Comunidades de Base.[8] As in the case of the

---

7. The Association of the Families of the Detained-Disappeared was taken in by CONFERRE, the international confederation of religious priests and nuns. CONFERRE is typically more progressive than national hierarchies, although it does house members of very conservative orders, such as Opus Dei or Legionnaires for Christ, as well. Although the Association of the Families of the Detained-Disappeared can continue to meet in the offices of CONFERRE, it has lost the visibility and national prominence that it enjoyed while housed at the Vicaría de Solidaridad (Montserrat Lopez, executive director of CONFERRE in Chile, interview, May 22, 1995).

8. According to Mariano Puga, one of the most well known progressive priests in Chile, the Vía Crúcis was first convoked through the Vicaría de Pastoral Obrero, but the Coordinador Nacional de Comunidades

coordinadora, the church's clampdown on the popular, lay-led Vía Crúcis was seen by grassroots activists as a clear withdrawal from support of grassroots activism and popular empowerment and a reassertion of vertical, hierarchical, and traditionalist control.

Other progressive ministries and practices also suffered blows, but survived. The Vicaría de Pastoral Obrera endures; however, it shriveled to a staff of only eight full-time employees by the mid-1990s (Alberto Gonzalez, executive director of the Vicaría de Pastoral Obrera, interview, March 14, 1995). The Academy of Christian Humanism gained independent status in 1988, cutting it and other research institutes off from church affiliation. Funding from international Catholic and non-Catholic sources dried up once the return to democracy removed Chile from the list of most needy and worthy recipients for aid, particularly regarding support for human rights activities that were largely affiliated with the church (Alexander Wilde and Cynthia Sanborn, Ford Foundation interviews, March 16, 1995).

Several progressive study centers still exist, such as the Centro Ecumenico Diego Medellín, Universidad Cardenal Silva Henríquez (formerly Blas Canas), Universidad Padre Alberto Hurtado, and Con-spirando, and they continue to house much of the continuing progressive debate and innovation. The late progressive theologian Fernando Castillo speculated that by the mid-1990s, perhaps 20 percent of the clergy remained adherents to the principles of liberation theology, yet they had been pushed to the periphery of the church by newly appointed bishops or changes within the hierarchy's priorities (interview, March 14, 1995). Progressives feel as though they have "lost the argument" over the public face of the church in democracy.[9] In fact, several international conservative Catholic movements—represented by, for example, Opus Dei, Legionnaires of Christ, and the Shchoenstatt community—have grown among businesspeople and journalists in Chile in recent years (Fontaine 2000, 253). Although these movements, which target the upper classes

de Base was the real organizational force behind its success. Cardinals Raul Silva Henríquez, Francisco Fresno, and Carlos Oviedo all sought ways to bring them under closer hierarchical control (Puga 2000).

9. The Vicaría de Pastoral Obrera conducted a survey in 1985 of 611 men and women who had worked in organizations supported by the *vicaría*. The explicit purpose of the survey was to determine what role people wanted the *vicaría* and the church to play in Chile's future. The overwhelming response, among union and non-church-related respondents as well as respondents in church-related grassroots organizations, was support for continued church activism and outreach to grassroots and popular organizations (VPO photocopy).

through the latter's exclusive preparatory and high schools, do not typically penetrate the popular world, they are extremely influential among the wealthy and the church hierarchy.[10] According to Fontaine, one measure of the conservative influence of these movements is the degree to which they control the public discourse in Chile. Almost all the newspapers and radio stations are "controlled by conservative businessmen or, directly or indirectly, by the Catholic Church or Church-related institutions" (280). Not surprisingly, a spirit of dejection plagues many progressives, who now feel relegated to the margins of the church's public discourse and activity.[11]

Brazil: Pockets of Popular Church Persistence

The overall trajectory of the Brazilian national church has certainly been similar to that of the church in Chile, yet the former's retreat from a liberationist stance was more gradual and more nuanced. While it has clearly retreated from its position as the "voice of the voiceless" and raising moral opposition to government, it has not forged a passive, dependent alliance with the state or renounced all social and political roles. Instead, as Kenneth Serbin (1999) argues, its position can more accurately be characterized as that of "moral watchdog." As a result, greater pockets of progressivism persist, although that line is clearly no longer dominant and support for the base communities has diminished.

The difference should not be exaggerated because the transition subjected the Brazilian church to many of the same pressures its Chilean counterpart encountered. Some were internal and resulted from a long-standing imbalance in power dating from the military era; the Brazilian church was always divided between liberationists and conservatives. From the 1970s until 1995, however, progressive bishops dominated the CNBB, making it one of the most

10. For example, Joaquín Lavin, who came close to winning in the 2000 presidential election, is a supernumerary member of Opus Dei. His campaign emphasized a platform that was pro-Western, family oriented, conservative in morals and religion, and pro-business.

11. The change in the church's public rhetoric also reflects a strong conservative shift within the ranks of the Chilean church itself, and not merely the influence of the Vatican or Vatican-appointed conservatives. The clear trend in Chilean vocations for the past fifteen years has been toward a more traditionally pastoral clergy. As Father Rodrigo Tupper, the director of the National Commission on Vocations, states, "The percentages of vocations from the upper or lower classes has not changed. What has changed is the general profile of the man taking a new vocation. Regardless of class background, the new clergy are generally much more devotional, with a narrower pastoral vision of the church" (Rodrigo Tupper, interview, May 11, 1995).

outspoken national hierarchies in the world. Liberationists, however, were always a minority among the bishops, so it was probably natural that the balance of power would begin to shift the other way at some point.

The Vatican also wanted to bring the troublesome Brazilian church to heel.[12] It helped to curb the liberationists through a variety of measures, many of which the women activists vividly recall. Most dramatically, the Vatican signaled its displeasure with liberationist tendencies in Brazil by officially silencing theologian Leonardo Boff in 1984. Lúcia links this action directly to the decline of base communities: "I don't see base communities in the future. Even more so after they silenced the voices of the prophets, Leonardo Boff—these people don't speak anymore. . . . Dom Adriano Hipólito doesn't speak anymore, dom Hélder Câmara doesn't speak anymore, the bishops who were progressive are retiring, dying." The impact of Boff's silencing (and his renunciation of his priestly vocation in 1992) may have been largely symbolic, but Lúcia is right that the number—and therefore the power—of progressive bishops is declining. The Vatican has helped along the natural processes of retirement and death by reducing their numbers through many direct interventions.

The Vatican's power of appointment has exerted a tremendous moderating influence on the episcopate. It quickly replaced progressive Cardinal Paulo Evaristo Arns of São Paulo when he reached retirement age, for example, but delayed the replacement of Rio's conservative Archbishop Eugênio Salles.[13] It has favored conservatives and moderates in its new appointments and promotions, most conspicuously when it replaced Recife's dom Hélder Câmara, the charismatic elder statesman of the liberationists, with conservative José Cardoso Sobrinho, who quickly dismantled many of dom Hélder's innovative institutions. Similarly, moderate dom Carlos Hummes replaced Cardinal Arns. Five of Brazil's eight cardinals were appointed by Pope John Paul II, and he has appointed them with an eye toward reestablishing Vatican control and cohesiveness (Coutinho 2001, 46).[14] Progressives are certainly a diminishing minority within the Brazilian episcopate overall (ibid.). The Vatican has used additional powers to reduce the control of remaining liberationists and marginalize them. Most important, in 1989 it dismembered the Arch-

---

12. Many authors mention this as a key factor, including Hewitt (2000, 5, 6) and Levy (2000 168).

13. "Catholic Church Remains Outspoken Despite Shifts," *Latinamerica Press*, August 20, 1998, 1. Salles's replacement was finally announced in June 2001.

14. Recently Hummes and dom Geraldo Majella became Brazil's seventh and eighth cardinals.

diocese of São Paulo, restructuring it to leave Archbishop dom Paulo with the most affluent areas, in which there were few base communities, while having him lose control of the Zona Leste and Zona Sul, two regions known for their base community activism.

As in Chile, the growth of Pentecostalism also pushed the Brazilian church toward a less activist stance. While Pentecostal churches mushroomed during military rule, the base communities had not proved to be particularly successful in attracting large numbers of the unchurched poor. Many bishops concluded that part of the base communities' "problem" was an overly political and intellectualized sensibility. The Pentecostals' more visceral, emotive spirituality seemed to have more appeal to poor laypeople. Although the church was not about to change its practices dramatically, it could try a "resacralization" of local church life—a return to the traditional sacraments, an emphasis on ritual, and a revival of folk traditions such as processions— in an attempt to stave off the inroads of the evangelicals. To the extent that the hierarchy continued to support base communities, it would do so with a new emphasis and an eye toward evangelical competition from the mid-1990s on. In addition, some conservative bishops began to explicitly promote the apolitical, devotional Charismatic Catholic Renewal (RCC) movement, whose practices share many characteristics with those of evangelical groups.

The transition to democracy itself had a neutralizing effect by reintroducing the complexities of party politics. In contrast to the entrenched Chilean political party system, with its well-established parties and deeply politicized civil society, Brazil's party system has been historically much weaker. Brazilian political parties did not play the same central role in the democratic transition as in Chile, and the major left party, the PT, grew out of the social movements rather than displaced them. Thus, although neither Brazilian political elites nor the bishops argued for the same deference to the parties' role as the proper interlocutor between citizens and the state as did their counterparts in Chile, the partisan competition inherent in democracy did reinforce Brazilian church elites' long-standing worries about the damaging effects of the appearance of church partisanship. The Brazilian church had always eschewed partisanism, and the period of the transition made it increasingly difficult to make a political statement without appearing to endorse one party or another. The base communities themselves faced this problem at the local level, as individuals had to maintain a level of neutrality that would hold the community together. The fall of the Berlin Wall made any association with a Marxist left problematic and led many liberationists to revise their views of the meaning and desirability of socialism, complicating their policy positions and public statements. In addition, the church sped up cutting loose the popular organizations it had created because, as the previous chapter showed, it never intended to preserve the space for avowedly political organizations or parties until they could retake their rightful place in society. It therefore encouraged grassroots groups to take over much of its role in promoting human rights and social movements (Serbin 1999, 211).

For all these reasons, the institutional church's support for base community involvement in social movements dropped precipitously as the cycle of movement activism entered its decline. Despite these pressures, however, the progressives' reversal in Brazil was not complete. Although they are now clearly less influential within the hierarchy, their ideas retain some influence within the church as a whole, and they are not as isolated as their Chilean counterparts. Although no longer a prophetic opposition, the church's position as moral watchdog preserves some of the liberationists' legacy. Moreover, the erosion of progressives' power within Brazil's much larger and more diversified hierarchy was a slow process, with many even today retaining some visible and significant posts.

The mixture of traditional and progressive voices in the pluralistic Brazilian hierarchy is evident in official church statements. Conservative domination is most noticeable in the hierarchy's emphatic statements on moral issues, such as abortion, which occupied little of its time and attention in the 1970s and 1980s. The church has advocated strenuously for protection of the family and a prohibition on the sterilization of women. It has fought to maintain religious instruction in schools and sought continued or renewed government support for many of its charities (Serbin 1999, 212–13). In contrast to its earlier mobilizations for direct elections and social rights, in 1997 the church organized significant demonstrations in opposition to a bill that would have obliged public hospitals to perform abortions; a right to a hospital abortion has legal standing but has never been enforced in Brazil. Although the progressives' old ally the PT sponsored the bill, there is no evidence to parallel the Chilean case of progressive bishops attempting to pressure PT politicians on the vote.[15]

Even in speaking of social issues, church leaders have generally tried to distance themselves from anything that could be seen as "politicized" or

---

15. "Emotions Run High over Abortion Bill," *Latin America Regional Reports: Brazil Report*, September 9, 1997 (RB-97-08).

"liberationist," stressing instead the moral and spiritual tenor of its positions. Recently, for example, dom Claudio Hummes commented: "It's evident that a conflict between the included and the excluded exists. We continue to denounce social problems, but with a basis in the Gospel, not in ideologies" (Coutinho 2001, 46). As in Chile, statements tend increasingly to move the notion of the "excluded" away from an emphasis on class and poverty and toward a broader category that includes drug addicts, prostitutes, the mentally ill, and other social "outcasts."

While conservative positions predominate, however, the progressive legacy persists. Progressives may be isolated or may speak alone at some times and on some issues, but the episcopate as a whole continues to offer quite critical pronouncements on social, economic, and political issues on a fairly regular basis. In 1998, for example, the church issued a strongly worded criticism of the government's handling of a drought in the northeast, with a number of bishops (including moderate dom Hummes) agreeing with dom Marcelo Pinto's assessment that the desperation in the region justified looting. A May Day declaration the same year, endorsed even by conservatives, attacked the government's neoliberal policies.[16] The bishops regularly discuss and write about such issues at their annual CNBB meetings. In 1997, for example, of three documents produced at the meeting, two dealt critically with social issues.[17] Such critical statements have been enough of an irritant to lead President Fernando Henrique Cardoso to accuse the bishops of interfering in politics.[18]

Similarly, Brazilian progressives are less clearly marginalized within the hierarchy than in the Chilean case. For example, progressives controlled the presidency of the CNBB as late as 1995, well past the end of the military regime. When the conservative elected in that year, dom Lucas Moreira Neves, was called to the Vatican in 1998, that body promptly voted in another progressive, dom Jayme Chemello. He was elected to a full four-year term in 1999. Another progressive, dom Marcelo Carvalheira, serves as vice president, while progressives head a number of work areas, including vocations and ministry, and laity and ecclesial base communities.[19] Overall, base

---

16. "Cardoso Criticized over Drought in NE," *Latin American Weekly Report* 5 (May 1998), 50; "Catholic Church Remains Outspoken Despite Shifts," *Latinamerica Press,* August 20, 1998, 1, 8.

17. Nevio Fiorin, interview, Rio de Janeiro, 10 July 1997. The third dealt with matrimony.

18. "Return of Progressive Church," *Latinamerica Press,* May 3, 1999.

19. Ibid.

community advisor Nevio Fiorin considered eight of eleven members of the
CNBB directorate to be progressives as late as 1997.[20]

We can certainly question how much real power is attached to these offices.
The office of laity and ecclesial base communities, in particular, is not likely
to prove to be a power base from which the base communities' resurgence
could be launched, even under progressive leadership. As Manuel Vásquez
(1997) points out, recent local-level attempts to recognize and regularize
base communities have usually gone hand in hand with a reduction in their
autonomy and a restoration of clerical authority (62). Nonetheless, unlike in
Chile, progressives in Brazil remain visible and have, at least in language
and rhetorical commitment, left a noticeable legacy.

Finally, the progressive legacy is visible in real institutional structures.
The CNBB opened a special office on social issues in the 1990s to facilitate
its moral watchdog role. More important, and more irritating to the government, through the Pastoral Land Commission, headed by dom Tomas
Balduino, the church as a whole actively continues to support and identify
with the most visible, controversial social movement in Brazil today, the
landless movement (Movimento dos Sem Terra [MST]). Further, the National
Bishops' Conference continues to maintain an office of base communities
headed by a progressive, longtime base community advisor Pedro de Oliveira
Ribeiro, and national base community encounters continue to be held every
three years. The most recent, in Ilheus, Bahia, in July 2000, drew more than
three thousand participants. Sixty-three of Brazil's 309 bishops attended.

Again, this does not necessarily translate into material support, freedom, or
strength for the base communities. On the contrary, there is a strong tendency
within the church to maintain the communities but "rein them in" with
tighter clerical control. And as feminist theologian Ivone Gebara comments,
"[T]he encounters, while important, are . . . a celebration or affirmation of
hope" rather than a sign of strength in or support for the base communities.[21]
We should be cautious in interpreting the signs that the progressive church is
still alive and holding some sway within the Brazilian church as a whole.
Nonetheless, the church's more gradual and nuanced retreat, as well as its
sociocultural model of base communities, lead Brazilian activists to a different

20. Nevio Fiorin, interview, Rio de Janeiro, 10 July 1997.
21. "Interview: Feminist Theologian Sr. Ivone Gebara: 'A Church with Different Faces,'" *Latinamerica
Press*, November 12, 1998.

perception from that of Chileans of the decline of protest. Although not hopeful that the church hierarchy will soon support social activism again, activists in Brazil are optimistic that base communities and church groups will remain a basis from which to launch organizing and protest.

Activists Interpret Declining Support

Chile: "There Was an Earthquake, Not a 'Change'"

Grassroots women activists experienced the Chilean Catholic Church's withdrawal from its notable social commitment during the dictatorship as a sudden, rapid, and wrenching abandonment—as is articulated in the preceding quote (Veroncia Pardo, base Christian community San Gabriel, Pudahuel). Virtually all the Chilean women expressed this sentiment—in fact, only one states that her base community remains unchanged in its activities and progressivism. In contrast to Brazilians, who experienced a gradual decline in their base communities, Chilean women all pinpoint a specific time at which they perceive that the church began its withdrawal, underscoring their experience of the change as dramatic and rapid.[22] As we will see below, while many women describe the change in their own base communities in terms of the coming or going of individual priests, the Chileans' dominant perception is that the withdrawal was a conscious choice on the part of the national hierarchy, and it can be traced to the church's response to changing national conditions.

Contradicting the conventional wisdom that the Chilean social movements, and grassroots women's activism in particular, subsided because democracy was achieved and women could "finally go home," our findings show that most women in the base communities blame the church for abandoning them. Although a number of women described the height of the protest movement as both exhausting and exhilarating, only a handful of respondents explain their communities' decline as the result of activists'

22. One-fifth (20 percent) report that the change toward a more traditional, hierarchical church began in the early 1980s, when traditionalist Juan Fresno replaced progressive Cardinal Silva Henríquez, founder of the Vicaría de Solidaridad and one of the most progressive church officials in the Americas. However, 76 percent date the change to around 1988–89, the period in which Pinochet lost the plebiscite that would have allowed him nine more years of rule, the presidential election occurred, and the democratic transition began.

exhaustion or some misplaced hope that democracy would solve their communities' problems.[23] Rather, the overwhelming majority of Chileans (87 percent) blame the church's withdrawal and the downturn in social activism on the church itself. Veronica Pardo's remarks below underscore the sentiment shared by the majority of Chilean women:

> Around 1989, the Catholic Church returned to what it had always been: a great, hierarchical, authoritarian and fairly rightist Church. It was more than a change; it was an earthquake. It replaced priests, bishops, and officials at every level with conservatives. Pastors who differed quite a bit with the direction of the Christian base communities were named. . . . People who participated were discredited as communists, infiltrators, whether or not they were believers. . . . Parish facilities would no longer be lent for solidarity or cultural activities. The church went back to looking no farther than its own belly button. . . . In truth, the church never believed in the social movement. Those who wanted social change were a minority.

Mercedes Montoya dates the change in the church to the visit to Chile by Pope John Paul II. "Before the transition process began, the pope's visit and the change in the archbishop brought changes to the community. The new priests wanted to end everything that the previous priest had built over many years. They even asked the people who had a greater social commitment to leave. They forgot the church's missionary purpose and imposed a traditionalist, fundamentalist church." Betty Sepulveda explains the church's withdrawal as starkly political: "The interests of the church hierarchy in Latin American and particularly in Chile aimed to consolidate the neoliberal system. . . . Progressive priests were admonished and sent to remote parts of the country, or retired."

The most painful and dramatic change experienced by the Chilean women stemmed from the rapid turnover in local priests as (often foreign)

---

23. Suzanne Leiser, a Canadian nun who has been active in Cerro Navia since 1970, is one of the few Chileans who describe the decline of social activism consistently with the conventional wisdom that many women who were in the Christian communities came to a moment in which they needed a rest from the war. "Democracy arrived and there were a lot of leaders who had spent the majority of their youth working for everyone else, and they had not married or had children. So they went home. Now, there are people who want to participate but they still have small children. This is an important thing that has happened with many people. They have a bad conscience for not participating, but I tell them that they also have a right to their life."

progressives were replaced with traditionalists. Ninety-one percent feel that their relationship with their priest has changed. Although a few women report that their parishes are enjoying a resurgence in base community activity because of new, progressive priests, almost all (93 percent) report that their base community's relationship with the parish priest has become more distant and hierarchical.[24] Flor Gonzalez, former participant in base Christian community Cristo Rey in Peñalolen, states that today "the community is like a group closed in on itself. The priest used to go see people in their houses. Today relations are cold and there is little communication. [Now], priests are changed every two or three years." Juana Rivera from La Legua reports that "Father Ramon said that 'you're not going to have an *olla comun* or *comprando juntos* here anymore.' He felt that people came to the church out of self-interest, to look for help. He wanted to see if they would come to pray without that incentive." María Ortega Soto from Huamachuco describes a more extreme change: "The priest said, 'Either participate in the church or leave the church.' He imposed his position and strongly urged that they throw us out of the place where we had been participating. Also there was a lot of pressure from conservative people to throw us out. . . . They threw out all unmarried couples, single mothers, and rehabilitated young people from the meeting place, La Caleta. In other words, they threw out everyone they found who were not 'good Christians.'"

A similar picture emerges from responses to a question regarding base communities' current levels of support from church sources. The majority report that support from the parish or priest has either decreased (32 percent) or stopped (52 percent), support from their diocese has either decreased (36 percent) or stopped (64 percent), and support from national or international church sources (including the *vicarías*) has either decreased (8 percent) or stopped (83 percent).[25] As discussed in the previous chapter, Chilean base communities depended heavily on priests for moral support and open access to meeting places, while they depended far more heavily than in Brazil on the *vicarías* for training and material and (to a lesser extent) financial support. Given the closing of the Vicaría de Solidaridad and the reduced visibility of

---

24. All the Chileans also report that their community's relationship with the bishop is more distant, and 87 percent feel the relationship with the national church is more distant.

25. The further the funding source from a respondent's local experience, the less likely she was to answer the question. Roughly half (48 percent and 52 percent, respectively) failed to answer if their base community currently receives support from their parish or diocese. Seventy-five percent failed to answer about support from national or international Catholic sources.

the other *vicarías,* the precipitous decline in national and international support reported by Chilean women is not surprising. The similarly dramatic decline in perceived support from the bishops and priests, however, under- scores the Chileans' perception that the changes in the church were not only a reflection of Vatican or even national episcopate politics, but also a real and fundamental change on the ground in parish after parish. Irma Parraguez echoes the experiences of the majority of Chilean women: "The priests changed in 1990. There was still plenty to do, but these new traditional priests changed things. . . . They closed the chapels. They said that young people could not meet there. A health group still worked from the chapel but these priests said it had to find another place. . . . The priests think that they own the truth. The congregation simply has to obey." Many of the Chileans report that the more socially and politically committed groups in their base communities were denied access to the neighborhood chapels, turning these locations—which often were originally built by local members—into exten- sions of hierarchical control. For example, Aurora Hernández describes her new priest's imposition of the church's hierarchical authority over the previ- ously participatory base community in her neighborhood: "There are no real CEBs [anymore]. Before, the communities called meetings and the priests attended like the rest of the people. Today, the priest has to approve of everything. As long as you don't overstep your bounds, there is no problem, [but] you can't talk about divorce, abortion, or politics."

In addition to there being virtual disappearance of support for grassroots activities that might be considered "political" or "social," almost all the Chileans report that training workshops facilitated by the parish or other, national church organizations today consist entirely of traditional, religious instruction—for example, catechist, traditionally pastoral, or devotional courses. Only 11 percent report that their base community currently receives training relating to anything beyond strictly religious instruction from their parish. Even more dramatic, given the historic role played by the *vicarías* and other international aid agencies during the dictatorship, no respondent reports any form of training or networking support from diocesan or national or interna- tional sources beyond strictly religious, devotional courses.

Without clear leadership from progressive priests and in the absence of a "preferential option for the poor" by the national hierarchy, many base Christian communities have simply disintegrated, leaving former activists frustrated, angry, and isolated. As Mercedes Montoya, currently a regional director for Servicio por Paz y Justicia (SERPAJ), describes, priests' leadership usually played a critical role in determining the level of social activism in a base community:

> The priest was the principle promoter of the base community. It was a contradictory relationship because it was not a mature community; therefore, the priest had to go slow, trying to satisfy everyone. . . . There were always struggles between the social activists and the traditional laity. The feeding centers [*comedores*] and charity work existed in the beginning years. Then the base community added the human rights committee and health groups, but they always lacked unity. One group came to accept a greater social commitment while the others always resisted social-political work.

Although base community activists experienced the change in the church toward a more traditional focus on pastoral and moral matters as a devastating abandonment, from the *church*'s perspective, the turn toward tradition has been quite successful. Although new vocations have dropped somewhat from their 1987 high, the 1997 number still far exceeded the 1977 number (Gill 1999, 33). Similarly, although many of our respondents have left their local parishes out of dismay over the church's traditional turn, they report that new members, including young women, are joining. The return to the church of those who had been uncomfortable with or afraid of church social activism has led to renewed vibrancy in many parishes. Many of our respondents report that parish-level groups are attracting new participants who are looking for traditional religious practices and formation. Marta Alvarez, a coordinator of the women's handicrafts workshops for the Vicaría de Solidaridad during the dictatorship and currently director of a community center that trains women in job skills, describes her parish: "During the dictatorship, many people were afraid of the social-political work that went on within the church. As a matter of fact, there were many arrests of people involved in this kind of work within the church. Many people who had stayed away out of fear returned with the change to a more traditional and safe church."[26]

---

26. The community center where Marta Alvarez works was founded in honor of her daughter, Araceli Ramos, who was killed in Temuco by agents of the military in 1988 along with another leader of the MIR. After her daughter's assassination, Marta had a personal encounter with the changed church. A priest accompanied her to Temuco to find a church that would offer mass for her daughter's funeral, but no Catholic parish or institution would agree to their request. Finally, they found a Methodist church willing to conduct the funeral.

Virginia Puga, who had been detained and tortured for eight days during the dictatorship, says that in Villa Francia, "the majority are new people, those who did not participate before because they thought that the church and the community were communist."

Some local churches continue to offer some technical training, although only in the spirit of providing individual help, not as part of a larger consciousness-raising project. Especially in the late 1990s, during a severe economic downturn that resulted in rising unemployment and poverty, young people again began attending church for the opportunity to take part in church training programs. For example, Alicia Cortez from Lo Valledur Sur reports that "there are a lot of new people and young people in the training projects, but they only participate in order to learn a trade, not for motives of solidarity like before."

Others report a new emphasis on consolidating and beautifying church infrastructure—new buildings, fresh paint, newly planted flowers and trees, and other physical improvements. Suzanne Leiser describes the return to her parish of many people who are pleased with the new, attractive parish building. "Before there was only a very small chapel. Now there is a large, beautiful, and flashy parish. Now people who left before to go to Lourdes [a large devotional site a couple of kilometers away] are coming back, and now they have this new church that is closer. They are the people who had been passive in the past."

The problem our respondents perceive is not that their parishes are empty; rather, they believe that their church has abandoned them in preference for a obedient, hierarchical institution in which the faithful, and women in particular, return to their proper roles as dutiful followers of church spiritual teachings. As Laura Herrera complains, "I feel very out of place among people [in the church today] who couldn't care less for social issues. . . . Their only concern is to have a nicely painted church with flowers inside."

Brazil: Erosion and Invasion

I think things have slowed down a bit, diminished, you know. From a certain time until now, I think the CEBs are at almost a standstill. The type of vision changed. The CEBs were a vision of a different church, very advanced in the minds of some people, and then suddenly it seems that's it. As if they had thrown a chill over them and then they were changing a little.

— MARIA EDWIGES

Like Maria Edwiges, most base community activists at the grass roots agree with their Chilean counterparts that their organizations are atrophying and receiving less and less support. They are as unanimous as the Chilean women in articulating that the decline has been pervasive. Many expressed the view that base communities, in fact, no longer exist. Cida Lima says of the groups in São Paulo's formerly activist Zona Leste, "The CEBs were broken and whoever says otherwise [is wrong]. Today there are people trying to preserve this, but with great difficulty." Célia is from the same area, and she agrees: "Today we don't speak of CEBs anymore. It's not worth speaking in terms of *comunidades de base*. We have churches, parishes in themselves." Charmaine Levy (2000) points out that conservatives have often targeted activist CEBs for transformation into parishes, specifically to exert more clerical control (171). And indeed, new priests and the new conservative bishop, dom Fernando, have transformed many communities in the region into "parishes" in an attempt to regularize their status and rein them in more closely to the church, a trend that has occurred elsewhere in Brazil as well.

Even where the church has not exercised official powers to dismantle base communities, however, there is a strong sense that they are a thing of the past. In another part of the Zona Leste, Sofia says, "There aren't any CEBs. Today there aren't." Maria das Graças, in the Baixada Fluminense of Rio de Janeiro sees the same trend in her region, where she oversees a number of mothers' clubs. "I think the CEBs have weakened. Nobody even talks about CEBs anymore." She adds, "Today there has been a great change in the church. It is difficult to work with CEBs within the church." Even Geralda, who has participated in several national base community encounters, concludes that if they are strong anywhere, it must be somewhere else: "You see that the CEBs fell and it seemed they would not revive. The CEBs fell so far it seemed they didn't exist anymore. The CEBs aren't strong around here. They're strong in the north, in Ceara. In Maranhão they're strong, in Espirito Santo a little strong." Although some clerical supporters of base communities, such as Clodovis Boff, try to put a positive face on the current situation, others agree with these women that the groups are in a general decline. Father Ed Leising, founder and director of the NGO in Rio de Janeiro called FASE, has worked closely with base communities since their inception. His view is quite clear: "The base communities have been crushed by the church."[27] Sister Ivone Gebara says, "Base communities are part of the past. They continue today, but [their presence] is very weak."[28]

27. Fr. Ed Leising, interview, Rio de Janeiro, 29 July 1997.
28. "Interview: Feminist Theologian Sr. Ivone Gebara: 'A Church with Different Faces,'" *Latinamerica Press*, November 12, 1998.

Activists view these changes with regret, depression, and disillusionment. Melania is nostalgic for that time of greater activism:

> Today I see the CEBs with great sentimentality. Looking back at the past, they say you can't be nostalgic, but I am nostalgic. Because I've talked to people and we aren't only violated by civil society, but also by the church. Because I am saying, I did the Latin mass, I did the conservative church, and I passed through that moment of the renewed church and that moment of CEBs, of strikes and all. Today I look back with great sadness, because I ask, "What are CEBs today, where are the CEBs of that time where people committed themselves to the *caminhada* [march]?"

Maria Socorro can even feel nostalgia for the period of the military regime: "I even have nostalgia for the time we had more hope, because when we had the military and we couldn't vote, we had hopes that better days would come. Personally, sincerely, I don't have much hope. Maybe elsewhere there are more active CEBs. Here we are in a kind of retreat." Maria das Graças says, "I feel a little lost in the church, and I see lots of depression in the health pastoral group, too." Lourdes, from São Paulo, adds, "Today we are a little discouraged in our participation." And indeed, almost a fifth of the women—Cida Lima, Sofia, Maria José, Emerenciana—have left their base communities definitively, while another fifth (six women) did not mention any religious activities among their current community commitments.[29]

The four who left the church were among the most strongly critical of its declining support for the base communities. As Cida Lima says, "We went to church to nourish our souls [as militants]. The church broke that—we didn't." In contrast to the Chileans, however, Brazilians are less unanimously critical of the church. They assess its role more gently, and they see the sources of change as more gradual and diffuse. There was apparently no "earthquake" in Brazil. Instead, the Brazilian women describe a slow erosion of support for base communities and a simultaneous decline of the social movements. Many continue to believe that faith and politics can be reunited within other groups in the Catholic Church.

29. In several of these cases, however, the interviewees mentioned elsewhere that they do attend mass or a neighborhood prayer group.

Their gentler assessment of the church's role in the decline of protest owes much to the sociocultural model of base communities. First, this decentralized model meant that there was no single support system for the communities that could be cut off, as the *vicarías* were in Chile. Moreover, the decentralization facilitated a lack of conflict between base and hierarchy. As Scott Mainwaring (1986) predicted, this nonconflictual model seems to have insured progressive persistence, within limits (173). Second, it exposed activists to a range of secularized movement groups. Nearly half the women named nonchurch sources of support during the military regime; having had outside support, these activists now view the decline of the base communities in the context of a larger movement decline. Finally, the sociocultural model prioritized popular religiosity and local issues, and many more of the Brazilian women (60 percent) remain active in the church. They still view their spiritual participation as part of a larger social project, and many believe that faith and politics can be reunited in aspects of local church work that focus on social issues.

The much greater range of dates that the Brazilian women give for changes in their base communities' activism is one sign that the church's withdrawal there was less abrupt and less universal. Some women, like Ilda, gave dates as early as 1982—still under the military regime—a period that several women in Drogus's (1997) earlier study also refered to as the "peak" of activism. Others cited specific dates from the movement for direct elections in the early 1980s, to the constitutional assembly of 1988, to Fernando Collor de Mello's defeat of PT presidential candidate Lula in 1990. Of sixteen women who gave specific dates for the change, six cited the late 1980s or even the 1990s, well after the beginning of civilian rule.[30] No one mentioned the end of progressive domination of the CNBB (1995) coinciding with a loss of church support: power was gradually shifting to the conservatives before this date.[31] Thus, the changes in Brazil were either more gradual or more specific to locality. The women expressed less sense that the church had simply cut off the base communities as a whole.

The women's views of their relationship with different levels of the church suggest that the changes varied across localities. As in Chile (91 percent),

---

30. The date for a transition to "democracy" is controversial in Brazil, since the first civilian president (José Sarney, elected in 1985) was indirectly elected. Nonetheless, Hewitt (2000, 5); Levy (2000, 168); and Vasquez (1998, 48) all cite 1985 as the beginning of the decline.

31. As we will see below, many women described the gradual marginalization of progressive bishops.

women in Brazil (88 percent) said their community's relationship with the priest has changed. They report less change in other relationships, however. Sixty percent say the relationship with the bishop changed (78 percent in Chile), while 56 percent say the relationship with the national church changed (69 percent in Chile). Moreover, Brazilians are much less unanimous about the direction of the changes. The bishops come in for the most criticism: 73 percent of those who saw a change said relations with them were worse. Women who experienced the change to a conservative bishop in the Zona Leste were particularly critical, seeing him as arrogant and distant. Sixty-three percent said relations with the priest had deteriorated. As in Chile, many of the women cited the advent of younger, more traditional priests who did not support community work. Cida Lima, for example, says that the new priests in her parish sought out new lay leaders, pushing aside people like her with long work in the community. Edna laments that no new priests are coming forward with a progressive agenda. The national hierarchy received the least criticism (42 percent said relations were worse.)

Similarly, although the overall story the women tell is one of declining resources for base communities, a larger number still report some support from the parish and diocesan levels.[32] Fifty percent say they receive aid from the parish and 36 percent mentioned the diocese.[33] Thirty-six percent mentioned training from the parish, and 44 percent from the diocese. Since some of the women reported only "training" or "education," much of this may have been purely religious. Given that 60 percent are religiously active and given the sociocultural model's emphasis on "faith and politics," Brazilians may be more favorable to such aid than Chileans. However, in contrast to the figure in Chile, one-quarter of Brazilians mentioned activities with more social content, such as speakers on "economics and politics," "unemployment," or topics oriented to "those who are poor." Maria Edwiges's diocese facilitated leadership and citizenship training by the NGO, the Center for Community Action (CEDAC), in her community. Although the pockets of persistence are small, as we would expect, Brazil's more decentralized model does seem to facilitate continuity with a more political and social agenda, at least in some areas where bishops or priests facilitate this.[34]

---

32. Only a handful mentioned other levels. As in Chile, clearly most were unaware of resources beyond the diocese.

33. Only two mentioned national aid and one, international aid.

34. Base communities with a social agenda have grown significantly in Brasilandia (SP), for example, since dom Angélico Bernardino's assignment there (Levy 2000, p. 174). In addition, three women mentioned

This local pluralism partly accounts for Brazilian activists' apparently warmer feelings toward the church. For example, some of the women come from dioceses still headed by progressive bishops, such as dom Mauro Morelli, who they believe continue to support their efforts, even though these efforts no longer seem to bear fruit. Others, like the women from the Zona Leste of São Paulo, still work with the same sisters who supported them during the social movement era. In only a few cases is the institutional Church's role in ending the base community experiment extremely clear. In the Zona Leste of São Paulo, the women clearly perceive the new conservative bishop and the many conservative priests he brought in after the archdiocese was restructured as a problem. As Célia says, "The revolutionary bishop we had was taken out, pulled out of the region. That was dom Angélico. A completely conservative bishop came, then everything changed." In the Zona Leste, at least, "the conservative side won." Cida Lima is more specific about how this happened: "We had trouble with the [new] priests there, because when they came, I thought they were disrespectful. Because when a new person comes, they have to see who the leaders are and who has a certain participation, but it was just the opposite. They went after other people. And they were trying to break us."[35] While many Chileans cited specific priests or bishops as problems, such complaints in Brazil came mostly from women from the Zona Leste.

The decentralized Brazilian model and the gradual nature of the church's withdrawal gave Brazilians fewer such tangible changes to criticize, but they are generally critical of the "bishops" for abdicating their leadership role. As Melania says, they always knew that only some bishops supported them and others did not, and this is still true; but after 1990, "in the church the bishops who were full speed ahead seemed to do an about-face and weakened too." Even here, however, the sense of betrayal is more diffuse than related to discernible actions, and the women often see attenuating circumstances. For example, most women who criticized the CNBB's conservatism referred in

---

aid in organizing interecclesial meetings. It is unclear what the content of this aid is, but interecclesial CEB meetings have always raised a variety of social issues.

35. As Manuel Vasquez (1997) points out, most Brazilian base communities always had a mix of liberationists and more traditional Catholics. The two groups often coexisted in an uneasy division of labor in the 1970s and 1980s, with the liberationists dominating the leadership. Today, more conservative priests often tilt the balance in the other direction, bringing the traditionalists into leadership positions. The resentment the liberationists feel is predictable and strong (58, 59, 63). For a description of the coexistence of groups with quite different religious outlooks and political philosophies in base communities in the Zona Leste of São Paulo, see Drogus 1997.

some way to the pope or the Vatican having tilted the balance toward conservatives there. Women in the Zona Leste are keenly aware that the Vatican, not the CNBB, dismantled the archdiocese and gave them a conservative bishop. Similarly, Maria das Graças says: "There was a time when the CNBB was active a little, but it changed. I don't know if the pope boxed their ears. Once in a while the bishops of the CNBB say something." Of the eight women who very specifically criticized or referred to the retrenchment in the CNBB, only two described this as a move by the leadership to undermine the base communities. Melania says that the CNBB "pulled the carpet" out from under an increasingly independent laity, while Lúcia recalls: "We fought hard when the CNBB said that the church had a supplemental role in activities outside the church. I remember that we started there. For me it was a little bit of that; it was when the hierarchy of the church retreated from this social role, entered more into religious problems. I think that's where the change began in the degree of participation." Most of the other respondents perceive the process of change in the church as pervasive, but less deliberate. The progressive bishops "were marginalized," they didn't betray or cut off the base communities, for example. Or, as Célia says, there is a new "dominant ideology" within the church that the base communities must overcome in order to be revived.

This sense of diffuse, gradual abandonment may account for the Brazilians' mixed response to the question of whether the base communities and their goals have changed. Only 68 percent of the women responded that the objectives of the communities had changed during the transition, compared with 96 percent in Chile. Although the Brazilian women admit that their groups are no longer politically active, many share Maria José's view that it wasn't the objectives of the communities that changed—as she says, "The objective of the CEBs is consciousness-raising, valuing the human being, finding our faith, integrating into society." Brazilian women have no large church directives to point to that prove that expectations of base communities have changed. Activists still believe in the mission. As in Chile, women in Brazil overwhelmingly—twenty-three of twenty-five respondents—believe that base communities still have an important role to play in their poor neighborhoods. What changed, in their view, is their ability to carry it out. Only a little more than half the women believe that their communities can act for change today.[36]

---

36. Hewitt (2000) found that only 27 percent of women expressed confidence in the church's ability to promote social justice; our respondents, however, seemed to believe that it *should* play this role (13).

While they point to fewer specific things the church did to hinder the communities, most Brazilian women argue more generally that what Célia calls the "dominant ideology" in the church has changed. The connection between faith and politics has been replaced by a more spiritualized ethos, and as a result the base communities as they knew them "no longer exist." In some cases, the change is a result of deliberate local policies designed to facilitate the growth of the Charismatic Catholic Renewal (RCC), a devotional group whose faith-healing and other practices are similar in some ways to those of the growing Pentecostal churches. The Zona Leste's new bishop, dom Fernando, has promoted the RCC in the region, as women there clearly know. Cida Lima, for example, notes the church's promotion of Padre Marcelo Rossi, the "aerobicizing priest," a charismatic priest in São Paulo with his own television show. If liberationists like Frei Betto had had such TV time, she suggests, they could have accomplished more. Sofia, also from the Zona Leste, says that the church abandoned the base communities to "compete with other churches," and that the priests and bishops today "only want microphones, TV"—a clear swipe at the likes of Padre Marcelo. Lourdes, from the same diocese, says, "I see more that people today, we invite them to meetings, invite, invite, and people don't even care. I see this more after the charismatic renewal. People are more into pray, pray, they don't see why we have to have prayer and action together."

Only a few women who have left the church altogether are uniformly critical of the RCC. Another small minority sees something admirable in its strong spirituality, while the majority of respondents sees it in a mixed light. Most of the women (sixteen) believe that—at least potentially—RCC members could work with liberationists. Three women cited the fact that RCC members participate in some of the church's socially oriented pastoral groups (such as the Youth Pastoral). Others saw the RCC's emphasis on prayer as potentially complementary. But although few rejected the RCC outright, the overwhelming majority of respondents viewed it with some degree of skepticism: open to the possibility of cooperation, but to varying degrees depending on the mix of "threat" and "complementarity" they perceive.

Most women believe that, promoted by the hierarchy or not, a more "alienated" religiosity is simply popular and appealing right now and that people will choose that over the communities' social gospel. Many women specifically mentioned the growth of the charismatics as a clear example of this. As Edna says, "In this context now, confronted with so much violence, suffering, so much loss . . . various sectors of the church have become more

Pentecostal, sort of." Despite their willingness to consider working with charismatics, many women fear their growth, seeing it as potentially divisive or threatening to the base communities' social projects. As Edna says, "If the church becomes completely charismatic, I see no reason to stay in it." Geralda laments that at the ninth national base community encounter in 1997, some of the worship was so similar to what she sees among charismatics that "it scared [her]."[37] Most believe that cooperation is possible, but difficult and even improbable.[38]

"Things have changed," Lúcia says. "In the communities people don't pay much attention to the gospel. It seems the gospel today, the word of God, is very spiritualized. And the questions of reality are left aside. They don't speak of uniting the two things." Maria das Graças concurs: "There was a change. Things receded a little, because the church was very involved with the social part and now it is more oriented toward prayer. It thinks it got too involved with the social, and lost the spirituality." This change is traumatic for many of the former activists. "You go to a celebration in the community," Lúcia says, "and get half tired out, because it's all 'up in the sky,' you know, and the practical questions of life are not perceived by the community." Similarly, Lourdes adds, "They are just there in their own prayer group and they forget a little. . . . I think that we have to have prayer and action together to feel more. I like it more [participating in other activist groups]. I've left off a little with church things." Edna's assessment is the most straightforward: the church has become "more Pentecostal."

The Brazilian activists understand that, as in Chile, this has been a boon for the institutional church: it has filled some churches, even if it is with people who "only pray." Several women pointed out that their churches are full, that their communities have actually gained new members: mostly women between thirty and forty years of age, with a primary education. In the upswing of the protest cycle in the early 1980s, these would have been good candidates for the base communities, but now they seem to be attracted to the charismatic groups. Some communities like Geralda's try to have the two groups coexist, in the interest of church growth. As a result, the women are keenly aware that the hierarchy is not likely to reverse this tendency any time

37. Scholars who argue similarly that the current economic crisis provides a more hospitable climate for charismatic religion include Vasquez (1997) and Chesnut (1999).

38. Evidence from elsewhere in Brazil suggests that activists and the RCC can coexist in a community (Thieje 1998, 230).

soon. As Célia says, "I don't think there's any will to change in the church today. Because it doesn't depend on the people who would like change. It depends on the hierarchy," which "today only values the charismatics."

Most Brazilian activists also connect these changes to factors outside the church itself, however. Because these changes seem to come as much from popular sentiment as from hierarchical policy, the Brazilians perceive them as something more akin to an invasion or infiltration, rather than as an "earthquake." In contrast to the Chileans, nearly all of the Brazilian respondents mentioned at least one nonchurch factor that they saw as explaining the decline in activism. They argue that social changes—particularly the growth of neoliberal ideology as well as it economic consequences—undermine the context for activism. It may even contribute to the "alienated" religion growing around them. Neoliberalism, according to Maria José, has left everyone lost, seeking immediate solutions, and thereby undermining the working-class solidarity the base communities propose. Maria Socorro concurs that "now you don't even know where to turn. People are unmotivated."

In addition, Brazilian women see their movements' decline as part and parcel of the political and economic changes that accompanied the transition. For example, several women described former church militants leaving their communities to work in parties, unions, and so on. Maria José says that after the *abertura* she put all her activist efforts in the union movement, because it simply took too much time to participate in the base community as well. Edna notes that "there was a great emptying of people who went to the popular movement, the political movement, the union movement. Now, those people can't come back to the communities" because of the changes that have occurred, especially the more charismatic orientation. Some women recognize that in the current political context, even revived "real base communities" would have little appeal for activists. "Today, if you are looking for participation," says Maria José, "you aren't obliged to seek the church, the communities." In a sense, the decline of base communities was a foregone outcome of a more open political system.

The transition complicated things for all social movements in other ways. The complexity of choosing between parties is part of the problem, according to Geralda. Edna argues that it is the limits and unresponsiveness of the current democratic regime. Melania sums up the discouraging confusion of the present political conjuncture: "At the time of the military we knew the enemy, knew who it was, even when we were infiltrated . . . and today, no. The enemy is invisible."

The women see the neoliberal economy as another factor discouraging participation. Most concretely, the economic situation is so difficult for many people that they have to take a paid job, or have to work extra jobs. As Edna notes, movement activism peaked at a time when relatively few women worked in paid jobs: "That was a time of women's participation because they did not work. In the political process, women had to leave home to work in the factories, and many went to study, thank God. But many went to earn their living and survive." Several of the women themselves, including Rita and Cida Morais, left off participating actively in their groups initially because they had to take jobs.[39]

Thus, many women place their movements' decline in the context of larger economic trends. Melania says, "I think that difficulties made people distance themselves and each was pursuing their own life, because difficulties come in the day-to-day and everyone has to survive on their own and defend their own. I see it this way: there was a draining of the movements, weakening of the church itself, of the associations, of the party too." Lúcia adds, "Today I see that they are more involved with who will give them something. For example, in the last elections, whoever pays, people go and help in the campaign. They don't participate in a party. They don't participate in political discussions of the party's program. The want to resolve the immediate problem, to arrange a little cash." Neide do Carmo links this change to generational change: "The people from that period are of a certain age; they aren't young, and their children seem to have been raised and educated in an era when everything was fear, and they aren't in the struggle today."

Finally, many Brazilian women commented that fatigue and age have simply taken their toll on the base communities and their related movements. Fatigue is not only physical and related to aging, but also psychological. As Lúcia says: "I think my way of seeing things changed, because I did not see a lot of fruit. Suddenly you wanted to eat the fruit, too, right away. And that fruit [of consciousness-raising and struggle] does not grow that quickly. So it's tiring. It tires others. It tires me. Many people desist from the community. You end up alone." Edna agrees: "I think it's fatigue, tired of the struggle. Because we spent a lot of time on struggles, and today we see the same problems." Several of the women, including Melania and Madalena, noted that they themselves had cut back to one or two selected

---

39. Their experience is confirmed by W. E. Hewitt's survey of São Paulo base communities, which found 44 percent of women members working in 1993, compared with 39 percent in 1984 (Hewitt 2000, 12).

activities because they were simply too tired to keep up their earlier level of activism. And indeed, as we noted earlier, the average age of the Brazilian activists is higher than that of those in Chile. Many of these women today are at retirement age. Some of their beloved colleagues have passed away. Such changes can be discouraging for those who remain. "The people I was accustomed to, they went on to other activities, some moved, some disappeared from this world, new priests came in. I always found it difficult and then I didn't get involved anymore," says Rita. "The leadership is always changing," adds Edna. "Some people die, some are tired, some are getting older, and nowadays new priests haven't come along." As their statements suggest, it isn't only the aging of their women colleagues that has put a damper on the movements, but also the loss of esteemed priests and bishops, such as dom Adriano Hipólito in Nova Iguaçu. Newer priests and bishops are much more likely to promote a traditional or even charismatic worship style, and the women can no longer depend on them for leadership and inspiration for social activism.

Conclusion

In both Brazil and Chile, the church withdrew support for the "new" actors who had broadened participation at the same time at which the cycle of activism accompanying redemocratization was slowing down. Although activism as a whole declined for many social, economic, and political reasons, the withdrawal of church support in both countries critically wounded the base communities and their ability to mobilize social protest. The church withdrew support more thoroughly and decisively in Chile, but Brazil's more gradual and nuanced retreat also had devastating effects on most base communities. The Brazilian church, however, had facilitated the creation of autonomous groups, and its more decentralized support for base communities meant that pockets of progressivism survive. Although the hierarchy is as unlikely as Chile's to revert to support for social activism, these new groups may have some potential for becoming a basis of activist networking. In particular, the tendency to see movement decline as natural and generalized, not as the result of specific action by the church, may actually be relatively healthy for the process of movement maintenance and network building. Brazilian women perceive and are disheartened by the decline of church support and activism in their country and communities, but they also find pockets of potential alliances, even within the church. They may not be optimistic about encouraging the hierarchy as a whole to return to a more progressive stance, but they do see some connections that can be made and sources of ongoing, if reduced, support for their efforts. The fact that they do so owes much to the gradual changes in Brazil, as well as to the church's strategy of decentralized support during the military regime, which allowed a variety of independent progressive groups to continue to operate despite the changes within the church.

Chileans, in contrast, feel more isolated and less optimistic about the possibility of making connections with other groups or institutions, in large part because the Chilean base communities were more dependent on centralized support from the institutional church, particularly the *vicarías*. Chileans remain quite knowledgeable about the issues facing their communities, and they recognize the need to organize both within and across communities. Most Chileans, however, continue to argue that the church *should* provide leadership in grassroots organizing because, as Alicia Ubilla says, "the church has the power to call people together to talk about what is happening today. [It should] make concrete criticisms of the economic model and commit itself to protect human rights." Maritza Sandoval agrees: "The church should . . . organize with communities from other neighborhoods. We need to organize large gatherings with people from other places about participation and to form women leaders." Because Chileans do not expect the church to return to its former social activism, many express a greater sense of unmitigated nostalgia about the past than do their Brazilian counterparts. For example, Ruth Saldías Monreal says wistfully at the end of her interview, "In spite of all the fright and trials, I miss those years for the sense of unity and the feeling that we were ready and willing to put our lives on the line to protect others."

Activists in both countries feel betrayed and disheartened by the changes they have witnessed in the church and in society since the peak of social activism. What remains to be seen, however, is how the women are coping with their understanding of events and their disappointment. Most are struggling to find new forms of activism. Edna says: "Many people today say, 'Ah! The CEBs are dying!' I don't think so. It's a type of passion. If you meet someone, it's that feverish thing, until that passion becomes love and then it begins to settle. I think that this way of the church being community—what was called CEBs—now is passing into that phase of settling down." Her optimism about the future of the base communities as a whole may or may not be warranted, but as we shall see in the following chapter, it is clear that the activists themselves are in a "phase of settling down."

FIVE

Keeping The Faith:
Empowerment and Activism in a New Era

Those who were in the CEBs and who did not adapt to this new model [of the church] went to activism in the political party, in the landless movement or in other movements. People didn't leave off on account of the church. I think the CEBs spread a bunch of people with the capacity to see things more clearly, to act in the union, in the popular movement.

— CIDA LIMA, BRAZIL

I became disillusioned with the community and the priest. I wanted to develop social programs, but it became impossible to continue that kind of work. I kept at it until 1998, when I finally left the parish in frustration. I also came to realize that the Christian communities discriminate against women. . . . I felt they were restrained and did not feel I could speak freely. I am no longer there, but it still hurts.

— ELIANA OLATE, CHILE

In Chapters 1 and 3 we described the sense of personal empowerment that the women—and especially the poorer women with no prior political experience—gained in the base communities. We have shown that women regard participation in the base communities as an awakening or a revelation, and they claim that the new experiences of speaking and acting publicly changed their personal lives and opened up new possibilities for them. In this chapter we examine whether and how that "awakening" translates into action as the wave of protest in which they were involved declines. Was the "intersection of biography and history" described in Chapter 1 a transformative experience with long-term consequences for women's political empowerment? Or have women retreated to earlier roles or been unable to find new outlets for their energies as the political situation has changed?

For activists, the current political juncture poses critical personal and social questions: How and where can their activism continue? What form can it take? Can it persist at all? Their decisions are individual. The church no longer attempts to mobilize groups of women for activism in either country. The sum of their individual decisions, however, is crucial for society, for it is the sum of decisions by them and activists like them that determines how much of the infrastructure of earlier movements survives. Their ability to find, maintain, or build new networks, however small or attenuated, will be critical to developing a denser civil society and potentially a new generation of working-class women (and men) who feel empowered to act collectively and have some organizational basis for doing so.

Ideas About Activism in a Time of Passivity

Most women contend that activism is as important as ever, that something must be done to improve their circumstances and those of their communities. In a context of declining activism, lost church support, widespread individualism, and largely unresponsive governments, however, the prospects for organizing movement activism, let alone those for movement success, seem dim. How do women imbued with an activist faith respond to these changed circumstances? How do they reconcile their expressed belief in activism and its fundamental importance with their understanding that the times are not propitious for activism as they knew and practiced it? We suggest four possibilities.

First, the disillusionment and despair that many women expressed regarding changes in the Catholic Church and the decline of social movement activism generally could lead to them to withdraw from activism and participation altogether. Women may retreat to other activities or into purely sacramental, traditional religious practices out of a sense of personal burnout and sacrifice in causes that never seemed to come fully to fruition, even though they may still believe that activism is necessary.

Second, the same causes might lead women to abandon more abstract politics, but remain engaged in religious activities with a social dimension. For example, they may focus their efforts more on local charity and self-help rather than on the development of neighborhood-wide movements or participation in larger political debates. Els Jacobs (2001) suggests that this is indeed what happened to many women in base communities in Rio Grande do Sul: except for the most politicized leaders, she argues, women actually welcomed the church's turn away from politics writ large in the 1990s. They were happy to return to the more local, personal practices of community- and identity-building that base community leaders previously would have characterized as mere charity.

Nevertheless, the responses of the majority of interviewees from both countries in the previous chapter suggest that, if they have retreated to local religious activities and charity, they have not done so happily. Instead, they

may be seeking a third alternative: new venues in which to carry on movement activism. Like the Freedom Summer volunteers interviewed by McAdam
(1988), the base community activists may be seeking new ways to recover the
"freedom high" of participation in a post-activist period. They may be finding
new outlets for activism oriented around new causes or in new groups, whether
or not related to their previous work in the base communities.

Finally, McAdam's research suggests a fourth alternative: activists may
take their leanings in new directions when the cycle of protest hits a downturn (212–32). Rather than just seeking new issues and new movements,
they may channel their activist commitments in new directions that are
more compatible with the current situation and with their current personal
circumstances. For example, activists may become involved in local electoral
politics, or they may choose professions that provide a basis for advocacy or
social justice work. These can be ways of acting on convictions honed in "the
movement" under circumstances (both personal and political) that make
movement activism itself difficult or impossible.

Because base communities in both countries were far from homogeneous,
we expect to find some women from each country following all these paths.[1]
While ordinary base community members or those who "went along" with
the liberationist project without ever internalizing its political dimensions
may have chosen one of the first two alternatives, it seems likely that women
who were leaders will have chosen option three or four. Women who were
leaders recall their experiences of liberationist spirituality and movement
activism in much the same way that McAdams's Freedom Summer volunteers
did: as a life-changing experience that left them wanting more. This is why
they are so dissatisfied with the turn the churches took in the 1990s. Therefore we expect that, while some members may have retreated from activism,
most of the women leaders we interviewed would have found or be seeking
new venues for participation or new forms of advocacy.

At the same time, however, the differences between the two countries
suggest that Brazilian and Chilean women may respond differently. Brazil's
sociocultural base communities, with their heavier emphasis on popular
religion and local action and their more socially homogeneous membership,

---

1. Indeed, we would expect an outcome similar to Klandermans's (1994) finding regarding the Dutch
peace movement. After its peak, some activists remained focused on the movement despite its decline, others
sought new venues for activism, and a third group desisted completely.

seem likely to produce more activists who will move with the larger church back toward a focus on "charity." The Brazilians' more forgiving attitude toward the church, noted in the preceding chapter, may increase the likelihood that more Brazilian women will continue to find their primary source of community participation in the church itself, even in less politicized ways. In contrast, Chile's more politicized communities seem likely to have produced higher levels of continued political activism, while at the same time their close connection to the institutional church means that women who want to pursue such activism will be forced to do so in new venues outside the church.

While Church support for activism has deteriorated in both countries, the networks and alternatives that are available depend partly on the legacy of the base communities' earlier practices. The kinds of links they forged and the degree of their dependence on central church structures help to shape the alternatives available to base community activists once the protest cycles of which CEBs were a key part have declined. Thus, we turn first to a brief description of whether and how the activists' communities have maintained links to other organizations before delving more deeply into the question of how the women themselves have responded to the decline of social movement mobilization.

Brazil: Building on Old Foundations

The Brazilian church's approach to base communities created, at least briefly, a flourishing web of local popular movements. In many areas, it also facilitated the linkage of these movements to the PT, which for many activists gained legitimacy from its association with the popular church and grassroots activism. Before we turn to an examination of what the women themselves are doing today, it is useful to gain an insight into whether and how they see these organizations in general. Do they still perceive the presence of the kind of network that existed during the transition? In their efforts to revive the activism centered in base communities, do they still identify possible local allies, and if so, who are they? To gain an insight into how they apprehend the organizational context of their communities today, we asked the women to comment on groups with which the local church organization still maintains connections. We also asked what community groups with which they are familiar could be mobilized to support new activism.

The Local Organizing Context Today

Despite holding the view that the base communities have forsaken their social calling and that they "hardly exist anymore," the vast majority of women declared that their church groups still maintain connections with a wide variety of community groups. Nearly 80 percent (nineteen of twenty-five) of activists said they knew of groups in their community that could support revitalized activism by the base community. Asked to list these groups spontaneously, the majority mentioned popular women's organizations, including the grassroots feminist group the Association of Women of the Zona Leste (AMZOL) in São Paulo, political parties, and other churches. Given our particular interest in groups that could form a basis for social movements, we asked specifically about ties to women's and other religious groups. Nearly half the women (twelve) said their community currently has connections with various grassroots women's organizations. Half of these women (six) were from several base communities in São Paulo connected to self-consciously feminist groups such as AMZOL and Catholic Women for Free Choice (Católicas pelo Direito de Decidir [CCD]). Women in other communities cited groups ranging from mothers' clubs to municipal women's offices, Afro-Brazilian women's groups, and self-help groups organizing such efforts as co-op bakeries and a recycling project. A surprisingly high 40 percent said they maintain ties with local Protestant churches, with which they sometimes carry out cooperative activities.

These two types of connections and their potential are explored in the following chapters. Here, it is important to note that despite the pessimistic assessment that the base communities "no longer exist," the communities, and even their more activist members, may be less isolated from others in their local areas who could support renewed activism. However they may have changed, many communities appear to be maintaining some links to other civic associations in their areas.

Further, the women state overwhelmingly that their local church communities maintain other ties, either to formal political parties or to traditional charitable organizations. Eighty percent said that their church still has connections with at least one political party, usually the PT. In most cases, this seems to involve primarily sponsoring activities such as community debates and forums prior to elections. Roughly 60 percent of the women said that their communities work on some kind of charitable or social project: drug prevention, union-related work, collaboration with government agencies, and poverty prevention. Many of the communities participate, for example, in the "Kilo Campaign," which is a project of food collection and distribution.

Finally, most of the communities have pastoral organizations. These are groups that involve laypeople in various forms of ministry; often they are oriented around a specific task or group that is served. Pastorals and their purposes range from the highly church-focused pastorals centered on cate-chism and tithing to the broader pastorals for women, youth, Afro-Brazilians, and so on. Each of these pastorals can include both exclusively religious and social content. For example, the catechism pastoral may include a social dimension by teaching a liberationist catechism or encouraging students to engage in consciousness-raising. The health pastoral might include activities ranging from bringing the host to homebound church members, to teaching nutrition classes, to supporting the staff at the local clinic in improving their facilities. Many focus on the provision of basic needs in the community (Jacobs 2001, 92).

Pastorals have taken over some tasks that would have been performed in previous years by the base community or a group from an associated move-ment, such as the health movement. They appear to have moved activities in a more generally religious and charitable direction and away from social activism, in line with the overall movement of the church. It is important to note, however, that the women activists regard these groups as networks that could support more social activism. Etelvina says the pastorals are "stronger than the CEBs" and have more continuity because they are better structured. Pastorals are not exclusively or only traditionally religious; as Célia says, at least some of the pastorals work "in the social area," although this varies a lot from one place to another. While Maria das Graças sees her branch of the Pastoral for Youth very clearly as enacting an antipoverty pro-gram, Célia believes that the pastorals in her region are hindered because the local bishop "puts everything social in last place." Similarly, Maria Melania says that any social pastoral could contribute to activism, but "it's a question of mentality."

Twenty-four of the twenty-five women interviewed mentioned pastorals as "other Catholic groups" that could support social movement activism. Many mentioned specific and more "social" pastorals as key potential allies; the Youth, Women, Children, and Health Pastorals were all mentioned in this vein. Many women seem to hope that the pastorals can build on their connections to social issues to move in a more activist direction. As Zelita says, the pastorals should foment action, because "prayer without action is worthless" *(oração sem ação não vale)*. Thus, the pastorals are omnipresent and a potential vehicle for activists, but the presence of pastorals—even those such as Youth or Health that might seem more "social"—does not necessarily indicate that a community currently is engaging in activism. In many places, they may represent a potential platform for activism rather than providing a current venue.

Finally, it is important to note that many of the groups with which the women report continued contact are actually outgrowths of the base communities' earlier organizing. This is true of a number of women's groups that are specifically named: AMZOL in São Paulo, the *catadores de lixo* ("garbage scavengers," a recycling project) group, and domestic-workers' union in Rio de Janeiro. Many also mentioned local or municipal community councils working on issues of health and education, especially, as important organizations with which they maintain contact. These councils themselves are, in many cases, as our interviewees point out, the fruit of the health and education or day-care movements organized largely by the base communities in the 1970s and 1980s. Maria Edwiges, for example, describes their municipal forum as "a conquest that the church itself fought for during the constitutional debate." Thus, the longer-term effects of earlier community organizing include the creation of local groups capable of taking on new roles or filling new niches and with which the activists and their communities now maintain ties. The very basis for networking within many local communities is itself a legacy of organizing that occurred at the peak of the social movement cycle.

Overall, the portrait of local church connections that emerges is one that is less consistent with highly politicized activism, and more consistent with a role in community- and identity-building. Organizing around more local charitable issues or mobilizing for "citizenship" activities such as political debates may be less dramatic than the kinds of social protests that took place in past years. Nonetheless, these activities provide a basis for new forms of mobilization, and most base communities seem to be maintaining local horizontal linkages that leaders could potentially activate for movements on behalf of their communities or even broader efforts. While the church as a whole and the local communities individually have moved away from more abstract political arguments and issues, they nonetheless maintain local connections and an interest in and commitment to local poverty concerns. Despite their general discouragement, many activists believe that these could provide some basis in the future for renewed movement activity.

Biography and History: Retreat to the Church?

If activists find that the local, social, and political context offers some rays of light, how, in their personal lives, have they responded to the changes that have occurred since the peak of the social movement cycle? We know from other accounts that many individuals, particularly men and the most activist women leaders, have gone on to various forms of political engagement. W. E. Hewitt (2000) found that 42 percent of men in São Paulo base communities participated in one or more civil associations in 1993 (15). More anecdotally, Ana Maria Doimo (1995) has documented the importance of former CEB members in a wide variety of popular organizations. Rebecca Abers's (2000) study of participants in "popular budgetary" organizations sponsored by local PT governments also shows that many of the people who volunteer to participate in these grassroots political processes are former CEB members. The list could be lengthened to show that many former activists continue to be variously politically active.

As the quotation from Cida Lima at the beginning of this chapter indicates, the women we interviewed stressed the way in which the base communities produced an outpouring of activists into other movements and organizations. In fact, twenty-four of the twenty-five women interviewed said that they know base community activists who are today active in political parties, women's groups, or other organizations such as the neighborhood association. In some cases, church activists continue to play a role in groups that the church helped form, among them the various community councils. For example, Neide do Carmo mentioned that people from the Children's Pastoral are always elected to their local social council because of the work they do. She reported that they are also more persistent than representatives of other NGOs in attending and trying to use the council to achieve changes.

Besides noting these more movement-oriented activities, many recalled specific individuals who went on to activism in the PT. In fact, the movement from base community membership to participation in a local PT group seems to have been the single most common path for activists, at least as far as our respondents are aware: eighteen women specifically mentioned former activists they know who are now in the PT. Several women mentioned former church activists who have run for or been elected to local office. Ilda's community elected a PT deputy who, she says, still maintains contact with the community. Geralda Francisca says more than one person from the base community ran for office, and they elected a former activist named Elisa to the city council. Maria Socorro says she knows a city council member, a state deputy, and local party militants who were base community members. Neide do Carmo says her city councilwoman is a former base community member, as is the municipal secretary of social welfare. A woman activist from Maria das Graças's community ran twice for city council. The path taken by these women's acquaintances thus seems to confirm the anecdotal evidence that many base community members became involved in party politics.

Accounts of "other activists" who went on to "other things" are suggestive, but they may overstate the extent of current activism, especially by more ordinary members and by women. For example, according to Hewitt (2000), only 12 percent of all women in São Paulo base communities participated in at least one civil association in 1993 (15). To get a better idea of the trajectory of women activists, we need to look at the activities of the women themselves. This will give us a more accurate idea of how many women from the base communities felt that the "intersection of biography and history" changed their lives in ways that required a continued commitment to some kind of action and how many have withdrawn into more religious or charitable work.

Our first two hypotheses suggested that women activists might, from disillusionment, fatigue, or other causes, desist from any kind of movement politics and concentrate instead on activities that are more traditionally religious, charitable, or both. There is no doubt that the Brazilian women remain highly involved in the church, despite their criticisms of it. Only six women report that they no longer participate in the church at all.[2] These women, among the most vocal critics of changes in the church, are also among the most active in social movement and political organizations. Thus, withdrawal from religious life for them is not a retreat into inactivity; rather, it seems connected to a choice to maintain greater political engagement. But the women who "choose" activism over church are a small minority—just more than 20 percent—of our respondents. Most have chosen instead to maintain some form of religious activity. Fourteen women, or just less than 60 percent, remain active in their local churches in ways that go beyond mass attendance. In many cases, they participate in church activities beyond their local communities as well.

Most of the women say that they continue at least to attend mass, but these fourteen women continue to engage in the kinds of "extra" religious

---

2. This is consistent with Hewitt's (2000) finding that women maintain stronger ties than men to the institutional church (14).

activities that they undertook during the days of the base communities. They are involved in community councils, mothers' clubs, and the new pastoral groups. Their choice of pastorals suggests that these women continue to place a high value on traditional religious practices: only four mentioned participating in the most self-consciously "social" of the pastoral groups. Others work with more strictly religious or church-oriented pastorals, concerned with such aspects as baptism, catechism, tithing, liturgy, and adult education (the Pastoral of Catechumens.) As mentioned above, many of these may have social dimensions, but whether they do depends largely on the local context. It is not clear from our interviews that any of these more sacramental or church-oriented pastorals they mention have a social or activist bent in their communities.

Many of the women who continue to be involved in traditional church work combine this with charitable activities. Food collection and distribution seems to be the most common charitable activity, whether arranged through an NGO, for example, Ação Contra Fome (in Ilda's community), or through the local branch of the Children's Pastoral (as in Lúcia's community). Neide's community distributes donated clothes, while Elsa's participates in Projeto ACAS, a popular housing initiative. Earlier, such charitable activities were often dismissed by liberationist pastoral agents as mere "assistencialism" and insufficiently political. Nonetheless, many communities did engage in such charitable work even at the height of political activism, so these projects can be seen as continuing the tradition of the base communities, although in a less politicized manner.[3]

While most of the women continue to engage in these activities, very few do so exclusively. In fact, only four women currently confine their activities to church-related religious and charitable work: Zelita, Neide, Etelvina, and Maria Pereira. That is, less than than 20 percent of the women engage only in charity. Three of these women seem to fit the pattern described by Jacobs (2001): active but not community leaders, they seem to be happy and comfortable limiting their participation to these more mainstream, and perhaps more feminine and less politicized, forms. Neide and Etelvina have gravitated toward work with children and did not mention any other kind of political activity over the past decade. Maria Pereira has confined her activities to helping with regional church assemblies, the ministry of baptism, and Bible

3. Both Burdick (1993) and Drogus (1997) discuss the role of charitable activity in base communities and the fact that many participants viewed their participation largely as charitable action.

circles. In her case, health influenced the choice of activities: she had hoped to attend Rio de Janeirs's Curso de Verão, a citizenship course offered annually, but was unable to do so because she was unwell. Zelita, by contrast, was active in the Movimento dos Sem Terra (MST) in the 1990s and in AMZOL. She has also always been active in the more traditional charitable organizations such as the Legion of Mary throughout her time in the base community. Only in past few years has she confined her activities to these groups.

Overall, then, only a handful of women confine their current participation to religious and charitable work. This seems to meet the needs of some. Others are responding at least in part to pressures of age or health. This kind of work, which still engages 60 percent of the women activists to some degree, is not, strictly speaking, social movement work. It is, however, part of the process of community building. Although less overtly and abstractly political than other kinds of participation, it may play a useful role in maintaining the basic health and density of civil society in a period of movement decline. But at least as important, this is not the only way in which the majority of Brazilian women remain engaged and involved. In fact, ten of these women engage in activism that is in addition to their participation in sacramental and charitable work in the church. Eight other women also continue to be politically active in their communities and beyond.

Finding New Paths

Eighteen of twenty-five Brazilian women—72 percent—have found some means of acting on their political commitments locally in this era of diminished movement activism. Fifteen, or 60 percent, continue to be active in some way beyond their local community. This is a striking finding for a group of poor women, most of whom have little education, many of whom are now elderly, and many of whom have significant health problems.[4] It seems unlikely that a random sample of women of the same ages and social and education backgrounds would produce a similar result. Yet how can they maintain this sense of commitment in a context of diminished church support, of political disillusionment, and of declining activism generally?

---

4. This is a higher rate of participation than Hewitt (2000) found for women in São Paulo (15). Hewitt's sample was not appreciably larger than ours (thirty-three versus twenty-five). Moreover, his was not confined to former activists, but rather looked at women base community members in general. This difference may explain the higher rate of participation that we found.

Most continue to seek some kind of outlet that offers work similar to what they did in earlier popular movements, as we hypothesized. Fourteen women, or nearly 60 percent, participate in some kind of local movement organization. Most of these (44 percent of all the women) participate in popular feminist groups or in other community groups that work with women's health, self-esteem, and other issues. Neide, for example, promotes courses on citizenship among the twenty mothers' clubs she oversees. Others participate in the local health movement, the black consciousness movement, an organization called Action and Citizenship, and a local group that works on transportation issues.

Besides being involved in these movement venues, women find means of participation in grassroots politics. Some of these are themselves legacies of the base communities' attempts to create sites for grassroots participation in local political decision-making, and the women involved in them are dedicated to maintaining these spaces for popular pressure. Several women participate in councils that deal with children's rights (Cida Lima, Célia, Neide); like the women in Rio Grande do Sul who were interviewed by Jacobs (2001), these women find themselves elected to local councils in recognition of their persistent work with children through mothers' clubs, pastorals, and so on (111). As Neide explains, the women from their church were chosen by other council members because of the work they do: "It's because of our involvement, of the work we do in our [mothers'] group that we were invited to be in the council. We were elected; the pastoral was elected by the other previous council members . . . in a public assembly they voted on the groups to make up this council for the next term. Then we were elected precisely because we also have this work." Maria Edwiges participates in a similar group, the State Forum on Social Assistance. In her view, this group, like the children's councils, grew out of the church's work. She has been a member for two years.

Councils are new venues for base community activists, but they are consistent with their communities' earlier work and also with the emphasis on grassroots participation. Activists value these venues, though they sometimes feel frustrated about their effectiveness. Neide feels that her group remains the most committed to ensuring that the council continues to do its work. Unlike other NGOs that have been elected to the council but that do not always show up, "the mothers' group is always present, always there, because we know what it's worth." Authorities may or may not heed the advice of popular councils. Neide is not optimistic about political change. But women who were involved in the base communities are anxious to at least keep these options for participation open. They recognize that, as Jacobs (2001) says, the councils present base community women with new social and political opportunities (118).

Neighborhood associations are another venue that shares many characteristics with sites of base community activism, and many base communities helped to form or influence these local groups during the communities' heyday. Only one woman, Maria Antônia, continues to list the neighborhood association as a current activity. She describes how her current activism grew from her experience in the base community:

> For me the community was the church, a space where we organized to pray and to also think a little about our reality. But then came the neighborhood association and I also engaged in that. That is to say, it is a community. In the neighborhood association I felt there was space for the political question. You can't organize people or resolve anything without more committed participation. Through the community I discovered the neighborhood association, and through the neighborhood association I felt the need to participate in organized politics . . . and that's when I affiliated with the party.

She was president of her local association for ten years. Melania is a former president of her association, though she is less active now because of health problems. Several others have also passed through these groups. Like the councils, they represented new ways for women to be politically active, and many base community members embraced them at least for a time.

Maria Antônia's experience of identifying ever larger circles of participation has been shared by at least some of colleagues. Perhaps the most surprising new venue for women activists is party politics. There have always been anecdotal cases like those mentioned above of women from the base communities running for public office, but our interviews confirm that the base communities were a gateway to party politics for many women. Only two women said they had no party preference. All the rest expressed some degree of involvement in the PT. Of these, eight said they were "sympathizers" but not members. Sixty percent of women say that they are members of (or affiliated with) the PT. Nearly 30 percent (seven women) say they are active in the party, or describe themselves as people who are party "militants," at least from time to time. Again, given that these are poor women and given their age, these are surprising findings.[5] Few women who were demographically similar to these former activists would describe themselves as PT militants. As electoral politics replaced social movement politics after the transition, these women clearly found an outlet for their political interests and demands in the party that had been most closely associated with the social movements and the liberationist church: the PT.

Overall, then, women activists have found a number of explicitly political ways in which to channel their energies; the clearest examples are continuing in the movements that remain active, getting involved in grassroots local politics, and joining in party membership. We should note that many have also found less overtly political ways of satisfying the desire, nourished by base communities, to work for social justice. Four women are now social workers, involved with health (community health agent Maria das Graças), children (Célia and Cida Lima), or battered women (Emerenciana). The most impressive exponent of this path is a fifth woman, Madalena, who at age seventy-two and with a primary education, has just completed a course enabling her to work with battered women as a legal advocate. Besides the obvious ways in which their work fits with their commitment, these women are sometimes able to find channels for participation through their work. As Célia says, "We professionals who have all that baggage [from the base communities] continue to participate in our workplaces." She is a member of a children's organization run by the nursery she works in, as well as of the Center for the Defense of Children.

In addition to those who have found formal job opportunities in social work, a few women have made their own opportunities. Lourdes has become involved with trying to teach people about alternative medicine and nutrition. Sofia and Maria José, two former union activists, now are engaged in trying to help women set up a cooperative restaurant. Unlike the cooperative bakery mentioned above, the restaurant is not connected with a church group. These two women are trying to start it on their own.

The picture that emerges is one of continued engagement in a variety of ways. Very few women have given up participation or retreated to the church completely. The few who have done so, such as Melania, express regret that poor health has forced this choice on them. Most continue to engage in charitable work. While locally focused and less political—the

---

5. For comparison, Hewitt (2000) reports that 80 percent of women and 90 percent of men in São Paulo base communities stated a preference for a "left" political party in 1993 (15).

kind of "assistencialist" work that liberationists frowned on—even this may contribute to building a basis for community in the future. In an even more impressive development, 72 percent of these women have found new forms of activism. They are not sanguine about the prospects of these organizations. They know that their party, their councils, and their movements face an uphill political battle in Brazil's current political climate, and they lament the fact that they are unable to recruit enough new members to make these organizations really strong. Despite these limitations and concerns, however, these women are finding ways to carry on political engagement and to keep the potential for new movement activism alive in trying times.

Chile: The Weight of Old Foundations

As in Brazil, in Chile a national web of social movement groups—linked both horizontally across neighborhoods and vertically into national networks—flourished during the period of the dictatorship (1973–89 in Chile). Yet, as we see throughout these chapters, Chilean women today are more pessimistic than their Brazilian sisters about the role of base communities in maintaining or building social movement networks. In fact, many of the Chilean women have left their base communities in frustration over the church's withdrawal of support for their former social commitment and prophetic stance. Consistent with the Chilean women's portrayal of the church's withdrawal to a more narrowly defined pastoral mission, only nine of the Chilean women who remain active in their parishes today name any other groups that work with their local base communities.

The Local Organizing Context Today

According to the Chileans, the problem is not the absence of potential partners or allies in either the local or national contexts. Almost one-third of the Chilean respondents name other groups that *could* support revitalized activism by local base communities, if the will existed to forge new partnerships. Chileans do not identify the same kinds of potential allies mentioned by the Brazilians, however. For example, none of the Chileans mentioned as a potential ally any religious groups—either Catholic or non-Catholic—and only one mentioned a political party. In fact, no one group, or type of group, received more than a handful of responses, and most were groups specific to a particular neighborhood, or *población*. The Chilean responses suggest that to a greater extent than in Brazil, social movements in Chile appear to have disintegrated into a myriad of more isolated groups, leaving former base community activists more frustrated and less sanguine about the future of social movement maintenance than the Brazilian respondents.

Chilean women's perceptions of their communities' greater isolation are grounded in the realities of the Chilean context. As discussed in the previous chapter, in Chile part of the church's conservative trend is a reaction to the explosive growth of non-Catholic, particularly Pentecostal, groups—making ecumenical cooperation anathema to the majority of the Chilean hierarchy. In spite of the innumerable grassroots social service activities associated with Protestant, Pentecostal, and other religious groups, Chilean women do not mention any other religious group as potential allies. The additional fact that Chileans did not mention Catholic organizations similar to the Brazilian pastorals reflects that the church in Chile withdrew more completely to a strictly pastoral mission than was the case for the Brazilian church.

In contrast to the situation in Brazil, where the PT grew out of the earlier social movements and therefore is seen as a likely political ally by grassroots activist women, the Chilean church's "protective umbrella" during the dictatorship concealed the historically deep partisan divisions in Chilean society. Particularly in the 1970s and early 1980s, partisan activists from across the political left joined base communities to seek protection from state repression and to find common cause with other social movement groups. But in the early 1980s, when political party leaders reemerged to take center stage in the national protests and subsequent negotiations with the military, partisan tensions within social movement groups again broke open.

The return to party politics affected the base communities in several important ways. As discussed in Chapter 3, the Chilean church's vision of its role as a "holder of the political space" during the dictatorship contributed to its decision, once party leaders retook the political stage, to withdraw more rapidly and completely from "social activism" than was the case in Brazil. More important, the historically strong party identification—once submerged beneath the common goal of ousting the military—again divides Chilean society, including Catholic base communities and their surrounding neighborhoods.[6] Although roughly half the Chilean respondents do not identify a

---

6. The tensions between party activists and representatives from the autonomous social movements erupted into public view in the 1986 meetings of the Unitary Congress of Pobladores, an umbrella group

specific party affiliation, it is unlikely that most do not have party loyalties. The half that do mention their party identification divide across the range of leftist parties: Socialist (12.5 percent), Communist (12.5 percent), Movimiento Independiente Revolucionaria (MIR) (10.4 percent) and Partido por Democracia (PPD) (8.3 percent). In contrast to its Brazilian counterpart, not only has the Chilean Catholic Church withdrawn more completely from its previous cooperative relationships with the political parties, particularly on the left, but no one political party or group represents the legacy of the social movements for former activists who want to continue the base communities' former "political" work.

The Chilean hierarchy not only withdrew from social or political work to a narrowly focused pastoral mission, it also reimposed on the church a traditional and patriarchal vision of the institution and its authority structure. Lay leadership was bent to the authority of the parish priest and diocesan bishop. Women's roles, in particular, were dramatically curtailed, with the renewed focus on women as wives and mothers rather than individuals who are economic, political, and social actors. Thus, while Brazilian women feel as though they can build on the social movement foundations laid during the dictatorship, the weight of Chile's pre-dictatorship foundations—a strong multiparty system, a well-established but deeply divided political system, and a self-consciously "apolitical" and pastoral Catholic Church—leave the Chilean women feeling isolated and pessimistic about the prospects of broad social mobilization in today's democratic setting.

Biography and History: Exit from the Church?

Whereas Brazilians see some rays of hope in their local social and political context, Chileans are not sanguine about the possibilities for social movement maintenance, at least within the context of the Catholic base communities. Few Chilean women report connections between their neighborhood base communities and other social, political, or religious groups; however,

---

originally designed to give grassroots groups an independent voice. The following quote, from a female co-founder of a handicrafts organization, highlights the perception that the parties were trying to reassert their control over grassroots groups: "I was invited to a congress of pobladores and I found it to be a fight among political parties. I thought I would see many pobladores from different areas and that it would be democratic. What I found was a joke. But, I like it because it was a lesson (about political parties). I always got confused about political parties. For this it was good, but what happened served no purpose" (quoted in Oxhorn 1995, 237).

almost all the women themselves remain active in some other form of organizational activity. Virtually all of them say that the needs of their communities are as great as ever, if not greater, and most are involved in more than one activist or solidarity organization. In fact, only two of the Chilean women reported that they do not belong to any community group or organization. One of these, María Angelica Molina, apologetically explains that she must babysit for her four grandchildren because her two daughters have moved back into her home. The other, Luisa Caro, a high school teacher, admits to only sporadic community work, lacking the time to do more, but she laments, "I feel really alone because there is no place for me to participate in communitarian activities."

As we can see, our first hypothesis proves even less true for Chilean than for Brazilian women. Chilean women have not "gone home" from exhaustion after the dictatorship or because they believe the return of democracy obviates the need for community activism. But where are Chilean women active today, especially given that they are more pessimistic than their Brazilian sisters regarding the possibilities for network building, particularly through Catholic base communities? A further examination of the range of the women's current activities shows that our second hypothesis, that some women returned to traditionally charitable, church activities, also proves largely untrue in Chile.

As in Brazil, some Chilean participants were always more motivated by traditional religious concerns than were other, more politicized and activist women. Because of the Chilean church's "protective umbrella," however, Chilean base communities attracted a larger share of politically motivated participants than did those in Brazil. The heavier preponderance of members interested in political work often helped transform the ethos of local base communities. As María Espina describes, the harsh years of military repression resulted in a dense mix of religious, political, and social motives in her base community:

> The Christian communities encompassed religious, political, and social interests. On the one hand, the motivation was religious because people needed something and someone to lean on. If something happened to you, people were there to support you. This brought in the social aspects because people got together to help each other. It was political as well because it was a safe place to

meet. . . . Mistrust was great because there were so many informants who turned people in. Coming together in the communities and the church was an act of faith. It was the only place you could act freely and express yourself openly.

In Chile, the perception of the church, and of base communities in particular, as a safe space not only drew some people to base communities who might have found other outlets, as they did in Brazil, but also politicized the Chilean base communities' religious mission. Clotilde Silva Henríquez describes base communities during the dictatorship as suffering similar state-sponsored persecution as the early Christian communities, a view that blurs the distinction between "religious" and "political" meaning and action. "Precisely because they were born during the dictatorship, the communities were born with the spirit of the first Christians who faced persecution. . . . Christianity was lived clandestinely just [as it was for] the first Christians . . . and the issue of martyrs was also parallel. So many friends were persecuted, shot, and killed. Many people came for the religious aspect and discovered other interests."

The conventional wisdom has it that once the political conditions changed, the more politically motivated or partisan participants left to pursue more explicitly political aims. Several of the Chilean respondents echoed this belief. María Espina says that although "concern for social problems has not been lost," people are more likely to choose overtly political channels for their resolution because "we lost our fear of being attacked by the state." Yet few of the Chilean women personally report leaving in order to pursue political activism. As shown in the preceding chapter, rather than choosing to leave their base communities to pursue other avenues for participation, the majority of those who left report that they felt "pushed out" by the new conservatism among priests and bishops. In some cases, conservative or traditionalist priests simply eliminated base communities, in order to put a stop to activities deemed too "political." Alicia Ubilla says regretfully, "The José Carpintero Christian base community ended in 1990. Our hope ended. Now I only go to mass once in a while."

As a result, fewer Chilean than Brazilian women report that they and others remain active in their parishes. Less than half (44 percent) of Chilean women remain active in their religious communities. Among those who left, an overwhelming majority (68 percent) report that the conservative church caused their exit.

Noemi Peña Igor is one of the only Chilean respondents who describes herself as active only in the religious life of her base community during the dictatorship, avoiding the more social or political activism. In spite of the fact that since 1991, under the leadership of Mariano Puga—one of the most openly liberationist priests during the dictatorship—the parish is far more sociopolitically oriented than before, Noemi still focuses on those activities that fit within traditional charitable or pastoral parameters. "Every Sunday we have 'Breakfasts for Jesus' for people in hard economic shape. We work a lot with drug addicts. The church has *ollas comunes* in three different areas. Now the church is promoting its 'La Legua Paints Its Face' campaign, for which we have obtained paint in different lively colors to paint the houses." Virtually all the rest of the Chilean respondents, however, are highly critical of what they perceive to be the loss of the church's prophetic voice and the reembrace of traditionalist charity. Lily Caja, for example, dismisses the "social work" carried out by many local parishes today: "'Social' today does not mean 'to denounce' but assistance and paternalism." Angelica Vasquez echoes her disdain for the paternalism of her base community: "The Solidarity Action group still exists but it reverted to paternalism, giving out food packages as a Band-Aid solution. The groups are made for women who don't work, because they meet at hours not convenient for working women. The Christian community is limited to sacramental concerns."

Of the handful of the Chilean women who list membership in religious groups as constituting their primary activities today, almost all are careful to distinguish their liberationist, versus their traditionalist, content. For example, Adela Ramirez says of her base community: "We still read scriptures and talk about our situations. [The group] has declined in terms of numbers, but we still connect faith with life. Groups are a lot smaller, but they are still going." Like Irma Parraquez, who belongs to a group called Oración Aterrizada (Grounded Prayer), these women and their continuing participation in the religious life of their parishes cannot be characterized as "religious" or "charitable" in the traditional sense. Rather, the women vehemently distinguish their commitment to link "faith with life" from the activities of other women who accept the patriarchal and hierarchical authority of the church. In a poignant statement that sums up many Chilean women's sense of alienation from the conservative Chilean church, Angelica Vasquez laments: "We have to recognize that we share the blame. We should not have left the church, but stayed to continue creating consciousness."

New Paths

Chilean women confirm both our third and our fourth hypotheses. They are active in ways that can be seen as an extension of their pre-transition activism and also in new directions that are more compatible with the post-transition Chilean social, economic, and political contexts. Before turning to an examination of Chilean women's new paths, however, it is important to note that a minority of women continue to participate in some of the same organizations that were associated with the repression enacted by the dictatorship. Human rights work was one of the activities most closely associated with women, and several of the respondents remain active in this area. Clotilde Silva Henríquez defines the importance of women in the Chilean human rights movement: "All the concern for human rights during the dictatorship was organized by women. Women organized, denounced, and mobilized. Most of the people killed and disappeared were men. Their surviving women opened up the issue of human rights. It is not a coincidence that women played such a prominent role in the human rights movement." Since the democratic transition, Chile has continued to struggle with the legacy of human rights abuses during the dictatorship, most notably in terms of bringing military leaders, and particularly General Augusto Pinochet, to justice. Perhaps it is not surprising that 10 percent of the Chilean women remain active in human rights organizations. For example, Laura Herrera Gonzalez continues to participate in the Organization of the Families of the Detained and Disappeared, and Juana Ramirez Gonveya is active in the Political Prisoner Collective. Alicia Cortez belongs to a human rights group called the Program for the Recuperation of Health and Human Rights (PRAIS), and Ana Acuña and Pilar Avendano Garrido belong to the Asamblea Pueblo de Dios, an organization dedicated to the rights of indigenous people. All these groups mobilize to mount pressure on the national government to resolve the issues left by military rule as well as to put in place legal safeguards and educational programs designed to prevent human rights violations in the future.

While some women remain active in the same organizations or activities with which they were involved during the dictatorship, most have found new avenues that are consistent with their previous commitments. The most obvious legacy among the Chilean women is a commitment to women's organizing *as women*. Today, 65 percent of the women either have found jobs

or participate in women's organizations or in entities whose primary beneficiaries are women. Six Chilean women are currently employed as popular
educators for adult women, two work in anti–domestic violence programs,
and several more work in local women's groups such as the Casa de la Mujer
or Casa Malen. The majority of the remaining respondents (60 percent), who
are employed in a variety of other occupations, list as their primary form of
community involvement participation in a women's organization—they are
involved in women's discussion groups, feminist theology discussion groups,
women's self-help organizations, women's training groups, various women's
workshops, and the like. Membership in women's organizations is spread
across all the *poblaciones* in which we surveyed women. Even though many of
the local women's organizations are confined to a particular neighborhood,
as is, for example, the Areceli Ramos Training Center, started by Marta
Alvarez in memory of her daughter who was assassinated by the military,
women across all the *poblaciones* belong to similar kinds of organizations.
Other women's organizations mentioned by the Chilean women include local
women's discussion groups, Casa de la Mujer (Huamachuco), Grupo Mujeres
Domitila (Recoleta), Mujeres Frente a la Globalización (San Joaquín), Colectivo
Feminista Autonomo (San Joaquín), Casa Malen (Pudahuel and Lo Prado),
DOMOS (Villa Portales), Grupo Araucaría de Mujeres (Lo Espejo and La Victoria), Casa de la Mujer (Lo Espejo), Domestic Violence Network (Pudahuel),
Mujeres Creando Futuro (Cerro Navia), Red de Mujeres (Renca), AIDS Network
(Conchali). In addition to these organizations that are active in one or more
poblaciones, several respondents mentioned Sol, an association that provides
artisan workshops for women throughout Santiago, and Remos, a network
of women's organizations that provides workshops and other training
opportunities in a number of areas, including globalization and women's
rights. Finally, several women participate in sporadic women's workshops
organized by government agencies such as the Servicio Nacional de la Mujer
(National Women's Service [SERNAM]) or the Program for Women and
Development (PRODEMU).

The significant percentage of the women who either have found jobs or
participate in women's organizations illustrates the degree to which participation in Catholic base communities empowered Chilean women and raised
their gender consciousness. Such a level of women's participation, especially
in specifically women's organizations, would have been inconceivable prior
to the dictatorship, both because of traditional gender norms and because of

a relative absence of grassroots women's groups. Although these activities confirm our third hypothesis, that women have found new avenues for participation that are consistent with their commitments during the dictatorship, the majority participation in grassroots women's organizations also signals something new. The extensive list of organizations cited above undoubtedly represents activities ranging from social or charitable to political, yet it also shows that building blocks for future social movements exist. Chilean women's greater sense of isolation and pessimism regarding the maintenance of social movement networks is not a result of the lack of grassroots organizations in which women are key players. Rather, the sociopolitical context, and particularly the demise of the church as the facilitator of network building, has removed the previous institutional structure within which grassroots groups could forge ties with one another.

Our fourth hypothesis, that women have channeled their activism into new, specifically political, directions in response to new opportunities afforded by democratic politics, also proves to be true for some Chilean women, albeit in local rather than national political arenas. In fact, none of the Chilean women lists work for a political party among their community activism, and Chilean respondents do not list political parties as potential allies.[7] This contrasts sharply with the Brazilians, virtually all of whom view the PT as a natural partner and 30 percent of whom describe themselves as active in the party. The apparent disconnect between the Chilean respondents and national political parties signals a change from pre-1973 Chilean politics.

To a greater degree than in Brazil, politics in Chile historically has been played out on the national stage. Intense electoral competition for control of the presidency and the legislature provided a national stage for social groups attempting to gain state recognition for their demands. Social movements were tied to national political institutions through intense partisan activity. During military rule, the construction of pro-democracy networks weaving together a wide range of issue-oriented groups further reinforced the focus on national politics. Yet, as Philip Oxhorn (1995) describes, the intense repression of the military era also undermined the traditional patron-client relationship between political parties and popular organizations. As grassroots organizations flourished in response to the social and economic needs

---

7. Juanita Riveros of La Legua listed working on Ricardo Lagos's presidential campaign in 2000 as one of her activities, but she is not a party activist.

created by military rule, social movements outgrew their historical dependence on political parties as channels through which they voiced their demands to the state and by means of which resources flowed back to local groups. By the mid-1980s, however, the political elite clearly sought to reimpose its control over the nature, scope, and pace of the transition. Oxhorn characterizes the relationship between the political parties and popular organizations as "clearly one of competition, in which popular organizations ultimately lost" (239)." With the reimposition of political party channels dominated by a small political elite, popular organizations and activists have been forced to choose between a return to a clientelistic relationship with the political parties or autonomy. Our respondents' current forms of activism suggest that they have chosen autonomy, even though the result is a keen sense of isolation and frustration.

The contrast with Brazilian women's activism in the PT does not imply that Chilean women have abandoned "politics." To the contrary, virtually all the Chilean respondents believe that their communities' problems—whether related to poverty, drugs, machismo, or other causes—are political in that their solutions require community mobilization to push for responsive and adequate public policy. Like their Brazilian counterparts, however, Chilean women choose their activities based on their perceptions of the real opportunities afforded by today's democratic politics.

In the Chilean case, these activists find local, rather than national, political opportunities more promising, particularly through the *juntas de vecinos,* or neighborhood councils. Eight women (16 percent) cite local *juntas de vecinos* as possible allies, and another four mention local municipal governments. Eleven women (23 percent) are personally active in *juntas de vecinos* in their areas, and have been elected to varying positions from block delegate to member of the administrative directorate. Several, like Alicia Sanhueza, have been active in their neighborhood councils since the 1970s. The fact that almost a quarter of the Chilean respondents are active in some way in their neighborhood council signals a change in political focus from mobilization in order to influence national policy-making to a more flexible, local approach. The *juntas de vecinos* are not new, and whether they represent an effective means for grassroots participation or an effort to legitimize and offload the costs of economic restructuring is debatable.[8] Nonetheless, the fact

8. *Juntas de vecinos* were created during the presidency of Christian Democrat Eduardo Frei (1964–70) as part of a massive government-sponsored effort, called Promoción Popular, to mobilize the popular sector.

remains that activists are attempting to use the local venues available to them in this new political and economic climate.

Conclusion

In spite of social movement decline in both Brazil and Chile, 72 percent of the Brazilian and 92 percent of the Chilean women continue to participate in some form of local activism. There can be no doubt that participation in the base communities was a formative experience for these activists, even coming as it did for some of them well into their adult lives. Particularly in Brazil, where fewer women have left the church, some remain active in grassroots work that can be viewed as largely charitable. In Chile, the retreat of the church to a stricter emphasis on traditionally pastoral concerns has left women who are interested in self-help or charitable activities to find alternative organizations. As our third hypothesis suggests, however, most women activists in both countries continue to seek ways to regain the sense of involvement they experienced in the base communities and the popular movements. And most find avenues for participation that are consistent with their commitments during the dictatorships.

In keeping with our fourth hypothesis, a smaller number (30 percent of the Brazilians and 21 percent of the Chileans) pursue explicitly political avenues for pressing the demands of their neighborhoods. While the Brazilians affiliate with and may work for a national political party, the PT, and the Chileans eschew partisan work for local participation in neighborhood councils, both avenues represent new responses to the opportunities presented by their democratic contexts. In both cases, the rates of participation in new political channels are higher than would be expected among the general population of demographically similar women.

What does the legacy of social activism mean for the prospects for democracy in Brazil and Chile? The extraordinary levels of grassroots activism among these women today is ample testimony to the empowerment and

---

Because they were intended to serve as clientelistic channels linking *pobladores* to the Christian Democratic Party, they engendered intense partisan competition, especially from the Communist Party and, to a lesser extent, other leftist parties. Under the military government, *juntas de vecinos* were viewed as mechanisms for local control rather than potential vehicles for effective demands. For a more recent look at the *juntas* and their effectiveness as representative structures, see Paley 2001.

personal growth they experienced through participation in their base communities during the dictatorship. In order for the sum of their personal commitments to signal the deepening of democracy in either Brazil or Chile, however, these women must find ways to build effective networks for channeling their demands to the state. In the following two chapters, we turn to the potential of grassroots activists for building partnerships with either Protestant groups or national women's organizations, both actors with roots in popular neighborhoods and substantial mobilization potential.

Catholics and Pentecostals:
Possibilities for Alliance

Cecilia Loreto Mariz, Maria das Dores Campos Machado,
Hannah Stewart-Gambino, and Carol Ann Drogus

Faith can separate, but reality unites people.

— MARIA ANTÔNIA, BRAZIL

We lived in a bubble that popped. Inside the bubble were solidarity, affection, and unity. All of this was lost.

— ELIANA OLATE, CHILE

Latin America experienced a number of dramatic changes during the 1960s and 1970s, including a new spirit of ecumenical cooperation. Especially after the wave of military coups, Catholic, Protestant, and Jewish leaders allied to denounce arbitrary imprisonment, torture, "disappearances," and other state-sponsored violence. Catholic progressives in a number of countries wove a network of solidarity and political resistance, particularly with the mainline Protestant bodies such as the Presbyterian, Methodist, and Lutheran Churches. Religious opposition to military rule and the abuses of dictatorship was especially noteworthy in Brazil and Chile, where Catholic, Protestant, and Jewish leaders cooperated in a range of national organizations, especially regarding human rights and aid to victims of state repression and terror.[1]

Myriad small Pentecostal churches, rather than mainline Protestant and Jewish congregations, form the dominant non-Catholic religious presence in the neighborhoods of most grassroots women activists, however. According to Cristián Parker (1996), "Pentecostals number 50–70 percent of Brazilian Protestants, and 80–95 percent of the Protestants in Chile" (143), with the majority of Pentecostals in both countries concentrated in the kinds of poorer, urban neighborhoods where our respondents live. Larger institutionalized Protestant churches have little visibility in the daily lives of the women in this

1. For descriptions of interfaith cooperation during the Brazilian military regime, see Serbin 1999. In Chile, the most visible ecumenical efforts occurred under the umbrella of the Vicaría de Solidaridad; see B. Smith 1982, and Vicaría de Solidaridad 1991. Less well known internationally is the role played by the Fundación de Ayuda Social de las Iglesias Cristianas (FASIC), a prominent ecumenical human rights organization founded in 1975 that drew on wider ecumenical participation than did the *vicaría* (Fruhling 1989).

study, whereas Pentecostal religious services can be found in storefronts, private homes, and small church buildings on streets throughout their neighborhoods.[2] As women activists look around them for potential allies and organizations with which to form networks, Protestant and, most likely, Pentecostal congregations who share their neighborhoods would certainly stand out.[3]

What is the likelihood of such local, interdenominational alliances being formed in Brazil or Chile to further women's political aspirations or confront community social problems? At first glance, such interfaith cooperation may seem unlikely, because the Pentecostal churches that are most visible in poor neighborhoods have historically rejected ecumenism and a rapprochement with the Catholic Church. Recruiting their members from among a Catholic population, they have typically strongly criticized Catholicism and its religious tradition. Until quite recently, Pentecostals also have declared themselves apolitical. Thus, they have pointedly distanced themselves from the social or political preoccupations that guide the actions of Catholic progressives, and they have often been regarded as an opposing, conservative religious tradition (Stewart-Gambino and Wilson 1997). According to this view, politicization among progressive Catholics and Pentecostals' emphasis on spirituality should reinforce a general interdenominational wariness that impedes partnerships or collaboration between Catholics and evangelicals.

However, changes within both Latin American Catholicism and Pentecostalism have created greater common ground for potential alliance than ever before. First, many Pentecostal groups have adopted more flexible attitudes toward morals and customs, loosening the rigidity that once separated them from their neighbors. Second, as Pentecostal congregations grow and institutionalize, they channel less energy into intragroup identity and often expend more on social and political engagement. Evidence of such an outward turn is mounting as many Pentecostals become more open to engagement with "worldly" politics, social welfare programs, and even larger social movements (Cook 1997). Pentecostal parties and elected officials are increasingly

2. The total Protestant population in Brazil is estimated at between 13 and 15 percent, with calculations suggesting that 9–10 percent of the total population, or around 75 percent of all Protestants, are Pentecostals (Pierucci and Prandi 1995). An estimated 15–18 percent of Chileans are Protestant (Cleary 1999; Sandoval, Allende, and Castillo 1998). The author of one 1992 study of Chilean Pentecostals found that there were probably fifteen hundred Pentecostal denominations in a country of approximately 14 million people (Prado 1992).

3. Afro-Brazilian religious groups are prominent and visible in poor Brazilian neighborhoods as well. Because no similar non-Christian or spiritist groups exist in Chile, we did not include questions about Afro-Brazilian religious groups, since we would have no basis for comparison.

visible throughout Latin America. As some of the women from Rio de Janeiro point out, their own governor and vice governor at the time of the interviews were evangelicals.[4] Greater willingness to become involved in community social issues or national political campaigns undermines a monolithic view of Pentecostals as apolitical and could become a basis for Catholic-Pentecostal cooperation (Parker 1996). Third, the Catholic Church's growing emphasis on enhanced spirituality reduces the distance between churches. Throughout Latin America, and in Brazil and Chile in particular, this trend is a direct response to the growth in Pentecostal believers.[5] The increasing popularity of the Catholic charismatic movement indicates both the laity's thirst for more expressive church services and Catholic leaders' desire to check the appeal of Pentecostalism. Thus, trends from both sides may potentially decrease the barriers between religious identities.

A final important point is that grassroots cooperation—unlike national ecumenical relationships that are highly visible and must conform to official theological doctrine—depends on the visibility and range of religious groups in the local setting. Individuals in neighborhoods with visible and socially active Pentecostal or Protestant parishes may be more likely to have a more differentiated, that is, less stereotyped, view of other religious identities. Proximity to neighbors and family members of different faiths and transit between various religious groups may lower barriers as well. In this case, local cooperation may prove easier to imagine for grassroots Catholic activists, at least on an individual or case-by-case basis, than it is for the institutions per se, or in neighborhoods with less Pentecostal or Protestant presence.

In this chapter, we explore Brazilian and Chilean women's attitudes toward Catholic-Protestant cooperation. Using a series of questions about the women's own experiences of ecumenical cooperation as well as the likelihood of inter-religious partnerships in their neighborhoods, we look for both the potential for ecumenical cooperation and the obstacles that limit local, as well as national, strategic alliances. While some obstacles, such as religious exclu-sivity, are similar across the two countries, Brazilians appear to be slightly more open to building ecumenical alliances than do Chileans. In the final section, we argue that differences between Brazilian and Chilean women's experiences of Catholic-Pentecostal cooperation are due partly to differences

4. The two officials were Anthony Garotinho and Benedita da Silva, respectively. In 2002, da Silva was governor—Garotinho had stepped down to run for president—and was running to remain in that office.
5. Andrew R. Chesnut (1998) goes so far as to call this the "Pentecostalization" of Latin American (particularly Brazilian) Catholicism.

in their political contexts, but more importantly to differences in religious context. The greater fluidity of grassroots Brazilian religious practice, as well as somewhat more openness to ecumenism in the Brazilian institutional Church, may account for Brazilians' greater openness to ecumenical cooperation.

Brazil: Religious Pluralism and Individual Cooperation

The most impressive result of our interviews is the confirmation that Brazilian base communities and activists are, in fact, forming networks, at least at the local level, with their Protestant neighbors. Ten women—40 percent of the respondents—declared that their Catholic groups do in fact cooperate with Protestants in their communities. Ilda's community bakery includes Pentecostals, and Catholics and Pentecostals in her community work together on trash collection and in the mothers' club. Maria Antônia's Catholic group joins with the Pentecostal Assemblies of God in running the local community center (Comunidade Viva, or Living Community) and operating its program for needy children. These partnerships reflect a real advance and a real gain in resources in poor communities. Although several women mentioned that they had not been as successful in mobilizing their Protestant neighbors for more explicitly "political" rather than "charitable" action, common community organizations provide an infrastructure for future cooperation in more "politicized" activities. These common efforts go well beyond what most neighborhoods would have seen in an earlier era, and their importance as new sites of civil society is considerable.

Significantly, most of the cooperation mentioned has taken place in Rio de Janeiro: seven out of the ten women reside there. This may reflect the greater proportion of Protestant churches in the Rio area, especially in the poorer neighborhoods of the Baixada Fluminense. Indeed, metropolitan Rio has the highest proportion of Protestants, especially Pentecostals, in the country, according to surveys by the Brazilian Institute of Public Opinion and Statistics (IBOPE) and Datafolha.

Although only 40 percent actually have worked with Protestants, the overwhelming majority of Brazilian women in this study express a desire to do so. Twenty-two of the total of twenty-five Brazilian women interviewed cite Protestants as possible or desirable partners for grassroots activities. They chose Protestants more often than other movements within the Catholic

Church as reliable potential allies, and saw only neighborhood associations and women's groups as more desirable partners.

The women refer to the denominations to which their Protestant partners belong, and as we shall see, even distinguish between denominations in terms of those with which they think partnerships are possible. They do not, however, usually seem to imply that the alliances are between congregations per se. Only one diocese, Caxias, offered evidence of institutional alliances. There, Geralda mentioned that the Methodists gave help, support, and training to groups in her community. For the most part, the actual alliances appear to be more with individuals than with churches or denominations.

Most who identify Protestants as possible partners typically express the desire to develop activities together with individuals, rather than an alliance between the ecclesiastical institutions themselves. In districts with high indices of violence, without basic sanitation, and with few investments in social infrastructure and education, such as the ones that exist where these women live, various Protestant, mostly Pentecostal, churches are a part of everyday life. Often the women live with family members who frequent Pentecostal congregations, so they are conscious of the heterogeneity of the local religious landscape and religious differences between friends or community members who share the same hardships of daily life. As a consequence, many Brazilian women have a sympathetic outlook toward members of other religious groups. Maria Melania describes the religious pluralism in her own immediate surroundings as an understandable response to the challenges confronting the Brazilian poor: "In our area here, most people are evangelicals. Only I and the lady in front are Catholic; the rest are Protestant. I see this as a need of the people. They are looking for something that solves their problems because most are searching for a solution to their problems. I have seen the growth [of Pentecostalism] around here in that context. It's really a moment of desperation, of search, of curing, because you go to the health post and don't get attended to. Then you go to pastor so-and-so and he cures you." Maria Melania's comments reflect a recognition that Pentecostalism can fill a spiritual or psychological need among the faithful that the Catholic Church often fails to address. She says that the exodus of some Catholics to Pentecostal churches shows that there is "much to be desired in our church, and people are looking for something they can't find in our church. Unfortunately, the Catholic Church has to take a smack on the hand because it leaves much to be desired. It's a holy and sinful church, and we sin a lot in that way, in our warmth, in our presence." Maria Melania says of Pentecostal neighbors, "We get along really well together . . . when someone comes asking for prayers, I open my doors and I even go with them as well, without any rejection." In a similar vein, Ilda describes her relationship with her neighbor, a member of the Assemblies of God: "When I moved here, I had no phone; I used hers. She gave me messages and offered to let me call from there. People from the church called, the priest called, and she gave me the messages properly. Now she sold her phone and I have one and she uses it when she needs it. When her children get married, she calls me to go to her church and attend the weddings, and I go. When mine get married, I invite them, and she and her family go, as well. In this way, we are friends." In fact, many women referred to such personal cooperative relationships with friends and neighbors to explain why they thought their groups could work with Protestants.

Differences in theology or religious practice do not seem to be insurmountable obstacles among individuals. For the majority of Brazilian interviewees who view Pentecostals as potential allies, such neighborhood and friendship ties can override their differences in religious identity. Lúcia's ties with neighbors allowed her base community to work with other women from the Assemblies of God, as well as Presbyterians and Baptists, in community infant-health programs. Sometimes interpersonal cooperation among individuals who are struggling to survive can soften what appear to be firm boundaries between rival religious identities. For example, Neide describes individuals moving back and forth between Catholic and Pentecostal groups. She says that she lives together with many people who are *crentes* ("believers," that is, Pentecostals), as several live near her home and receive the *cestas basicas* (food baskets) distributed by her community. According to her, these poor families chose "Pentecostalism and attend the Assemblies of God (and the Baptist church), but since they don't have social assistance there, they come and seek it here in the community."

Brazilian progressive Catholics have always stressed that socioeconomic conditions will overcome other differences of identity that might separate the poor. Indeed, religious identity does not appear to be a rigid barrier to cooperation, at least at the individual level. Brazilian activists tend to see their Protestant neighbors as autonomous from their churches, and therefore able to be mobilized as individuals, even if their pastors and churches are unwilling to join in a particular project or cause. Nonetheless, they perceive some denominations as potentially more open to cooperation than others, and they are particularly critical of some denominations, especially Pentecostals and the neo-Pentecostal Igreja Universal do Reino de Deus (Universal Church of the Kingdom of God [IURD]).

Distinguishing Potential Allies

Although the Brazilian respondents refer to Protestants, evangelicals, and Pentecostals almost interchangeably, many refer to denominations to explain the success or failure to develop cooperative relationships in specific circumstances. In general, they perceive the historical mainline congregations (Methodists, Presbyterians, Lutherans) as more likely allies than Pentecostals (Assemblies of God) and, especially, neo-Pentecostals (IURD). Three of the five women who mentioned specific churches they could envision working with named Methodists, for example. In fact, of the seven who specified churches with which their CEBs do work, six named mainline Protestant denominations: Methodists (three), Presbyterians (two), and Baptists (one). In contrast, two stated specifically that they could not work with the Brazilian neo-Pentecostal Universal Church of the Kingdom of God (IURD). Only Ilda mentioned actually working with people from the IURD. Several others mentioned Pentecostal denominations such as the Assemblies of God as possible allies.

The mainline Protestant denominations the women tend to name are growing in poor neighborhoods, but they are less visible and are growing more slowly than Pentecostal and neo-Pentecostal churches. Some of the preference for these denominations may come from experiences such as the ones the women mentioned, but since fewer than half the women had direct experience of working with Protestant denominations, their distinctions may be based more on a general impression of various denominations than on actual experience. Catholics often see Methodists, Presbyterians, and other mainline Protestant churches, for example, as theologically closer to progressive Catholicism and, therefore, "more open" to Catholic-Protestant partnerships on social issues than Pentecostals would be. Maria Antônia, president of an association of residents in Nova Iguacu and a militant in the PT, states that Methodists and Presbyterians "work with the idea that we are all citizens with rights and duties."

In some cases, the denominations Brazilians mention, such as the Methodists, have "mainstreamed" some of liberation theology's values.[6] Baptists and

6. Interviews with Methodist lay workers at Colegio Bennett and Instituto Central do Povo, Rio de Janeiro, June 1997.

Methodists are prominent in the progressive and socially active Aliança Evangélica Brasileira (Brazilian Evangelicals' Association [AEVB]).[7] The women may also be aware of specific Protestant "personalities" and activities.[8] Edna, for example, infers a proximity of views between the two churches from the close friendship and partnership between her Catholic bishop in Caxias and the local Methodist bishop. The evangelical governor and vice governor of Rio de Janeiro at the time of the interviews were from left parties—then vice governor Benedita da Silva, in fact, from the liberationist-friendly PT. Thus, many women have a sense that some denominations are closer to or further from their social and political orientation.

Pentecostals and neo-Pentecostals, in contrast, evoke more mixed reactions. Many women admire these groups' ability to mobilize a highly committed laity, and most of the Brazilian respondents describe positive experiences of cooperation with Pentecostal neighbors or friends. Nonetheless, Pentecostals also awaken criticism and resistance among the Catholic women who were interviewed. They identify specific constraints as well as concrete opportunities for cooperation in their neighborhoods. Most of these relate to religious rather than political differences. Religious differences are manifest in a range of contentious issues, from the style of worship services to the theological meaning assigned to community problems. Some religious differences merely make progressive Catholics uncomfortable, straining the interpersonal relationships that undergird cooperation, while some—like religious exclusivity— appear to be insurmountable barriers to partnership.

Many progressive Catholic women are uncomfortable with what they perceive as overly emotional Pentecostal worship. Zelita, who visited an Assemblies of God church at the request of the Pastoral of Health in the Zona Leste of São Paulo, says, "They shout too much. . . . God isn't deaf. I know everyone has their own way of praying, but they shout too much." Most of the women who identify themselves as progressive Catholics share her discomfort, and many believe that emotionalism and enchantment indicate a lack of political and social conscience. This belief is consistent with the Marxist discourse of liberation theology in the minds of many. However, many of the same respondents who express discomfort with the religious

7. AEVB chose a Methodist to succeed its Baptist founder as president in 1997 (*Avante* [newspaper of the Methodist Church in Rio de Janeiro], June 1997, 21).

8. In Martins 1991, José Pedro Martins describes the social-change work undertaken by a variety of historic denominations.

style of Pentecostal services also cite positive experiences and even interpersonal alliances with Pentecostal neighbors or friends. Thus, while a source of tension, differences in religious styles do not in themselves appear to be an insurmountable barrier to Catholic-Pentecostal alliances.

Cooperation becomes more difficult when Pentecostals couple emotionalism with an explicit rejection of "politics." Maria José, speaking of her relationship with new *crente* neighbors, says that with some, "it's possible to discuss politics, with others it is much more difficult because they don't think there is much to do other than pray. They're stuck in that 'Jesus saves.'" But she acknowledges that "some accept discussing day-to-day difficulties, even though they are Protestant." Like others, Maria José distinguishes between Protestants, classifying mainstream Protestants, the Baptists, for instance, as more open-minded and disposed to talk about politics or problems in the community. She characterizes members of the Assemblies of God, by contrast, as "more traditional and narrow-minded [*bitolados*]." According to Maria José, the Assembly member is the Protestant who

> only sees the question of salvation . . . participating so he is saved. So, he's the kind of person it's difficult to count on to get together and demand things. Even within the factory, everything is the will of God, everything is solved by praying. So this was a great difficulty for us in our attempts to negotiate with the factory and the boss. So you have great difficulty in counting on the Protestant because of this limited vision that he has. They say everything is the will of God; that's conformity. That's the greatest difficulty.

In this case, Maria José believes that the Pentecostals' style of worship coupled with spiritual fatalism regarding the ability of individuals to influence the world stands in the way of Catholic-Pentecostal grassroots alliance. The majority of the Brazilian respondents made some reference to groups or individuals whose rejection of "worldly" or "political" engagement make local cooperation impossible. The largest obstacle to cooperation, however, is a sense of religious exclusivity, or constant Pentecostal criticisms of Catholicism. Maria José says that she cannot accept the fact that to establish a relationship with the people from the Assembly of God, "a person must convert to their faith, accept that type of life practice."

As critical as many of the respondents are of Pentecostals, specifically members of Assemblies of God, they are far more derogatory about members of the neo-Pentecostal IURD, whom they see as "fanatics" and "alienated."[9] This church and similar neo-Pentecostal churches encounter the most resistance among Catholics. These churches provoke a strong reaction among Catholics for many reasons, including their leaders' public criticism of Catholicism as a false religion. Perhaps more important, the IURD's theology offends progressive Catholics, with its claims of an ability to cure all diseases; its practice of exorcism; and its "prosperity theology," which promises financial success to those who show their faith by donating as much as they can (Serbin 1999). Many progressive Catholics, like these women describe the leaders of the IURD, along with the leaders of the similar neo-Pentecostal Renascer Church, as "exploiting the faithful." Maria de Socorro states that she has a cousin in the IURD for whom she is "afraid":

> I am afraid because it is a church that alienates people a lot and that attacks our church. Instead of talking about the good things they are doing, they just speak ill of the Catholic Church. . . . I know many people in the IURD and they become very narrow-minded [*bitolados*] when they join that church. Let me give you an example: I was disappointed in my daughter's medical treatment and these people who were my colleagues came to the house saying that if I went to the Igreja Universal [IURD] she would get better because the pastors there cure people. . . . I responded that if I received the grace of her getting better, she would get better with me being in the Catholic Church. It would have to be in my church that I received that grace. They said that I was defying God.

In this case, Maria not only views the Igreja Universal as rigid; she also accuses the pastors of manipulating the vulnerability of the poor, who constantly face poverty-related crises, exploiting them to heighten their loyalty to an exclusionary religious identity. By preaching that God only ministers

9. According to Everett Wilson (1997), neo-Pentecostal groups attract middle-class or upwardly mobile individuals with a message focused on health and wealth: "Although all neo-Pentecostal groups tend to be similarly contemporary in their styles, each has its own variation on the same themes. All emphasize empowerment in the form of prophetic authority expressed in emphases on miracles, healing, exorcism, and prophecy. . . . Pentecostal leaders suspect that considerable numbers of their better-established recent converts and many upwardly mobile young people from Pentecostal families have made the switch, finding in these groups desirable companionship and extended social contacts as well as more relaxed standards of dress and conduct" (146).

to the faithful of the Igreja Universal, pastors deliberately foster a religious identity that rejects contamination by, much less cooperation with, members of "rival" faiths.

Many Pentecostals comfortably separate religious identity from sociopolitical identity, strongly prioritizing the former and often rejecting the latter as "worldly." Many progressive Catholics, in contrast, believe that their religious identity necessarily calls them to political action. In the discourse of liberation theology, to be a Christian means that one must commit oneself to the struggle for social justice in this world. Not surprisingly, then, religious or theological differences between Catholics and Pentecostals take on political meanings that further complicate the possibilities for building alliances. The Brazilian interviewees consistently convey frustration that Pentecostals wish to be "apolitical," even when they may belong to an evangelical group that is heavily involved in community social work. Consistent with the findings of John Burdick (1993) and Rowan Ireland (1991), the women found their Pentecostal neighbors far more willing to mobilize around "social" ventures, such as constructing health posts or assisting children, than around more "political" issues such as the construction of a prison in the Caxias region or attending to partisan struggles in Baixada Fluminense.

Progressive Catholics, however, typically do not distinguish between "social" and "political" activism. They consider work on community social programs (community health, child care, soup kitchens, domestic abuse, drug treatment, and the like) as solidarity work, and as such, inherently political. Moreover, many identify their work on specific projects with their adherence to a larger political, even partisan, agenda. Our respondents express great dissatisfaction that their own willingness to maintain a dialogue with their Pentecostal neighbors, even accepting invitations to *crente* celebrations, is met with constant refusal to join in what Pentecostals view as "political" Catholic activities.

A few of the most politicized respondents, mainly from São Paulo, fear alliances with any church came at the cost of political autonomy, which could diminish their effectiveness. Maria Aparecida, one of the founders of the PT in the district of Itaim Paulista, expresses this fear clearly:

> We wanted to offer a service to the population, independent of what church one went to. Then, one of those people who was in the CEBs and who was one hell of a leader of the women's movement, Gil, who lives here in the Baixada in Parque Paulistano, came up with

an idea: "Let's form a directorate, and I participate in the Protestant Church, and that church will cover the costs.". . . I said, "Hold on a minute, if we didn't hand ourselves over to one church, the Catholics, then another, the Protestants, isn't going to grab us."

In general, however, most Brazilian women do not share the preoccupation with guaranteeing their political autonomy. Instead, many women from Rio de Janeiro view aid from Protestant groups as a positive gain for the social movement. This optimism may be fed in part not only by the concrete examples that they see locally, but also by some small examples at the level of the national church.

National Examples of Ecumenism

The Brazilian Catholic hierarchy, like most in Latin America, frequently expresses grave misgivings about the growth of Protestantism in the region. In fact, Pentecostal growth is usually seen as an indication of problems, either in the church or in society, rather than as a potential indicator of social health (Oro 1996, 95). The CNBB has developed a plan to reevangelize lay Catholics in which the "resacralization" of local parish life—turning away from liberation theology and stressing the sacramental and the enchanted again—is viewed as a means of "competing" with Protestant denominations. It would be a mistake to view the Brazilian Catholic hierarchy as a whole as particularly ecumenical or welcoming of Protestant denominations. Indeed, the national hierarchy as a whole sees Protestants as a threat to be reckoned with, not as potential allies.

As Daniel Levine and David Stoll point out, "Anxiety over keeping grassroots groups loyal to the church hierarchy inhibits alliance-building with other groups like themselves" (1997, 91). The bishops, then, as well as local priests, are unlikely to encourage the women's optimism about forming alliances with local Protestant denominations, or to model such cooperation on the national scale. Nonetheless, the diversity of opinion within the Brazilian church leaves room for more ecumenical spaces, and it is perhaps significant that some of the most visible of these are associated with the liberationist branch of the church. Indeed, Ari Pedro Oro (1996) argues that progressives within the church have generally adopted the attitude that religious diversity is inevitable and must be accepted; he adds that this is one of the two predominant views of Protestantism within the church as a whole (95–96).

In addition to seeing some individual models of such collaboration, such as the friendship between dom Mauro Morelli and the Methodist bishop that Edna mentioned, many women in Rio de Janeiro have had personal contact with organizations such as the Institute for Religious Studies (ISER) and the Center for Biblical Studies (CEBI). These organizations, originally affiliated with the liberationist Catholic Church and providing support to the base communities, now reflect a more ecumenical component, despite retaining a largely Catholic character. Moreover, the national meetings of base communities have strongly and resolutely adopted a more ecumenical tone. As a report on the 1997 meeting in São Luis do Maranhao noted, that meeting included afro-brazilian religionists as well as Protestants, and leaders of each group shared the altar with the local bishop in the opening ceremony. The official prayer, written by the well-known liberationist bishop dom Pedro Casaldaliga, referred to the presence of the three major religious groups in Brazil with its closing salute: Amen! Alleluia! Axe! (Junqueira 1997, 63).[10] By the meeting in 2000, an official document, "Letter to the People of God from Members of Non-Catholic Churches Participating in the Tenth Interecclesial," indicated that seventy-two members of the Lutheran, Methodist, Baptist-Nazareth, United Presbyterian, Independent Presbyterian, Episcopal, and Evangelical Congregational Churches participated ("Letter to the People of God"). That letter referred to these groups' unprecedented participation in the Catholic Church's annual lenten "Brotherhood Campaign" that year. In addition to taking as its theme, "A New Millenium Without Exclusion," the campaign included an "Ecumenical Solidarity Collection" on Palm Sunday (Martins 2000).

The Catholic Church's ecumenism should not be exaggerated. Overall, the church has been subject to many of the same conservative trends as the rest of the region and has similarly encouraged a retrenchment to more conservative and traditional practices, in part to compete with the thriving Protestant communities. Nonetheless, there are pockets of diversity within the church that continue to espouse more liberationist views, and many of these have also been more vocally ecumenical in recent years. This may be a source of encouragement to women who look upon their Pentecostal, or at least Protestant, neighbors as potential allies.

The Brazilian women see the obstacles to such alliances as formidable ones with both religious and political sources, but they also can see concrete

---

10. See the comments on ecumenism in the preparatory documents in Lesbaupin 1996.

examples of successful local alliances in some cases. They remain convinced that such alliances are worth pursuing with at least some Protestant groups, although they are often unsure of exactly how to pursue them. In contrast, both political and religious barriers to partnerships are greater between the Chilean respondents than the Brazilian interviewees.

Chile: Religious Segregation and Barriers to Cooperation

In stark contrast to the 40 percent of Brazilian interviewees whose base communities had some degree of cooperation with local Protestants, the comparative figure in Chile is low; religious denominations in Chile appear to remain much more isolated. The few cases in which Chilean women mention cooperation with Protestants all occurred during the dictatorship. Not one Chilean respondent describes an incident of local cooperation between Catholics and Protestants today. Chilean groups simply have not made even the limited connections with another prime organizing site in their communities—Protestant churches—that at least some of the Brazilians have achieved, even on an individual level.

The Chilean women are also overwhelmingly skeptical that they could make such connections. When asked about entities that could ally with grassroots Catholic activists to solve local problems, only a few Chilean activists mention Protestants or Pentecostals. Chilean women's pessimism regarding alliances with Pentecostals is not born of an ignorance of Pentecostalism, however. Chile has one of the highest percentages of Pentecostals in Latin America, and as in Brazil, the vast majority of Pentecostal faithful live in urban *poblaciónes* alongside Catholic activists like our respondents. Virtually all the Chilean respondents state that they know Pentecostals in their neighborhoods, but these relationships seem to be much more superficial than the ones the Brazilian women describe. At least in the Chilean case, the hypothesis that greater local Pentecostal visibility leads to reduced stereotyping, and, therefore, a greater potential for ecumenical cooperation, is not borne out. Although it is likely that Chileans experience the same, or a similar level, of personal friendship with neighbors of different faiths, the Chilean women's stories notably lack the kind of detailed descriptions of positive relationships with Pentecostal neighbors and friends that color the Brazilian surveys. Adela Ramirez, for example, states that "our chapel shares electricity and water with an evangelical temple, and we buy the bread that they make." She quickly adds that this is not evidence of a cooperative relationship, however; rather, each church keeps to itself, because "evangelicals work on the basis of fear and the apocalypse. They are close-minded."

Religious and Political Constraints

Like their Brazilian counterparts, the Chilean respondents cite theological differences between Catholics and Pentecostals as a major obstacle to joint work in their communities. Maria Espina sums up the view of most Chilean women: "There is so much ignorance because of a lack of understanding of the theological aspects that separate us, and of those aspects that unite us as well. Fanaticism and rivalry are strong." For example, Naemi Peña Igor states that Protestants "reject Catholics. They say we are sinners." Eli Molina, who participates in one of the few parishes in our survey that remains socially progressive, echoes the Brazilian respondents' frustration with a Pentecostal exclusivity that prohibits effective cooperation. Eli's parish and the base community work in alliance with a number of groups, from unions and women's organizations to local government departments and political parties. The range of her base community's cooperative activities demonstrates the participants' willingness to work with other groups to address local needs. Her parish has not succeeded in building effective alliances with any of the small local evangelical sects, however.

> Our relations with the neighborhood council are good, and we work together on projects. The Network of Women Against Violence gives talks and workshops about women's rights and violence prevention. We host political debates with candidates during electoral campaigns. Church members who belong to unions talk to the church. . . . Many people participate in a number of things, which gives this community so much life. . . . There are no large Protestant churches in the neighborhood, only evangelical sects that are very closed groups. Evangelical pastors are masters of their churches. Once we invited a pastor to participate with his congregation in an activity in our church and he replied, "Each to his own, and we will still be neighbors."

Juanita Riveros, who like Eli is from a socially active parish that has tried to work together with local Protestants, states that Pentecostal pastors are "not very tolerant. They just want to get us into their churches. They have little social concern."

Like the Brazilian respondents, the Chilean interviewees complain that Pentecostals eschew "politics," preferring to trust in God to solve community problems through individual salvation. According to Ana Acuña, "Most of them, and all of them in this neighborhood, believe that destiny has made our lives the way they are, and we just have to accept that destiny." Thus she says, "Although [Catholic priests and Protestant pastors] worked together during the dictatorship . . . [now] they are in a separate world, and they never come in contact with each other."

Constraints Within the Catholic Church

Unlike their Brazilian counterparts, not all the Chilean respondents placed the primary blame on the religious intolerance of Protestants. In fact, roughly an equal number faulted the Catholic Church. Lily Caja states that "the mentality of the Catholic church is that those who have different religious beliefs have nothing in common with us. There is little tolerance." Alicia Ubilla concurs: "The [Catholic] church has the power to call people together to talk about what's happening today. . . . [But] Catholic priests have not even given a thought to ecumenical work." Ruth Saldías Monreal states, "Some evangelicals cannot bear to sit next to a Catholic. But the same goes for the Catholics. There is a lack of understanding on both sides."

The difference between Brazilian and Chilean women's assessment of potential alliances with Protestants rests on Chilean women's view of the dramatic reimposition, by the Chilean national hierarchy, of a traditional, authoritarian model of church authority. As discussed in Chapter 3, the Chilean hierarchy viewed the democratic transition as an opportunity to return the church to its traditional, pastoral mission. As a result, the majority of Chilean bishops asserted that the church's central role in the flourishing of new social movements must end, the boundaries between the church and "political" activity must be sharpened, and the fluid authority structure of the base Christian communities must be tightened under hierarchical control. Church leaders explicitly encouraged political parties, trade unions, and other interest groups to return to their roles as channels for citizen demands so that the Catholic Church could withdraw to its primary mission—the salvation of souls through the sacramental life of the parish. Indeed, the majority of the Chilean respondents remember explicit instructions from bishops and priests to refocus the

efforts of the church away from the social and political activism of the dictatorship. As a result, the Chilean respondents not only perceive Pentecostals as
hostile to "political" work, they also face rejection from their own priests and
bishops. Rogelia Molina describes the change within her church and its effect
on the process of working with Protestants:

> We could work together [with Protestants] to solve problems we
> have in common. But both religions are close-minded. . . . We felt
> the changes after 1985 when all the Colombian priests were replaced
> by diocesan priests. The changes were handed down by Rome, which
> was afraid of losing power because laypeople had such force. . . .
> Laypeople used to organize the liturgies and almost did not need
> priests. The new diocesan priests ended the lay role as protagonists. . . .
> Relations are very formal. The priests seem way up there and it is hard
> to reach them.

Eliana Olate describes a similar transformation in her parish and base
community:

> The changed position of the church was imposed on the Christian
> base communities. It reflected what was going on in the country.
> Many people with a high social commitment stayed, but they
> became marginalized. . . . Today, people wait for the priest to tell
> them what to do. For them, it is important to feel that the priest
> approves of what they do. . . . This priest is very anti–other religions.
> He creates a climate that does not foster ecumenical work. In Bible
> study classes, he criticizes the beliefs of other religions.

In both Rogelia's and Eliana's cases, the perceived inability to work with
Protestants in their communities is intertwined with the church's imposition of a strict hierarchical authority structure within which a conservative
priesthood insists on exclusive religious identity and obedience from the
faithful. Both Rogelia and Eliana believe that their base community could
work with Protestants on local issues of common concern to both Catholic
and Protestant neighbors, but that such cooperation would have to depend
on relationships built between laypeople. According to Chilean women,
however, the church abruptly reined in such lay leadership around the time
of the democratic transition.

Like Rogelia and Eliana, Ana Acuña sees the possibility of working with Protestants in solving her community's problems, but she also sees the official church hierarchy as the major obstacle to such alliances. Ana, who today participates in an ecumenical human rights group, explains:

> In the 1980s, we worked together with Protestants. . . . [But] after 1989, the priest would say, "These are different times. The church has to go back to its traditional mission." The message was loud and clear. The church had ceased to be the place for social work. Many people who were more advanced politically lost their faith. . . . The priest says that he wants communities to grow, but he views them in a very paternalistic light. . . . The priest is at the center of everything, and the people have to come fill up the church.

Ana sees the reimposition of traditional hierarchical authority within the church as intertwined with the church's rejection of "social work." Most women use the phrase *social work* (broad grassroots mobilization organized through and within Catholic base communities) to connote not only previous political opposition to military rule but also community efforts to deal with the food, health, or safety needs of neighbors. The Chilean hierarchy's rejection of "social work," therefore, reduces the field of potential lay participation in community work to a task of merely being required to "come fill up the church." Furthermore, a rejection of community, lay-led social work on the grounds that it is outside the mission of the church makes cooperation with Protestants, even evangelicals whose churches provide social services to their members, difficult on more than just theological grounds.

In Chile, more evidence of the possibility of a Catholic-Pentecostal institutional alliance can be found at the national, rather than local, level. Because of the relatively high profile of the Consejo de Pastores (Council of Pastors), a national Pentecostal umbrella organization born during the dictatorship and vocally supportive of General Pinochet throughout military rule, conventional wisdom rules out the possibility of Catholic-Pentecostal alliance (Cleary and Sepulveda, 1997; Lagos 1982, 1985; Lagos and Chacón 1987).[11]

---

11. The Council of Pastors annually sponsored a "Protestant Te Deum" in the large cathedral of the Iglesia Metodista Pentecostal during the dictatorship to publicly thank General Pinochet and the military for saving Chile from the communists. This event was regularly broadcast on television, giving the military the appearance of strong support from Chilean Pentecostals. Yet, in spite of the public's perception,

In 1982, however, a rival organization called the Confraternidad Cristiana de Iglesias, whose stance was far more prophetic in its criticism of the military dictatorship, was founded by other Protestant leaders, including a number of prominent Pentecostal pastors. According to Juana Alborñoz, a Pentecostal pastor and president of the Confraternidad Cristiana de Iglesias:

> The Catholic Church played a very important role in defense of the people [during the dictatorship], but other churches also heard the call to raise our prophetic voices against injustice. . . . Chile had been a country of much hope and expectation. Overnight we were besieged by a pain worse than war. . . . Pastors of the Methodist, Presbyterian, Apostolic Pentecostal, and various other Protestant churches, with support from the World Council of Churches, came together to form the Confraternidad de Iglesias, to add our voices to those of other churches that already were denouncing human rights violations. The Confraternidad was born because we just could not remain silent after the murder of union leader Tucapel Jimenez, the burning of Carmen Gloria Quintana and Rodrigo Rojas, and other atrocities.[12]

For Pentecostals raised in the belief that their faith calls them to eschew "worldly" commitments and to keep their eyes on the afterlife during their earthly pilgrimage, a decision to join with others of different faiths to combat injustice in this world represents a dramatic shift in perspective. Pastor Alborñoz describes the theological changes in her own life in the following way:

> When I was a child, it was thought that we only needed to learn to read and write, nothing more, because the world had no relevance in our lives. We were supposed to work and live our lives to reach the eternal homeland, God's dwelling place. Such were our lives in 1973, and the military coup violently woke us up. Some Protestant churches, such as the Methodists and the Lutherans, already were

---

a 1991 survey by the Centro de Estudios Publicos (CEP) found that the majority of Pentecostal believers had a negative opinion of Pinochet and considered themselves politically independent, with only 15 percent identifying themselves as sympathetic to the political right (Fontaine Talavera and Beyer 1991, 102–12).

12. The cases of Tucapel Jimenez, a union leader murdered by the state in 1982, and Carmen Gloria Quintana and Rodrigo Rojas, both students doused with gasoline and set alight by police during a street demonstration in 1986, served as powerful symbols of military brutality during the pro-democracy movement throughout the 1980s.

known for their social commitment and their work in the community, but not the Pentecostals. In 1973, we came to understand that Pentecostals are also part of this suffering people. We saw how our communities also were make up of workers, fighters, people who were persecuted and imprisoned.

Pastor Alborñoz acknowledges that the schism between pro-Pinochet Pentecostal pastors and those, like herself, who felt called to join other Protestants and progressive Catholics in denouncing the regime represents a significant theological rift between Pentecostals. She states:

We wanted to show that the churches that prayed for Pinochet did not reflect the beliefs of the entire evangelical world. The majority of Protestant followers were poor, without a decent home, without opportunity for education. People would tell me, "My pastor preaches support for Pinochet but we are suffering; I don't sleep well at night because I'm afraid they will come take my husband away." It was during that period that Protestants also founded [other human rights organizations such as] the [Servicio Evangélico para el Desarrollo] SEPADE and [Social Service Foundation of Christian Churches] FASIC.

Organizations such as the Confraternidad Cristiana de Iglesias, as well as the Centro Diego de Medellín and Con-spirando, both of which enjoy ecumenical participation, suggest that some Pentecostal leaders became more open to working with other groups, even Catholic groups, to achieve ends of mutual concern. Chilean women see less evidence of such an openness at the grassroots level than do Brazilian women, however. In addition, Chilean women view the Catholic hierarchy as far more rigid in its condemnation of ecumenical "social work" than do Brazilian women. For Chilean women, the church's rigidity is seen not simply as a function of the prejudices or shortcomings of individual priests or bishops, but rather as an integral part of a national strategy to redefine the role of the Catholic Church in post-transition politics and society. The national hierarchy's more complete withdrawal from "politics" and greater capacity to enforce conformity throughout grassroots parishes is cited repeatedly as the primary obstacle to working with Protestants, even in cases where such alliances had flourished during the dictatorship.

Importance of Political Context

Although both Brazilian and Chilean Catholic activists view cooperation with Pentecostals as problematic, the boundaries separating Brazilian women's various identities (religious, class, partisan, racial, gender) appear more fluid than for Chilean women. Based on a shared sense of socioeconomic hardship, Brazilian women express a greater willingness, and even a desire, to work with Pentecostals. They reject cooperation only if met with an attitude of religious exclusivity. One reason for more permeable boundaries of personal identity in Brazil may be that the rapid growth of Pentecostalism coincided with the flourishing of new social movements, seen in such phenomena as Catholic base communities, women's organizations, progressive political activities culminating in the founding of the PT, and others. Given Brazil's weaker history of democracy and less developed political party system, many of the contemporary institutions of modern Brazilian democracy have not reached the same degree of penetration of civil society as have their Chilean counterparts. Disparate movements (religious, civil, and partisan) grew alongside one another under the shadow of dictatorship. Individuals moved in and out of organizations looking for effective ways to cope with the economic, but also psychic and spiritual, hardships imposed by harsh military rule. Thus, identities based on membership in particular religious, partisan, or social movement groups did not harden as broad alliances were formed across multiple boundaries. Perhaps it is not surprising that Brazilian women express a general attitude of openness to cooperation with other groups and unwillingness only in specific circumstances with particular groups.

A number of additional factors reinforce the tendency to greater openness on the part of the Brazilian women. First, as Cecilia Mariz has demonstrated, Brazil has a longer-standing experience of religious pluralism than have other Latin American countries, and Brazilian popular culture encourages a religious ethos in which there is a high degree of transit between and across religious groups (Mariz 1994). Catholic base communities tend to be much less open to such transit than are other religious groups, but the idea and the acceptability of religious pluralism nonetheless may be greater among Brazilian Catholic activists than among Chileans because of this ethos. In addition, as we have seen, the Brazilian church is less monolithic than the Chilean. Pockets of liberationist discourse persist and these have actively encouraged ecumenism over the past several years.

Thus, the Brazilian church's message on ecumenism is mixed, not uniformly hostile. The women's attitudes may therefore depend less on the presence of a particularly ecumenical priest or bishop, although as Edna's testimony indicates, such individuals also have an impact on laypeople's attitudes.

In contrast to what exists in Brazil, the boundaries between religious and political identities have remained relatively fixed in Chile since the early twentieth century. As discussed in earlier chapters, Chilean political culture has been divided between an ideological right, left, and center since the 1930s, with virtually the same parties competing for votes within a fairly stable division of the electorate into rough thirds of the population. Given the historically far greater degree of politicization of Chilean society vis-à-vis Brazil's, partisan identity in the former tends to reinforce other identities, including religious identity. Throughout the twentieth century, Chilean religious identity, particularly Catholic identity, coincided with, rather than cross-cut, partisan identity. For example, although the Chilean Catholic Church carefully steered a formally independent course "above politics" prior to the 1973 coup in order to avoid the appearance of partisanship, the Catholic Church, in fact, was strongly identified first with the Conservative Party and later with the Christian Democratic Party (B. Smith 1982; Stewart-Gambino 1992). As a consequence, religious identity in Chile always has contributed to a deeply politicized civil society in which individual identity tends to be more rigidly fixed by membership to fairly stable segments of society.

During the dictatorship, when political parties and other traditional channels for citizen demands were driven underground, boundaries between individuals participating in the new social movements, in which Catholic base communities played a central role, more closely resembled the fluidity of the Brazilian context. However, most sociopolitical actors—political parties, interest groups, and the church—all explicitly chose to return to the pre-1973 democratic model; consequently, the spaces for fluid alliances were dramatically reduced as elites returned to "normal politics." Most important for this study, the return to "normal politics" was actively and explicitly encouraged by a national Catholic hierarchy exhausted by years on the front lines of the opposition to the military and eager to adopt a more traditionalist line. Chilean women, like their Brazilian counterparts, remember cooperation with Pentecostals during the dictatorship as positive; however, the return to "normal politics" resulted in a reimposition of traditionally exclusive boundaries of identity, strengthening the obstacles to intergroup, or in this case ecumenical, cooperation.

The return to the Catholic Church's traditional mission meant not only a withdrawal from the social and political commitments inspired by liberation theology, but also a renewed commitment to compete head-on with the church's principal religious rival, Pentecostalism. Unlike in Brazil, with its wide range of religious pluralism, in Chile the Catholic Church does not have to compete for the souls of the faithful on multiple religious fronts. Mainstream Protestant churches, while deeply rooted historically in Chile's immigrant populations (particularly those of British and German extraction), are relatively stable populations that do not actively proselytize Chilean Catholics. With virtually no African-based religious traditions and no real threat from mainstream Protestant or Jewish proselytizing, the Catholic Church is primarily concerned with protecting the faithful from the appeal of the explosively growing Pentecostal congregations (Parker 1996). Sociologist Katherine Gilfeather (1992) characterizes the Chilean Catholic Church's stance toward Pentecostals since the democratic transition as "sectarian proselytism," suggesting a heightened degree of religious competition. The starker competition with Pentecostals further hardens the boundaries between religious identities, underscoring the Chilean respondents' belief that both Catholic and Pentecostal leaders stand in the way of local or national alliance.

The small size of the Chilean episcopate allowed the Chilean hierarchy to withdraw more rapidly and more uniformly from the prophetic stance adopted during the dictatorship.[13] The sense that the Chilean church changed almost overnight from a pillar of the new social movements to a conservative, traditionalist institution concerned almost exclusively with "the defense of family values and public morality" (Kamsteeg 1999) is shared by virtually every Chilean respondent. In their eyes, the Catholic Church's insistence that parishes and base communities withdraw from "social work" to a traditional, sacramental mission is redolent of Pentecostal apoliticism, and they express as much frustration with their own Catholic bishops and priests as they do with exclusionist Pentecostal pastors. Chilean women's acute sense of isolation results from their alienation not only from Pentecostals in their neighborhoods, but also their own Catholic hierarchy.

Nevertheless, it is important not to overemphasize the apparent differ-

---

13. As pointed out in earlier chapters, several of the most progressive bishops during the dictatorship remain in Chile, but they are isolated within a much more uniformly traditionalist national hierarchy than in Brazil, where a larger number of progressive bishops and priests remain active throughout the country.

ences between the Brazilian and Chilean respondents in this study. Although Brazilian women express a greater openness to partnerships with Pentecostals, like Chilean women they voice ambivalence or unease about particular groups or circumstances. Their accounts of their failure to forge cooperative relationships with some Pentecostal groups in their neighborhoods demonstrate that each instance of partnership must be negotiated through difficult and complex local and national realities. And in both countries, the entry of Pentecostals into the political sphere does not necessarily imply their adoption of the political line preferred by progressive Catholics. It is true that many Pentecostal pastors no longer instruct their followers to reject participation in political or social movements, allowing the faithful to more effectively participate in electoral disputes and political debates. Yet, in many cases, politically active Pentecostal churches reproduce patterns of political clientelism that are consistent with traditional Brazilian and Chilean culture. Thus, Pentecostals' political loyalties may be inconsistent with the views of progressive Catholics, underscoring that each instance of cooperation or alliance is contestable and must be assessed individually.

Conclusion

As activists seek to create new alliances that will enable them to pursue their goals, they are likely to look about their neighborhoods for potential supporters. Finding allies among those who share their day-to-day conditions is especially important, because such horizontal networks may be more durable and self-sustaining than vertical links to more powerful groups, including their church hierarchies (Levine and Stoll 1997, 75). Protestant churches, whether "historic" or Pentecostal, are potentially strong allies because of their social reach and ability to mobilize people. Individual Protestants, like active Catholics, are much more likely to be involved in civic activities than is the nonpracticing population (Gill 1999, 18). They share not only the Catholic activists' daily living conditions, but also a sense of self-esteem borne of the conviction that, as children of God, they have a right to a decent life.

Bringing these two groups together in neighborhood-based networks is important for the health of civil society and the future potential of social movements in both countries. If the groups can overcome their religious and political differences and fears of "losing" members to the other side, civil society will be greatly strengthened. If not, as Levine and Stoll (1997) point out, "At best, the results are dense but segregated networks of groups; at worst, potential nuclei of civil society are strangled at birth" (91). The likelihood of bridging such gaps seems greater in Brazil, for all the reasons of political context, religious culture, and institutional church politics out-lined above. Even there, however, integration of the networks so far remains at the personal level, and when most activists speak of working with "Protestants," they envision working with friends, neighbors, and relatives rather than with institutional churches. Chileans are more pessimistic about even such basic connections; Catholic and Protestant networks in Chile seem likely to remain "dense but segregated," as Levine and Stoll put it. The Chileans may be more realistic in their assessment that the institutional church, adding to other obstacles, would likely put a stop to any formal alliance of grassroots networks.

Activist Women and Women's Activists:
Possibilities for Networking with Feminist Groups

We became "feminist" the moment that we were able to open a Casa de la Mujer. The fact alone that the house is called "Casa de la Mujer" already associates us with feminism. . . . But in the *población* we use the term "popular feminism" in that we struggle for the whole family. We have tried to work with bourgeois feminists, but we clashed with them. They are professionals, while in the *población* men and women are working class. . . . Feminism has a bad connotation [in the *población*] because of the class differences.

—AIDA MORENO REYES, PRESIDENT OF
CASA DE LA MUJER HUAMACHUCO, CHILE

I consider myself a feminist in the fight for the good, the common struggle. A feminist fights for the well-being, the good, of the collective. I don't think feminism is necessarily making specific programs for women.

—SOFIA, FOUNDER OF A WOMEN'S SELF-EMPLOYMENT GROUP, BRAZIL

As potential allies of grassroots women activists from the base communities, classic feminist groups differ from Protestant groups in many ways. Perhaps most important, classical feminist organizations, unlike Protestant churches, typically are not located in the women's neighborhoods and do not share most aspects of their life conditions. Nonetheless, alliances with feminist groups are plausible on several grounds. First, feminist scholars argue that women's activism of any sort leads to a broadening of the issues, including women's issues, that engage them. If, as Lynn Stephen (1997) and others suggest, the distinction between "feminist" and "feminine" or "practical" and "strategic" gender interests does not hold, then alliances with feminist groups around at least some issues are possible (12). Second, the empirical flip side of this theoretical claim is the continued heavy participation of our women activists in explicitly women's organizations or groups, whose main constituents and clientele are women, noted in Chapter 5. Only some of the groups they work in are "popular feminist" organizations, but women do participate in both "feminine" and "feminist" groups. Third, Latin American feminists who emerged during the military regimes (the so-called second wave) developed new, more encompassing, specifically Latin American definitions of feminism. Although largely white, middle class, and university educated themselves, second-wave feminists showed sensitivity to and consciousness of the class issues that divide Chilean and Brazilian women. Their awareness of diversity within the women's movement led them to self-consciously espouse the notion of grassroots feminism (Lebon 1998, 180–81; Stephen 1997, 12; Valdés and Weinstein 1993, 186–92). Fourth, the discourse of grassroots feminism often had real, practical consequences in creating linkages between feminist and popular women's organizations. A number of feminist scholars have recently argued that networks of grassroots women's activists and feminist organizations have emerged and are being maintained in both Brazil and Chile.[1]

Despite their plausibility, alliances between popular women's activists, such as those from the base communities, and more classic feminist groups can also be problematic and difficult to maintain. Many women from the popular classes throughout Latin America continue to resist adopting the label *feminist* (Lievesley 1999, 140). Those who do adopt it often give it a new meaning. As Sonia Alvarez (1988) has noted, the logical consequence of the "decentering" of Latin American feminism is its "resignification." "On the one hand . . . feminist interventions in the larger women's movement arguably have had important cultural-political effects; yet, on the other hand . . . feminism is being resignified as it is appropriated by women whose life experiences differ significantly from those of the founding mothers of Latin American feminism's second wave" (302).[2] Differing life circumstances—particularly social class and religiosity—can lead women to espouse a specific, "resignified" feminism that fits with those conditions. Continued resistance to the very term *feminist,* however, may come from some of the same sources as resignified popular feminism. Both resistance and resignification pose challenges for collaboration across class lines.

Feminist ideas and discourse have made great strides in both countries. Most important and impressive, both women who agreed and those who disagreed with feminist ideas shared a discourse of gender equality and rights. Self-described feminist Emerenciana states, "We have to teach our sons so after they're married they won't be *machistas.* Men and women are equal." Edna considers herself a feminist "of a different type." She says, "I see feminism in another way. The feminist discourse is that we all have human rights in every sphere, regardless of whether we are male or female. In all categories, the same rights." Even Etelvina, who rejects feminism as "too radical," says she prefers to think in terms of "gender relations, rights,

---

1. See, for example, Stephen 1997; Schild 1998; Alvarez 1998.

2. Identifying class as a source of resistance to the term *feminism* is not the same as saying that reluctance to embrace feminism is somehow a "'natural' outcome of their class position" (Sternbach et al. 1992, 212).

equity." Alicia Ubilla, a social worker in a center that assists victims of domestic violence, voices a somewhat guarded endorsement of feminism that is typical of the minority of Chilean women who call themselves feminist. Her response shows that she is careful to delineate the parameters of her own definition of feminism. "Feminism means a gender identity. You look at the situation from a gender perspective. Biologically, I am a woman, but my gender role is culturally imposed. I am a feminist in the sense that being a woman is not a reason for stopping me from doing things."

Both countries offer instances of resignification as well as resistance to feminist identity, a testimony to the important role that feminists played in making it possible for poor women to organize around their rights, including their rights as women.[3] In many respects, the issues women raise and their attitudes toward the feminist movement are similar. Only Brazilian women, however, were willing to declare themselves even resignified "feminists"; 72 percent of Brazilian women were willing to accept the name feminist even though they qualified the term. In contrast, although 73 percent of Chilean women indicated that they agree with some feminist ideas, they declare that they are not feminists. We should not exaggerate the differences between "resignification" and "rejection" by focusing on a willingness to accept a label. At the same time, however, these subtle differences in opinion along with institutional and political factors do influence the potential for cross-class women's alliances. In this chapter we seek to clarify the extent to which women from the base communities have actually maintained and formed alliances with feminist organizations and the likelihood that they might do so in the future.

Brazil: "Feminists of a Different Type"

Brazilian women assert overwhelmingly that their communities could work with feminist groups. In fact, they endorse feminist groups as possible allies more frequently than any other choice. Madalena, a member of the grass-roots feminist organization AMZOL, is the most enthusiastic: "The feminist group is the one that works the best. They should work together [with the base community]."

3. See Rosado Nunes 1994, 191–92.

Current contacts and networking are limited, but Brazilian women do report more actual networking between their base communities and feminist groups than do the Chilean women. While half reported connections with various "women's groups," one-quarter mentioned connections with specifically "feminist" groups. All those who mentioned feminist groups were from São Paulo, however, and all these women mentioned AMZOL, the popular feminist organization that is itself an outgrowth of the base communities.

The connection with AMZOL is immediate and personal; individual women from the base communities founded AMZOL and continue to participate in it. At the same time, however, women not otherwise involved in AMZOL also perceive it as a group that collaborates with the base community. AMZOL represents the kind of resignified feminism that women in the base communities feel more comfortable with. It now covers a much broader area than the few neighborhoods that were involved at the founding, and so it does represent an expansion of networking for the women in the base communities. However, it does not represent a direct connection with "classic" feminist organizations rooted in other classes and other locales. Connections with these organizations, to the extent that they exist, are mainly channeled through individuals in AMZOL.

AMZOL and individual members do have such connections. The feminist União de Mulheres (Women's Union), for example, has trained several base community members active in AMZOL in advocacy and support work with battered women. Madalena, as well as two other former base community members who were not reinterviewed for this study, successfully completed the course to become "promotoras legais populares" (popular legal assistants) working with battered women at the Centro Maria Miguel, founded by AMZOL.[4] In addition, base community women in AMZOL have worked with the feminist health organization Sempreviva Organização Femenista (Feminist Movement Sempreviva [SOF]).[5] None of the women mentioned SOF or the União de Mulheres as feminist organizations that could work with the base communities, however, despite these connections.

Women did name two other groups as potential partners. One, Rede Mulher (Women's Network), is a feminist organization in São Paulo that worked extensively with grassroots women's organizations in the 1980s and

---

4. Nilce de Oliveira, personal communication to Carol Drogus, October 10, 2001; http://www.dhnet.org.br.

5. Nathalie Lebon, personal communication to Carol Drogus, April 20, 2000.

1990s. Sympathetic priests gave Rede Mulher access to mothers' clubs in the Zona Leste in the mid-1980s, and Rede eventually played a crucial role in the founding of AMZOL. Later, however, the two organizations severed connections. The one respondent who mentioned Rede Mulher is not actively involved in AMZOL. It is important, though, that AMZOL seems to have legitimized the idea of working with feminist organizations, and that women in São Paulo (though not Rio de Janeiro) were aware of the existence of specific groups.

Women in São Paulo also mentioned CDD (Catholic Women for Free Choice). CDD has interacted with AMZOL and has links to some grassroots organizers in the base communities. Its avowedly Catholic position gives it additional credibility among grassroots activists and church members, despite its pro-choice stance. CDD grew out of a liberationist perspective and shares a language and framework for viewing the world with activists from the base communities, even though they may differ on the issue of abortion. In fact, the CDD claims that it maintains growing links with progressive sectors of the church, including priests, parishes, and pastorates.[6] Moreover, many CDD activists (including former nuns) have a great deal of experience with and sympathy for poor, uneducated women and their worldview, and at least one outside observer has concluded that they have better, less tense relations with them than do secular feminists.[7]

One legacy of the decentralized nature of the Brazilian popular church may be the clear difference between Rio de Janeiro and São Paulo women's connections to classic feminist organizations. In addition to the willingness of individual priests and dioceses (like the ones in São Paulo's Zona Leste) to open up contacts with feminist organizations, the lower visibility and lesser strength of Rio's feminist movement no doubt contributed to this difference as well. Only women in the Zona Leste (AMZOL's home) had contact with feminist groups and could name specific groups as possible allies. In contrast, only Ana Lima from Rio said her group had worked with feminists in the past. On the contrary, another woman, Geralda, specified that her group "had never worked with feminists." Although the Rio women were quite open to the idea of working with feminists, they failed to name specific groups. Melania said no feminist groups existed in the area, while Neide do Carmo said she didn't know which groups they might be able to work with.

---

6. See the CDD website (http://www.cddbr.cjb.net).

7. Nathalie Lebon, personal communication to Carol Drogus, April 20, 2000.

In the past, decentralization partially shaped women's exposure to feminism. The slow, uneven erosion of the popular church may have left pockets of progressivism whose proponents, like the ones cited by the CDD, might collaborate with feminists in the future. The institutional church, in any case, is likely to be a key factor in such potential alliances.

The Institutional Church and Women's Organizing

Despite the role that it played in mobilizing popular women activists initially, the Brazilian church has been no friend to feminism. The popular church never explicitly aimed at organizing women; indeed, it sometimes placed obstacles in the way of their organizing on the basis of gender. The liberationist church never addressed specific women's problems, such as reproductive health (Rosado Nunes 1994, 200). Nor did it produce a discourse that could counter the essentializing language of the traditional church. As Drogus (1997) notes, "[T]he CEBs often remain silent on gender issues, subtly reinforce existing gender ideology, or politicize domestic issues on a class basis that obscures gender issues" (161). Many women at the grass roots have become critical of the church's discourse, and particularly of the inequalities of power that women face within the church. For example, the "bloco feminino" at the eighth national encounter of CEBs in Santa Maria in 1995 vocally criticized the church and demanded greater equality for women. Indeed, AMZOL itself grew from such a critique and a sense of exclusion within the church (Drogus 1997). Thus, we might expect the Brazilian Church to be an important obstacle to feminist identity.

Indeed, Brazilian feminists, often hold up the church as the source of a moral and religious agenda that is oppressive to women. Some argue that both the church and secular leftists deliberately misrepresent feminism in ways that inhibit the development of critical gender consciousness among popular women—the progressive church and the Left doing so by portraying gender solidarity as inimical to class solidarity; and the church as a whole doing so by admonishing women "against adopting 'bad' feminist beliefs, such as abortion and the right to sexual self-determination, as these are seen as intrinsically bourgeois and likely to 'divide' the united struggle" (Sternbach et al. 1992, 212; Franco 1998, 7). Moreover, since the transition to democracy, the church has taken on a more visible public role in its opposition to important feminist issues. Although the Brazilian church lost on the issue of divorce, it has been vocal and successful in its continued opposition to abortion.

The church in Rome chastized and silenced for two years the well-known feminist theologian Sister Ivone Gebara for her writings regarding abortion. Moreover, the PT dropped its commitment to abortion in order to accommodate its allies within the liberationist church (Haas 2001, 263).

The church has not wavered from its official opposition to feminism. Within the church, a discourse hostile to feminism remains dominant. Women such as Etelvina, who participate in the church's Women's Pastoral, express this clearly; she says bluntly, "This definition of feminism—we don't use it in the Women's Pastoral." However, in contrast to the Chilean case, no other Brazilian woman blamed the church hierarchy or expressed the fear that individual priests or bishops would veto cooperation with feminist organizations. Feminists trying to work with grassroots women's groups have been critical of such interference in the past, and it certainly has occurred. Numerous instances in which liberationist pastoral agents cut off discussions of sexuality or reproductive rights are documented (Alvarez 1990). Brazilian women activists, however, did not seem to view the church as a direct threat to cooperation with feminist organizations.

This sense that the church can accommodate such cooperation despite its official differences with feminism may reflect the legacies of the sociocultural model and gradual erosion of the popular church that we described earlier. In fact, despite its outspoken opposition to abortion, the church has also sent some rather mixed signals on other issues relevant to women. The CDD does maintain contacts with progressive parts of the church, including the Dominicans in São Paulo. Moreover, the church as a whole continues to officially recognize and support the Pastoral da Mulher Marginalizada (Pastoral for Marginalized Women [PMM]). The PMM originally worked with sex workers, but its agenda has grown broader and more influenced by liberation theology over time. It has become an advocate in the church on such issues as sexual abuse, domestic violence, and changes to the penal code. Tensions between the PMM and church hierarchy persist. The pastoral is, nonetheless, one of the continued visible pockets of the liberationist tradition present in the Brazilian church (Guider 1995).

Such examples and local pockets of progressivism may contribute to the women's belief that, in at least some cases, their communities could collaborate with feminist groups without fear of interference. Since most women qualify their definitions of the kinds of feminist groups and projects they might work on, they also envision collaboration that would not be threatening to the church's most deeply held values and that, therefore, would be less likely to be challenged. For example, Geralda said it would be particularly useful for feminists to raise consciousness about domestic violence—an issue that the CNBB itself has already vetted in a 1998 national brotherhood campaign. Ilda specified that they could work with any feminist group "in favor of full life, whether in the uterus of the mother or after birth." Maria José thought feminists should discuss discrimination against women, an issue certainly within the discourse of the liberationist church, at least. Other women stated less specifically that they could work with "less radical" groups or those who were not "bra burners" (Maria das Graças, Maria Edwiges, Etelvina). Only Elza claims that they could work "with any group, without restriction."

The women may be realistically appraising limits that church officials would place on them by restricting the range of feminist groups with which they envision working. They did not, however, identify the church and the priest as the ones dictating the boundaries of collaboration, even in such areas as the Zona Leste where they acknowledged many problems with their current clergy.[8] The subtle religious and cultural influence of the church may be at least as important as clerical fiat in restricting such alliances. Religious belief, like the different life conditions of the working class, is certainly a dividing line between popular and second-wave feminists (Lebon 1998, 185). Many of the women activists cited the attitudes of poor Catholic laywomen rather than direct church intervention as an obstacle to cooperation. Moreover, many of the activists themselves accept only some parts of the feminist discourse or adopt a "resignified" feminism influenced by both their religiosity and their class position.

Rejection and Resignification of Feminism

An AMZOL member told CDD organizer Maria José Rosado Nunes (1994), "The women in the Mothers' Club have a different mentality from the women in the association [AMZOL]. In the mothers' club it's one way; here, it's another. In the association, we can discuss everything, but in the mothers' club, no; there's always one who gets mad, no?" (194). Specifically, women in AMZOL complain that women in the church groups will not discuss issues related to sex, contraception, abortion, and so on (ibid.). More broadly,

---

8. This is also where, in fact, AMZOL had difficulties and disagreements with the former, liberationist bishop, dom Angélico Bernardino (see Drogus 1997).

AMZOL member Rita says that she would like her base community to work with feminist groups, but "it's not clear how this could happen, because many women don't understand what feminism is." The women activists seem to be asserting that cultural or ideological barriers are the greatest obstacles to other women's interaction with middle-class, secular feminist groups.

Relations even between women in church-based groups and popular feminist organizations appear to be somewhat strained. A pastoral agent who has worked for many years with AMZOL reports that women in the churches—both Catholic and Protestant—are no longer embracing the feminist struggle as the older leaders from the base communities did. Moreover, the few women in the feminist groups who maintain connections with the church groups are now more likely to be academics, for example, theologians, rather than women from the "base," many of whom have left the church.[9] Her observation is supported by the fact, noted in Chapter 5, that among our interviewees, the women active in AMZOL were most likely to say they no longer participated in their base communities. Thus, although some women in AMZOL continue to "bridge" church communities and feminist groups, the network is tenuous, as churchgoing women increasingly seem to resist feminism, while popular feminists increasingly drift away from the church.

Nonactivist women in the communities are not the only ones who resist discussing feminist issues that touch on sexuality and reproductive rights. The popular church's commitment to a sociocultural model that respected popular religiosity meant that it could gather people with widely differing religious and political views, leading to divisions that still persist among women activists on gender issues. Activists in Brazil range from a handful of adamant, pro-life nonfeminists, to a group that accepts some feminist ideas but is wary of sexuality issues, to a group that more fully embraces a class-based resignified feminism, to a handful who declare themselves feminists "without qualification."

Only three of the activist women completely reject feminism. Four declare that they are not personally feminists but that they agree with some feminist ideas or that feminism helps women. Ten are willing to accept the *feminist* label despite some disagreements. Eight unequivocally supported feminism. Despite their differences—whether they reject, partially accept, resignify, or accept feminism—common themes related to religious morality and social class cut across their discussions of feminism.

9. Nilce de Oliveira, personal communication to Carol Drogus, October 21, 2001.

Abortion and concerns about sexual impropriety are present throughout the spectrum of responses. Neide is part of the regional and diocesan coordinating committees of mothers' clubs and the Women's Pastoral. She says she is not a feminist, but adds, "I agree with feminist ideas. The only thing I disagree with is abortion, free abortion." In contrast, her opposition to abortion has not prevented Rita from joining AMZOL and accepting the label *feminist* as a badge of pride. Similarly, others who at least partially agree with the ideas of feminism more vaguely expressed moral and familial concerns about it, whether they were rejecting or resignifying the term. These concerns often encompass a fear that women would sink to "men's level" in terms of sexual behavior. Although she agrees with some feminist ideas, Maria Melania says, "A feminist to me is one who thinks like men, her husband cheated on her, so 'I'll cheat on him, I'll do the same.'" Geralda Francisca, who considers herself "a little bit feminist," nonetheless feared that feminism leads not to liberation, but to "libertinism." "The only thing I disagree with today," echoes Ana Lima, "is abortion and sexual freedom." In all, five women expressed some concern about moral behavior besides the problem of abortion, for a total of nine women (35 percent) who had some reservation about feminism stemming from religious or moral values.

Class also influences women's views. Maria José does not label feminism "bourgeois," but she rejects it on class grounds because it "excludes" larger social questions. Although Célia says she agrees with many feminist principles, she comes closest to articulating the critique of bourgeois feminism, saying: "There are some terrible feminist 'encontros' [encounters]. I participated and I noted that it was just the same machismo, completely closed people fighting for a purely egoistic cause. Some questions weren't broad; they were even bourgeois." Although only two Brazilian women articulated class specifically as a reason for their ambivalence about feminism, however, class—or at least the divergent life circumstances of poor women and second-wave feminists—certainly enters into the women's reactions to feminism in other ways. For example, the majority (sixteen, or 54 percent) of women declared that poor women face problems that are distinctive from those of poor men, just because they are women. Nonetheless, a third of these women began their responses by noting explicitly that the class basis of their problems was the same for men and women. Nathalie Lebon (1998) points out that popular feminists, and poor women generally, are acutely conscious of the ways in which their life circumstances and fates are intertwined with those of poor men. As Lourdes put it, "The financial problems are the same, but others are not." Elza Valeria adds, "Unemployment affects both, but women are discriminated against as women." In addition, nine women thought men and women face similar problems; all mentioned problems related to class, especially unemployment. Several mentioned that, when poor men suffer these problems, they indirectly affect women, through family problems associated with men's alcoholism, for example.

Many of the women we interviewed, like Lebon's respondents, resignify feminism in more male-inclusive, collective terms. Five women specifically describe feminism—or at least the feminism with which they identify—as being about women's activism on not only their own behalf, but also that of others. Sofia Díaz is clearly ambivalent about feminism precisely on the point of dividing the general popular struggle and the women's struggle. She first rejects the word *feminist,* saying, "I never assimilated that word in my life. . . . I never divide men and women. My path has always been a common fight, without forgetting that women have specific problems." Later, however, as her recognition of the specific problematic of women grows, she declares herself a specific type of feminist: "I consider myself a feminist in the fight for the good, the common, struggle. A feminist fights for the well-being, the good, of the collective."

Célia gives the collective dimension a more specifically class turn:

> Look, today we don't have to be feminists in that restricted sense of just thinking about women's problems, because both poor women and poor men are passing through the same situation and so we must fight for justice for men and women. I agree with feminism in that larger sense, of men and women struggling for a better society, because it does no good to have women on one side fighting alone, and men on another fighting alone, and blacks on another fighting alone, understand? You have to have everyone suffering injustice fighting together. I believe this is part of the feminist principles, because if not it would be the same as machismo, dividing people.

Like Célia, Geralda Francisca, a black activist, adds the dimension of race to the collective nature of the struggle. After declaring herself "a little bit of feminist," she backtracks and says she is in favor of the feminine, not the feminist, in part because "the struggle should be for equality, equality of blacks and whites, men and women, rich and poor."

Arguably, this preference for a general/collective rather than specific/individual struggle also informs the women's expressions of ambivalence regarding what they perceive as "anti-male" versions of feminism (Lebon 1998, 185). Maria Socorro's husband "says [she] seem[s] like a feminist when [she] start[s] talking." "I am in favor of us women," she declares. Yet she worries about a feminism that "wants to take over men's space," and especially their jobs. "If we take over all their space, what remains for men?" she asks. Maria Socorro has worked outside the home and is proud to have done so. She thinks women "can act in anything." But for her, employment is one of the major problems facing both men and women. It thus makes little sense to endorse a struggle that might place women's claims to an individual right to work against those of the more general popular struggle for decent, stable employment. Her version of feminism attempts to reconcile the two. Ilda is very clear about the connection between her rejection of allegedly anti-male elements in feminism and class. She declares, "I consider myself a feminist, because I fight," and says women can't allow men to dominate them. But she adds: "I only disagree when women are against men. I think this way: we must walk together. We're all *povo* [common people], poor people united, thus we can win."

Only six women (24 percent), all in AMZOL, unqualifiedly accept the name "feminist," while two others feel they can no longer call themselves feminists because they are unable to participate fully in the struggle. Rita, whose ill-health limits her activism, says: "When I was in the struggle, fighting for my rights, I was a feminist, but now I've taken a break." Cida Lima is typical of the small group of women who embrace feminism without demurring: "I always thought of myself as a feminist. People always call me 'machona' [a macho woman]. . . . On the question of fighting for feminism, one of my rules is to fight for women to have their role, their space. I think all feminist demands are just."

AMZOL's agenda has broadened considerably since its founding to include, for example, domestic violence. It continues to be an organization respectful of women's religiosity (promoting feminist spirituality and theology courses, for example), however, and continues to be run by, and to define itself as an organization of, working-class women. For Brazilian women who fully embrace the label *feminist* and participate in the popular feminist organization AMZOL, this *is* feminism. Others who say they are "feminists but" embrace this specific definition of feminism, but believe that not all self-described (or media-described) "feminists" share their view. Women activists who oppose feminism believe that this modified version is the only one they could potentially embrace, and they appear to believe that most "feminists" do not espouse this view.

The base communities' sociocultural agenda, as well as different opportunities for contacts with secular feminist groups, permitted some women to remain extremely conservative in their thinking on gender, while others have to varying degrees adopted a popular feminism that is resignified by class, religion, or both. A handful, among them Cida Lima, even have gone on to declare themselves feminists "without qualification." As their contacts with the CDD show, this last group of women came out of the base communities with enough self-confidence and trust in their own thinking to question even fundamental church positions on issues such as abortion. Overall, despite the reservations expressed in either rejection or resignification of the term *feminist,* the base communities produced a large number of activists who say they can find at least some common ground with secular feminists and who are willing to work with them within the limits of a popular feminist agenda.

A Common Feminist Agenda?

Brazilian activists show a remarkable openness to working with secular feminist organizations on issues that fit with their resignified, popular feminist agenda. Historically, second-wave feminist organizations such as Rede Mulher have often been eager to work with popular women's organizations as well. Although the willingness seems to be there, however, the connections have proved difficult to make and maintain, as exemplified by the AMZOL members' failure to mention the União de Mulheres and SOF as possible partners, and the Rio de Janeiro women's inability to name any specific feminist organizations.

Part of the difficulty seems to stem from the divergent agendas and needs of grassroots women's groups and classic feminist organizations. The often local, grassroots agenda of poor women activists no longer meshes with the national-level policy orientation of many classic feminist organizations. Brazilian popular activists had difficulty identifying specific feminist policy issues with which they agreed. Only a few women raised specific policy issues related to women: pensions for housewives, equal pay, contraception, and vaguely defined laws "against discrimination" or "protecting women's rights." While six women (24 percent) mentioned discrimination in the workplace, only five other policy issues—equal pay, day care, retirement, women's health, and domestic violence—came up at least once, and never more than twice.

Brazilian women are also skeptical that such big policy changes can be achieved. Twenty-one women (84 percent) see some role for the government in solving the problems of women like themselves. Nonetheless, nearly half the women (ten) who believe government can and should help, believe that it would not do so. "Yes, it should," says Célia, "but the government is not interested and wants to perpetuate this system of injustice." Similarly, Maria das Graças comments, "The government can help, but the money is misused and there is a lack of political will." Three others also expressed skepticism of the government's real willingness to help women, saying specifically that if it wants to, it should enforce the laws already on the books.

Rather than advocating big national agendas for change, working-class Brazilian women see "women's problems" in primarily local and cultural terms. Focused as many are on local community issues, some hope that feminists can help in concrete ways. Several suggested "material support for the work we develop" (Elza) or "sharing projects" (Cida Morais). "Just joining forces would be a big contribution," according to Neide. These comments are not conclusive, but they raise the possibility that this openess, like the openess to collaborating with Protestants, reflects the Brazilians' lesser concerns about autonomy and indicates greater need and desire to find others with resources to offer.

Only four women, however, suggested some kind of material collaboration. The majority hoped primarily for orientation or consciousness-raising that would help with the sociocultural problems they believe women confront. Eleven women (44 percent) mentioned "machismo" in some way as the primary problem women face. Many women cited machismo's impact on women's lack of access to employment, education, and power. Nonetheless, rather than addressing these issues through policy, most women envisioned working locally with feminist organizations on consciousness-raising in some way. Maria Antônia would like to work with any group, "bringing women to believe in their potential and capacity. Working with the idea and methodology that everyone is a citizen with rights and duties." Ana Lima, who worked with a feminist group earlier, imagines that they could help with "consciousness-raising and demanding a solution to the problem of valorizing women." Geralda Francisca, though quite critical of feminism, nonetheless believes feminists could help in her community to raise consciousness around issues of domestic violence.

Unfortunately, as the women's movement has developed over time and partly in response to the new incentive structure created by the democratic transition, feminist groups have become less and less interested in and capable of providing the specific kinds of support that these grassroots women's groups desire. Feminist politics in Brazil have become partially institutionalized with the creation of Women's Secretariats. At the same time, funding for autonomous NGOs has become more difficult to secure and more dependent on formulating research or other projects with observable "output," requirements to to satisfy donors. While it may make sense from grassroots women's perspective to focus on consciousness-raising rather than national-level policy issues, feminist groups have increasingly come to focus their efforts on research and policy, rather than consciousness-raising and have moved resources and attention away from grassroots work in recent years (Lebon 1998). For example, SOF, the feminist health organization that had connections with AMZOL, has moved its offices to a more central area of São Paulo and has reduced its staff. Funding requirements have often also led feminist NGOs to focus less on grassroots work and more on quantifiable projects of interest to funders (ibid.).

Such obstacles may prove to be temporary, influenced as they seem to be by the availability of resources and political opportunities rather than by conviction. The fact remains that Brazilian feminist organizations maintain a commitment to including popular women and their concerns, and the popular women activists at least claim to be open to future collaboration. Diverging interests and agendas that are partly a product of the current political conjuncture may be at least as significant an obstacle to stronger cross-class women's ties as institutional and ideological factors. If conditions change in the future, however, it may become easier for women's organizations with different class bases to find a common ground and form alliances.

Chile: Activist Women, Not "Feminists"

Chilean women, even more than their Brazilian counterparts, are extremely active in women's organizations. Approximately three-quarters of them work in social service or solidarity organizations that focus on women's needs or are composed primarily of women. Another ten report that they participate in at least one other women's organization. The range of organizations is great, including both grassroots women's groups and popular feminist groups, regional or national organizations that deal with specific issues such as women's health or domestic violence prevention, and programs associated with or funded by government and other national organizations.[10]

Despite these personal affiliations, however, no Chilean respondent reports connections between her base Christian community and national feminist organizations. In contrast to what holds in Brazil, even women in popular feminist groups do not perceive their women's organization as interacting with their church communities. In fact, several women such as Ana Acuña now participate in independent, grassroots religious groups, among them the Asamblea Pueblo de Dios and the Group of Christian Women in Villa O'Higgins, both groups founded by and for Catholic grassroots activists who feel that the space for women's activism has been closed in their local parishes. Very few report that they know of other local popular women's organizations that have any connections to national women's networks. In contrast to the Brazilian women who are active in AMZOL, most Chilean women who are active in popular feminist organizations explicitly reject the possibility of working with national feminist organizations. With few exceptions, popular women express a significant amount of hostility to forging greater cross-class alliances with feminists.

This hostility is somewhat surprising, because the majority of Chilean women identify closely with what could be considered a feminist political agenda. Thirty-six women (75 percent) cite workplace discrimination as one of the three biggest problems for Chilean women today; twenty-three (48 percent) cite the lack of equal employment or general opportunity; eighteen

---

10. The number of different grassroots and popular feminist groups represented in the Chilean sample is greater than in that of Brazil. These groups include Casas de la Mujer that are located in a number of *poblaciónes* and local women's groups such as the Grupo de Mujeres Decididas and Mujeres Creando Futuro in Cerro Navia; Grupo de Mujeres Domitila (named for Bolivian Domitila Barros de Chungara) in Recoleta; Centro de Capacitación y Formación Aracelí Romo (named for the founder's daughter, who was assassinated by the military) and Grupo Araucaría de Mujeres in Lo Espejo; Mujeres Frente a lo Globalización (which combines groups across several communes); Grupo Araucaria in La Victoria; and a Grupo de Mujeres Cristianas in La Florida. In addition to these local groups being available to the women, a couple of Chileans participate in Casa Malen, founded by Maryknoll sisters in 1986 in Pudahuel to serve the mental health and personal-development needs of *pobladoras*. Several more participate in the activities of either Conspirando, a feminist theology center, or local religious groups such as the Asamblea Pueblo de Dios, a citywide group for women who felt pushed out of the Catholic Church. Further, many of the respondents are employed as social workers or popular educators in programs concerning women's health, personal development, domestic violence prevention, or training.

(38 percent) list violence against women; seventeen (35 percent) list women's lack of access to adequate educational opportunities. Only twelve (25 percent) list any problem that can be characterized as a private-sphere concern, such as women's double responsibility for work and the home or marital difficulties. They also overwhelmingly believe that the government ought to address women's issues. In response to the question, "Can the government help solve any of the women's problems that you have mentioned?" 20 percent answer affirmatively and the remaining 80 percent assert that the government ought to help solve women's problems but has failed to do so. In other words, all respondents believe that the issues faced by women in contemporary Chile are political matters of public policy, not merely issues of general culture or private relationships. Although Chileans also mention the problems associated with cultural machismo, they identify women's problems as political issues with political solutions to a far greater extent than do Brazilians. It appears, therefore, that Chilean popular activists not only identify specific women's issues that are congruent with the feminist agendas of national women's organizations, but also see these issues as ones to be fought in the political arena.

This is a strong indication that common ground for collaborative political organizing exists, yet Chilean women reject this possibility overwhelmingly. This outcome—a mixture of confident political critique with a rejection of collaboration—can again be partly traced to the history of Chile's base communities. The first evidence of this legacy is the women's perception that the institutional church is a critical obstacle to cross-class women's organizing.

The Institutional Church and Networking

In Chile, one often hears that the Catholic Church is the chief impediment to women's organization. According to this view, the Chilean Catholic Church, one of the most traditional hierarchies in the region on gender roles, dominates public discourse regarding women's issues, particularly issues relating to personal morality such as reproductive rights, divorce, abortion, AIDS, or sexual choice. Traditional values associated with women's roles as wives and mothers remain strong in both official and popular Chilean Catholicism, and much of Chilean society still regards submissiveness, obedience, self-abnegation and faithfulness as women's primary virtues. (Fontaine 2002, 277–82).

Women activists concur that the church impedes women's organization. Eleven Chilean respondents (23 percent) state that the major obstacle to collaboration between base Christian communities and other women's organizations is the conservative makeup of the Chilean hierarchy. Ana Acuña, who left her parish community after years of activism (including serving on the Coordinating Committee of Popular Christian Communities in the 1980s), today remains active in an interfaith human rights group. A student of feminist theology, she organized a group of Christian women in her neighborhood that celebrates its own rituals. Not surprisingly, Ana can envision working with secular women's organizations. However, she states that church authorities believe that "women are not supposed to do anything other than teach children. When we formed a group of women to do meditation and inner contemplation, the church called us 'rebels.'" Alicia Ubilla, a social worker who works with victims of domestic violence, personally welcomes working with secular women's organizations, but agrees with Ana: "Women's organizations are viewed [by church authorities] as trespassing the boundaries set by the church for women, as mothers and wives." Maria also sees doctrinal rigidity of individuals in the church hierarchy as the most serious obstacle to greater coordination between women's organizations and popular women in grassroots base Christian communities: "It depends on the parish priest or vicar. . . . Some are very rigid and prefer that we don't address certain issues. Such was the case even during the years when the church was more open to human rights issues. The church has never been known to acknowledge that women's rights are also human rights. Very few people [in the church] are willing to let us discuss sexuality, reproductive rights, and health." For the majority of women who identify themselves as Catholics, and particularly for those who remain active in their own religious faith, the church's traditional stance on women's rights and roles makes collaboration with feminist organizations difficult. This is especially true for the nearly half of our respondents who continue to participate in their parish-level base communities, in spite of their disagreement with the church's stand on women's issues.

However, although all the Chilean respondents agree that most church officials oppose collaboration with secular feminist organizations, slightly less than one-quarter cite church opposition as the major obstacle to collaboration. Eleven respondents (23 percent), the same percentage that blame the church hierarchy, mention women's general distrust of feminists as a major obstacle to greater women's organizing. Another thirteen respondents (27 percent) identify the central obstacle as traditional cultural values among women themselves. In total, then, half the respondents in our survey place the blame on general women's attitudes rather than on church officials.

Although greater church openness to grassroots collaboration with women's groups certainly would strengthen local networks and hence civil society, it appears that major obstacles to greater women's networking also are located in the larger culture and divisions in Chilean society.[11]

Eli Molina's dismissal of the possibility of developing a collaborative relationship with feminist organizations is revealing. Her parish, San Pedro y Pablo in La Granja, is one of the few that remain socially active and progressive. Since 1988, her parish priest has encouraged community activism, and the parish supports a variety of local organizations promoting efforts such as a health clinic, an alcoholics' group, homeless assistance programs, and employment schemes. The parish also sponsors a number of activities to empower women, such as talks and workshops by the Network of Women Against Violence about women's rights and violence prevention. Yet in spite of an activist outlook and a history of working to help women in the parish, Eli rejects out of hand greater collaboration with feminist organizations. She says that, although "the church organized an event to celebrate International Women's Day, people mistrust institutional women's groups. Bourgeois feminists are not accepted."

Eli's experience suggests that, as in the Brazilian case, some windows of progressivism that could accommodate feminist collaboration exist, but Chilean women seem less aware of or less confident in them. This may be because, in the aftermath of the "earthquake" that shook the Chilean church, the pockets of progressivism are less visible and more isolated than they are in Brazil. Juanita Alvarado works at Sol, the organization, mentioned earlier, that provides women's workshops, as a popular educator conducting training workshops for women's groups and does call herself a feminist without qualification, yet even she points out that people "criticize the woman who participates. They call her a woman of the street [callejera], although they receive the benefits of that woman's participation." Juanita's comments confirm that Chilean activists share their Brazilian counterparts' perception that cultural values and conservatism among women like themselves who are in the church, but who have never had the experience of activism, obstruct collaboration as much as the institutional church.

11. A 1998 survey conducted by the International Social Survey Programme (ISSP) shows that Chileans rank among the world's most conservative populations regarding women's roles, abortion, and religious belief. See Fontaine 2002, 277–79.

Social Class and "Bourgeois Feminism"

Although roughly the same percentage (about 70–75 percent) of women in each country say they agree with some feminist ideas, Chileans and Brazilians frame their responses differently. While Brazilians say they "agree with feminism, but . . . ," their Chilean counterparts are more likely to indicate that they agree with some feminist ideas while often proclaiming that they themselves are not feminists or are only feminist "in the good sense of the word." Chileans and Brazilians cite similar reasons for their resignification or rejection of feminism: fears about values and morality, fears about dividing the popular struggle, and concerns about being anti-male. For the Chileans, however, the underlying current of class tension is much more palpable, and it translates into a stronger rejection of the feminist label.

Class is a major social division that helps define the contours of national politics and social movements in any country. Seventeen years of military rule intent on "depoliticizing" Chilean society through violent repression of political parties did not significantly alter the fundamental class basis of Chilean politics. Today, the Chilean political system remains divided into rough thirds, with the political left, right, and center parties still defined largely by class issues. Although visible manifestations of class antagonism such as the 1960s–early 1970s violent street clashes no longer force tensions into constant public view, our interviews show that class identity continues to dominate popular women's political attitudes and agendas.

The strength of class identification heightens popular women's distrust of national women's organizations, which they view as composed primarily of middle-class, "professional" women, and reduces the short-term likelihood of widespread, cross-class coordination of women's associative networks. This distrust of professional women's organizations, grounded in long-standing class tensions in Chilean society, was strengthened further by rifts between women's groups during the dictatorship and democratic transition.

During the early days of the dictatorship, both *pobladoras* and middle-class or professional women organized a variety of new groups.[12] The majority of working-class women's organizations were primarily geared to help women respond to widespread human rights violations and the economic crisis

---

12. Several excellent histories of the Chilean women's movement include Valdés and Weinstein 1993; Valdés 1994, Matear 1997.

produced by the military's neoliberal policies. Middle-class and professional women from the political Center and Left tended to organize in groups affiliated with political parties or in more explicitly feminist organizations that drew on developments in international women's movements. At the time, popular and middle-class women alike recognized the benefits of working together on the common goal of resisting the military regime and promoting democracy. Several middle-class feminist organizations worked closely with popular women's organizations in a broad front that combined a gender critique with a focus on the material needs of the *poblaciónes*. These included DOMOS; the Comité de Defensa de los Derechos de la Mujer (CODEM), which was associated with the radical party Movimiento de la Izquierda Revolucionaria (MIR); and Mujeres de Chile (MUDECHI), which was associated with the Communist Party.[13]

By the mid-1980s, however, middle-class and professional women's organizations split into several tendencies that distanced them from popular women's groups. Organizations primarily associated with the political parties concentrated on negotiating women's rights after the transition. Groups such as Casa de la Mujer La Morada sharpened their radical, feminist identities, becoming linked in the public eye with support for lesbian rights.[14] Academic and professional women from the political center organized into the Concertación de Mujeres por la Democracia (1988) that eventually led to the creation of a new governmental agency for women's issues, SERNAM (Servicio Nacional de la Mujer). Popular women viewed the central goals of all of these tendencies as middle class interests, leaving *pobladoras* to continue to struggle for individual and community survival on their own. Today, professional women's groups continue to express a willingness to work with *pobladoras* based on their perception of a shared history of opposition to the military regime, at the same time that popular women display a significant degree of distrust of national women's organizations given their perception that middle class women betrayed the interests of poor women in the democratic transition.[15]

13. Distrust of the motivations of political-party elites also led to the creation of the "autonomous" feminist tendency, producing feminists who eschew affiliation with partisan or other national groups that are seen as manipulating affiliated women's groups for national—or male—purposes.

14. According to Gaviola, Largo, and Palestry (1994) La Morada's association with lesbianism in the public eye was the result of a 1984 interview granted to the Chilean magazine *APSI* by a lesbian group (Ayuquelen) that rented space in the center. The interview took place in La Morada, and the press played on the connection to popularize the notion that "feminists are lesbians" (136).

15. For example, Isabel Duque, a staff member of Isis International and currently the executive coordinator of the Feminist Network of Latin America and the Caribbean Against Sexual Violence, voices an

Adding to the tensions between women's groups is a division between *pobladoras* stemming from early popular feminist groups that were born during the dictatorship. In addition to the myriad local women's human rights, self-help, and subsistence groups that appeared in the *poblaciónes,* some *pobladoras,* including some from the Catholic base communities, began to organize around an explicitly "popular" feminist agenda, particularly in the Movimiento de Mujeres Pobladoras (MOMUPO). Although these groups often worked together in opposition to military rule, tensions always existed between *pobladoras* who organized around a focused class/human-rights critique and those in "popular feminist" organizations such as MOMUPO whose critique highlighted gender inequality.

Because of the history of deep rifts between women's groups, it is not surprising that our findings show that although some women express attitudes that appear consistent with the church's views of marriage, the family, and sexuality, their cultural conservatism intersects more strongly with their class identity than with their religious identity. Alicia Cáceres, for example, rejects feminism using the language of "family values" and dominant norms concerning sexual preference, yet her assertion of a traditional family model is couched in class terms: "I don't like feminists. Both men and women are exploited by the system. . . . Feminists seem to denigrate men as machos. They only want a woman's fight and they only want to have sex with other women. They lose family values. I know of feminists who have turned lesbian, abandoning their men and little children. [Working-class] men and women must depend on one another." Alicia's assertion that she knows people who have chosen to "turn lesbian" is consistent with the church's condemnation of homosexuality as a sinful personal choice, but she frames her rejection of homosexuality in terms of men being equally "exploited by the system"

---

optimism about grassroots activist-feminist collaboration based on a perception of gains made during the dictatorship that contrasts sharply with the more negative responses from our interviewees. She believes that "[the women's movement] began with concrete demands for the family's survival, but it became a strong women's movement concerned about issues that affect women, working together with feminists. . . . The issue of domestic violence, for example, took on greater force during the late 1980s. On the one hand, the feminists were pushing to bring the issue out from the private sphere and situated it as a critical public issue. On the other hand, the women from grassroots organizations began to say publicly that they did not have to put up with beatings from their husbands. . . . Feminists and women's NGOs were entering the social network and had a presence in popular neighborhoods by this time. . . . Together with feminists, popular women began to come out of the dark and entered the public arena" (interview, February 10, 2000). For similarly optimistic views regarding cross-class women's alliances, see Valenzuela 1991; Chuchryk 1994; and Navarro and Bourque 1998.

and children being dependent on their parents in the harsh economic realities of a neoliberal market. For Alicia, "family values" prohibit personal choices that destroy the family's ability to survive or to resist economic exploitation, not choices that violate the church's insistence on female submissiveness, obedience, or self-abnegation. Her defense of "family values" does not preclude a strong sense of women's rights—in fact, elsewhere in the interview, Alicia lists ongoing gender discrimination and women's double workload both in and out of the home as the biggest challenges currently facing women like herself. Rather, her rejection of feminism is a rejection of choices that she believes working-class women cannot afford and ought not desire.

Similarly, many of the Chilean respondents reject sexual promiscuity or immorality that violates dominant norms concerning marriage and family; yet, again, their statements intertwine culturally conservative attitudes with class consciousness. Mercedes Montoya, a regional director of SERPAJ who continues to participate in her local Christian community, echoes the rejection of personal choices that diminish working-class solidarity: "In my opinion, feminism is divisive. It should not be reduced to free sexual choices. The reality of the working-class woman is different." For Maria Ortega Soto, the librarian at a Casa de la Mujer, the legacy of the military-imposed neoliberal development strategy is an individualism that destroys working-class solidarity: "There is confusion about the idea. Feminism has to do with all the things that a woman can be. But many women confuse freedom with promiscuity. . . . These days women, people, not just men, stoop very low. . . . Women also have become alcoholics, drug addicts, and some are very aggressive and violent. It is the scum that the dictatorship left us." Instead of asserting women's equal rights, Maria maintains that feminism has become associated with the destruction of families and communities resulting from the military-imposed economic model.

Women activists consistently condemn the growing individualism and consumerism associated with the flood of cheap foreign imports, which are encouraged by the state's economic model, and reject choices or behavior that undermine class solidarity. Carmen Lopez's comments reflect not only the concern about the immorality of declining class solidarity but also the especially deleterious effects on poor women:

> The neighborhood is worse today than during the dictatorship because no one cares about anyone else. . . . The situation was very critical before, but at least people had somewhere to turn to—*ollas comunes,*

workshops, etc. . . . . Today, people who lose their jobs are on their own. . . . . Women are more enslaved by consumerism. They work more but consumerism lures them and they have high expenses. Even though many women fought hard in the [19]70s and [19]80s, they don't complain about earning less than men.

Expressions of anxiety about increasing individualism and consumerism, along with the perception of feminism's failure to recognize or value class solidarity among the poor, show that Chilean *pobladoras* believe that although "the reality" of middle-class women may allow them to make personal decisions based on their individual interests or pleasures, "working-class reality" requires class and family solidarity for survival. Maria Mafalda Samaniega is one of the founders of Las Domitilas, a *pobladora* group organized throughout Santiago after the church withdrew its support for grassroots women's groups. In her case, the interplay of popular class solidarity and gender identity led to a resignification of feminism, as they have for many in Brazil: "We are feminists, but not loose women who keep switching boyfriends and practice free love. . . . We shouldn't be above the man but fight alongside each other. Our Domitila women's group believes that women have to educate ourselves, but not separate ourselves from men."

Although religious values enter into the women's rejection and, in some cases, resignification of feminism, women's main objection is that they perceive feminist discourse as lacking a clear class analysis of gender issues. Expressing unease about feminism in a reaction typical of many popular women, Ruth Godoy says: "Feminism does not seem to be grounded in the true situation of [working-class] women. . . . Feminism is for another social context and class." Maria Teresa Díaz offers a more explicit class critique of what she perceives to be the "feminist" discourse: "This is a situation of domination, but it is not only the result of a patriarchal society. The neoliberal economic system is also a factor. Feminists try to explain everything in terms of gender, but that is not always the case."

Running through many of these women's hostility is the perception that the lack of adequate class analysis is a sort of "luxury" of the middle class, or "elitists who had all their needs taken care of" (Carmen Lopez, 1999). Quite a bit of resentment was expressed about middle- and upper-class women who do not include class oppression in their discourse, because they are the beneficiaries of a dominant stratum in the class structure. Eli Molina offers the clearest expression of this perspective: "Feminism is not a response to the true problems of [working-class] women. These are problems of class, not gender. Feminists question the patriarchy but not the class system. There are no conflicts between a couple in working-class areas; poverty affects both of them the same way. Whether or not you identify with feminism depends on your reality as a woman, but if you see the reality of a working-class area, you cannot talk about feminism." Although class differences are an obstacle to women's organization in any country, they are a particularly daunting obstacle in Chile. The perception that middle-class and professional women define "women's issues" in terms of their own class interests (in opposition to working-class interests) makes it very difficult to overcome long-standing class hostility, in spite of apparent consensus on specific issues. Moreover, the neoliberal economy has widened the gap between rich and poor, pressing increasing numbers of working-class women into domestic service in the homes of the wealthy, further reinforcing class divisions between women and strengthening the obstacles to broad organizing by women.[16]

The assertion by Chilean popular women of the importance (even predominance) of class analysis to explain oppression denotes that they perceive solidarity and organization of both popular men and women as more important than cross-class women's organization. For example, two-thirds of the thirty-five respondents (73 percent) who said that they agreed with some feminist ideas specifically qualified their own feminism as not "anti-men." Victoria Plaza's comments are typical of those who qualified their feminist identity: "Feminism relates to my gender and the right to the same opportunities, same pay, and [same] rights as men. Feminism does not mean that we step over men. . . . I consider myself feminist in the good sense of the word." The idea that one is a feminist "in the good sense" is echoed by Maritza Sandoval: "That word is usually misinterpreted. For me it means fighting for the rights of women, but not that we fight against men, which is what many people, including my own husband, believe. . . . I don't believe in fighting to be better than men, although in some things we will be better than they are and in other things, they will be better. We need to work together. . . . I am a feminist in that sense of the word."

16. Ruth Godoy, a Communist Party member, shows how class divisions between women caused by domestic service can become reinforced by other social cleavages—caused by race, ethnicity, nationality, and so on. "There is no work, and women have no place to leave their small children. . . . Many Peruvians have come and accept work as domestics for less pay than the Chileans do. Many Chilean women cannot find a place to work or they earn less pay."

What is striking about these responses is the degree to which class identity overshadows gender identity. Working-class women do demand attention to women's issues such as job discrimination, equal pay, and equal opportunity; however, they see gender oppression alongside class oppression, in which both women and men are victims. Likely potential allies, therefore, are defined by shared class identity (men and women) rather than gender. The following quote from Laura Herrera points to the shadow that class casts over gender identity. At first, she appears to advocate organizing around gender identity: "We have to recover the organizational base of women, which in former years was the source of denunciations. Without a national women's organization, the government will not take us into account." Yet as she continues her remarks, class identity eclipses gender: "We all have equal rights, but I'm not so sure whether women need special rights just for them. . . . In fighting for rights of all Chileans, there is no need to place women's rights above those that pertain to everyone. All of us [working-class men and women] suffer from discrimination, lack of educational opportunities." Women such as Marta Alvarez, who focus primarily on economic sources of discrimination, often dismiss *gender* as a meaningful category: "Feminism means nothing to me. There is a type of feminism whose main enemy is men. There is another that fights to liberate women. But in a country where men and women are both enslaved by the same chains of poverty, we want to liberate not only ourselves but our children and husbands also. . . . The chains that bind us are poverty and the neoliberal system that attacks men and women alike."

Chilean women share with their Brazilian sisters a critique of feminism based on social class and religiosity. In both cases, it leads to some rejection and some resignification of the term. Although Chileans' rejection of feminism appears to be stronger than Brazilians,' this does not necessarily indicate greater social conservatism. On the contrary, Brazil's sociocultural base communities and more gradual transition appear to have created many socially conservative women activists, while Chileans appear somewhat less socially conservative and more radical in their class critique. Since the same critiques seem to lead to both rejection of and a resignified popular feminism, the long-term prospects for collaboration across class lines may be better than they appear to be on the basis of women activists' rejection of "bourgeois" feminism. However, the same class barriers that color their perception of feminism also appear to present institutional barriers to cooperation.

Institutional Barriers: "Official" Feminism and Class Resentment

Chilean *pobladoras,* who could identify with many policy issues of national feminist organizations, nonetheless reject working with these groups, especially government or government-funded women's agencies. According to many observers, the creation of SERNAM by the newly democratic Aylwin government (1991–94) was considered to be one of the biggest achievements of the Chilean women's movement after the dictatorship. The Chilean respondents' attitudes regarding SERNAM, however, best exemplifies those tensions between women's groups that strengthen barriers to broad organizational efforts.

Quite a few of the women who were leaders of middle-class women's organizations during the dictatorship either took jobs in SERNAM or moved into positions in other government agencies. Since SERNAM cannot be an advocacy organization, however, many activists accuse it of co-opting and ghettoizing women into positions in which they must be careful not to overstep the boundaries set by law. Tension is strong between those who believe that they can affect positive change from within the government and those who proudly assert their autonomy in order to press for more fundamental change. Clotilde Silva Hernández (coordinator of SERNAM's domestic violence prevention program) accuses so-called autonomous feminists of espousing a discourse that not only creates additional splits among women but also strengthens working-class suspicion that further undermines the women's movement: "Feminism has little meaning anymore. In Chile, there was a split between feminists. The more radical feminists question those of us who work in government. They have a theoretical discourse that jolts grassroots feminists. If you choose not to marry, be free and single—those ideas do not sit well in working-class sectors. . . . Consequently, the fight between feminists made feminism lose prestige."

In addition to creating a distinction between those who work with the government (accused of being "co-opted") and those who retain their autonomy (accused of being too "radical"), SERNAM's practice of contracting out much of its research to nongovernmental centers further exacerbates class tensions between women. Since the transition to democracy, foreign aid dropped precipitously. Women's groups, like other groups in civil society that depended on external funding for their activities during the dictatorship, have had to scramble to adopt new strategies for survival since the transition. Access to SERNAM's research contracts has allowed some women's NGOs to adapt more readily to democracy than many grassroots activist groups, whose members typically do not have the educational background necessary to secure research contracts. Access to SERNAM's research contracts further professionalizes national women's organizations, while driving the wedge deeper between national organizations and grassroots popular activists.

Chilean popular women's resistance to professional women's organizations, either independent or government-sponsored, was clearly evident at a follow-up meeting (October 9, 1999) at which several of the women in our study met to discuss the possibility of rebuilding networks between popular women activists. At the end of the meeting, Juanita summed up the consensus that *pobladoras* needed to organize as much as ever, both to pass their own experience down to new leaders and to pressure the state to respond to ongoing social and economic grassroots problems: "Then, in one way or another, there is pretty much agreement . . . about where to go from here . . . a meeting that could have various objectives: to share experiences, to find out what other neighborhood groups are doing, to learn about current events, also to formulate some sort of declaration, for example concerning human rights, and to include other people to share their experiences." Yet Eli and others immediately followed Juanita's comments with a strong rejection of pursuing an organizational strategy that would include alliances with national or governmental women's groups. The class basis for their rejection is unmistakable. Eli said, to the approval of others:

> I wouldn't want to invite two types of women [to such a meeting]. [First,] the women who took the feminist line during the dictatorship and afterward left their organizations in the lurch. For the feminists, all of the popular women's experience was cheapened and forgotten as past history. [Second,] I also wouldn't like to discuss or share opinions with women who . . . are working in government ministries and who tout the official story. For me, that would be a waste of time because one has to be constantly trying to convince them of what you are saying—when in reality popular women are autonomous and worthy women, and we constructed democratic spaces for women from the grassroots. I want to feel free to say that if the meeting becomes a space where we have to stay quiet in favor of plurality or diversity, I am not convinced that I want to participate. I want us to start with the recognition that we are *pobladora* women, we are a movement of popular women. That would be the point of departure.

Alicia concurs: "I agree that we should avoid anything that is run by women who don't respect or who aren't in solidarity with all women. I am worried a little that it shouldn't be a group that is too, too undefined, but when we start to talk about making proposals it makes me shiver. I am afraid of transforming this into something very intellectualized."

These comments highlight many women's reticence about expanding linkages to women's organizations that are not exclusively composed of *pobladoras*. Although professional women believe that they are successfully reaching out to *pobladoras* and helping them to grow in their awareness of themselves as women, most of our respondents view these efforts as attempts to erase the "worthy and autonomous" histories of *pobladoras'* accomplishments. Their resentment stems from the dominance, both in the mainstream press and in much academic discussion, of the "official story," a revisionist history in which elite negotiation is responsible for the democratic transition. Popular women reject the official story. They also are skeptical about professional women, whom they perceive to have traded on their participation in broad women's coalitions during the dictatorship to secure (usually government) employment, leaving popular women waiting for the supposed benefits of the neoliberal market to "trickle down." The strength of the resentment can be heard in Alicia's warning about becoming "too intellectualized"—a reference to professional women whose contribution to the women's coalitions during the dictatorship were not the flesh and blood offered by popular activists and their families. Middle-class women are perceived to have profited nicely from well-paying "intellectual" jobs, leaving the on-the-ground activists to fend for themselves in communities still wracked by poverty, unemployment, and political marginalization. Chilean *pobladoras* clearly view renewed women's organization as vital, but only on their own terms and not in vertical linkages with national or governmental women's organizations. Juanita sums it up nicely at the end of the meeting noted above: "The important thing is the desire to meet again. As we go along, we are going to be figuring out what we want to do. One thing is clear—we are *popular* women who work in sectors of the *población* and who have experience [to share]."

Conclusion

It is tempting to see Brazilian and Chilean women as the mirror images of one another on the basis of their responses to feminism. Brazilians say they are "feminist but . . ." in the same proportion that Chileans say they are "*not* feminist but . . ." This may tempt us to describe the Brazilian pattern as "resignification" and the Chilean response as "resistance," leading then to the conclusion that collaboration across class lines with feminist groups would be easier in Brazil. Such a conclusion, however, oversimplifies the picture in important ways.

First, both Brazilian "resignification" and Chilean "resistance" are expressed in very similar terms and come from very similar sources. Women from the popular classes in both countries refer to both class and moral or religious objections to a feminism that they see as somehow out of sync with their life circumstances. In fact, Brazilian women's objections seem to be more likely to stem from Catholicism and a religious conservatism that feminist observers have tended to see as more intractable than the class-based objections of the Chileans. Thus, distinguishing between "rejection" and "resignification" is unlikely to go far in suggesting the probability of alliances between these women and classic feminist organizations.

Second, and in keeping with the first point, Brazilian women are more open to feminist alliances than are Chilean women, but the former actually participate in popular feminist organizations at a lower rate. Although about a quarter claim that their *base community* maintains contact with feminist organizations, and although they seem willing and eager to engage in such collaboration, Brazilian women are actually less likely than Chileans to be personally involved in popular feminist organizations themselves. Moreover, all the popular feminists are clustered in one region with a very particular history of progressivism and openness to feminist collaboration. Chileans, in contrast, participate in a wider variety of women's organizations—including several that define themselves as "popular feminist" groups—but see no connection between their church groups and feminism and reject ties between their popular women's groups and national feminist organizations.

In a sense, then, we could argue that Brazilians appear to have done slightly better at network formation and maintenance, while Chileans appear to have generated more individually empowered women's activists. The Chilean women have gone on to form more of their own groups, but have not maintained networks as effectively. Several factors explain these differences, including differences between the classic feminist organizations in both countries and differences in political culture. Here, however, we would like to suggest that the way that popular women participated in social movements via their base communities has been an important factor in the subsequent development of their networks in this economic downturn and has also influenced the patterns of attitudes and activism.

Contrasting the Brazilian sociocultural and Chilean radical models of base communities helps us make sense of the way women activists have responded to feminism and to the possibility of creating networks with feminist organizations. Looking at Brazil, for example, we can see the influence of the more decentralized base community model. All the actual networking with feminist organizations has come in São Paulo (where classic feminist groups were strongest), in a region known for its particularly progressive clergy. Moreover, the sociocultural model of base communities accommodated women who participated without becoming highly politicized, and who often remained religiously conservative and close to the church, alongside women who became more politicized and who, in some cases, became "popular feminists." While some feminists left the church, others remain, hopeful that perhaps the pockets of progressivism they perceive might allow popular feminist organizations and church-connected women's organizations to reintegrate in the future. Brazilian women activists' remarkable openness to the idea of working with "feminists" may make this a real option in the future, at least in some areas. In contrast, Chilean women seem to have experienced greater radicalization and politicization, and the class basis of their political views means that even those who emerged from the base communities as popular feminists are skeptical of cross-class women's alliances. Yet the degree to which Chilean activists identify women's problems as political issues that require political solutions could provide the basis for negotiated alliances with the relatively well established women's organizations in the future. Given the deep class divisions between feminists and popular feminists, however, such alliances are likely to remain issue-based and specific for the foreseeable future rather than evolving into a broad political front. In addition, the traumatic history with the institutional church that the activists have experienced leads them to conclude that even popular feminist groups are unlikely to be able to make connections with church base communities or women's groups.

In both cases, the current political situation also seems to have led to a divergence of interests and agendas between popular and classic feminist organizations. Those organizations continue to espouse the idea of cross-class collaboration and inclusion, however, and it is remarkable that more than 70 percent of grassroots women activists in both countries say that they agree with at least some feminist ideas. As Madeleine Adriance (1995) argues, women who passed through the communities experienced substantial changes in their beliefs about gender, whether they call themselves feminists or not. Women activists who came to consciousness through the base communities in both countries express their convictions that women have equal political rights and that women must organize themselves politically. Despite the current difficulties and limits of networking, then, women in both countries may form a potential base for alliance with feminist organizations around at least some issues in the future.

EIGHT

Legacies of Activism:
Personal Empowerment, Movement Survival

Brazilian and Chilean women activists from the popular classes have shared, to a large extent, a common trajectory. Their experiences have been closely intertwined with the history of the liberationist church, for it was in the base communities that most got their initial taste of activism. They mobilized in various ways during the democratic transitions, only to watch in dismay as the movements in which they participated collapsed under the weight of circumstances beyond their control during the democratic era. This common history has often itself been interpreted in rather broad brushstrokes. At times those brushstrokes have painted an optimistic picture of the ability of new social movements, such as that emanating from the base communities, to fundamentally alter the lives and societies of Southern Cone activists. At others, they have depicted an image of lost opportunity, in which the women's risks and efforts at organizing came to little or naught once elections were held.

As Judith Adler Hellman (1995) has pointed out, studies of social movements often make three claims about what they can do: (1) transform consciousness or empower actors, (2) win concrete gains for their protagonists, and (3) contribute to democratization in a vital way (174). Much of the debate about interpreting the trajectory of base communities and their related movements in the Southern Cone has focused on the first and third points: empowerment and democratization. Too often, as Hellman argues, these terms themselves have been left vaguely defined. Again, too often, they have been cast in an either-or light. Did base communities empower women or not? Did they contribute to democratization or not?

In this book, we have sought to develop a more nuanced understanding of the legacy of liberation theology and of popular women's organizing in the base communities. We have used several means to do so. First, we have focused on the women activists themselves and their own perceptions of the trajectory that they, their church, and their movements experienced, rather than telling the story from "the outside." Second, we began from the assumption that the base communities and the movements they inspired should be seen as part of a cycle of protest during redemocratization. This assumption allows us to go beyond either-or debates about the contribution of these movements to democratization and frees us instead to define and delimit a more varied legacy. Finally, we have adopted a comparative approach. Looking at activists in both Brazil and Chile has enabled us to begin to examine the ways in which political and religious context affected not only movement organizations and their trajectory, but also the lived experiences of women activists.

In this chapter, we return to the themes of personal empowerment and alliance-building. After summarizing the long-term effects of activism in each area, we make some cross-national comparisons to show how context has affected the legacy of the liberationist church for future activism. In the second half of the chapter we return to the question of evaluating the impact of earlier activism for building civil society, connecting our study to debates about the role of religion in civil society and the effect of women's movements on democratization.

Surviving the Doldrums: The Long-Term Impact of Activism

The social movement activism that accompanied redemocratization in both Brazil and Chile was extremely intense. Although we know and the women mention that base communities spent considerable time building trust, passing on political information, celebrating religious services, and reflecting on the Bible, the activists often convey a sense of almost frenetic activity in those heady days of opposition. Marches, protests, and meetings on scores of issues seemed to follow one after another. Indeed, the Brazilian activists sorely needed the ubiquitous "agendas" that they carried to keep track of their many activities.

Life—perhaps particularly political life—cannot always be lived at such a pitch, however. Inevitably, circumstances change, opportunities evaporate, activism becomes institutionalized and routine. In short, for any one of a number of reasons, the "feverish" movement Edna described, noted in Chapter 4, subsides into more ordinary, day-to-day routines and is replaced by "politics as usual." Perhaps this is especially true for periods of activism that accompany redemocratization, because the return of elections signals precisely the return of routine politics, rather than a place for the "extraordinary" mobilizations needed to challenge the military regime. Movements and their hallmark protests become less and less visible, but as we have argued earlier, invisibility does not mean that they have left no legacy. We can see that legacy in the lives of most of the activists in both countries today.

Biography and History: Personal Empowerment

If studies of base communities have largely agreed on any point, it is on the claim that much of the impact of movement activism has been in individual transformation. As Hellman (1995) noted, many claims have been made about "transformed consciousness" or "empowerment" as a result of participation in social movements (174–75). Daniel Levine (1986), for example, in one of the earliest studies of the groups, argued that base communities had a transformative effect on their members' values (14). More recently, he and David Stoll have distinguished between "empowerment of ordinary people," an objective they believe the base communities achieved fairly well, and the creation of enduring organizational groups to achieve tangible benefits, a task at which they were less successful (Levine and Stoll 1997, 64–65). Similarly, feminist scholars often argue that social movement participation transforms women's gender consciousness and empowers them in a variety of ways.

As Hellman (1995) points out, however, "Although there is a broad consensus that important forms of learning and attitudes change when the new subjects join the new movements, beyond these vague assertions we have no intersubjective indicators of what these changes are" (175). In the absence of longitudinal studies of attitude change, for example, most researchers fall back on interviews in which activists describe their increased knowledge of politics, sense of efficacy, or ability to handle new kinds of activities. These statements seem to show "empowerment," implicitly defined as political knowledge and sense of efficacy (175).

If we take seriously the words of our respondents as they tell their own stories, such statements are, indeed, a good indicator of subjective empowerment. And these statements certainly abound in interviews with participants in base communities. All the Brazilian women and most of the Chilean women claimed that they had little political knowledge or interest before their experience in the base communities. With the exception of the Chilean women political activists who sought refuge in the base communities, the women do express a subjective sense of greater knowledge, efficacy, and, ultimately, power as a result of their experiences of activism.

Hellman rightly points out how hard it is to prove that such a vaguely defined "empowerment" has occurred in a meaningful way, however.[1] At

---

1. McAdam (1999) also points to the difficulties involved in studies attempting to show a causal effect of social movement participation on later activism and attitudes.

best, these individual accounts, though they occur over and over in different interviews, countries, and scholars' accounts, are strongly suggestive that some kind of change in the lives of participants occurs as a result of activism. Our study, while confirming other such accounts, allows us to go beyond individual claims of changed consciousness to argue that activism had concrete and long-term effects on the lives of the women involved. As McAdam (1988, 1999) found in the United States, activism appears to have affected their subsequent behavior. While Hellman (1995) is right that we cannot argue persuasively that the women's political views changed in any particular, concrete ways, we can argue that activism led them to paths that their lives would have been quite unlikely to take in other circumstances.

As we saw in Chapter 5, 60 percent of the Brazilian women and nearly all the Chilean women continue to participate in some kind of movement organization. They have found new venues in which to organize and continue their efforts, most often through grassroots women's organizations. While we lack the control group that would allow us to make more definitive claims, such a high level of participation could not be expected from a random group of women with similar backgrounds. Since very few of the women had prior political or activist experience, we can infer that intense activist experience tends to change people in ways that lead to continued personal activism and work for social change.

Such personal trajectories are surely one of the invisible legacies of the base communities and the redemocratization protest cycle. It is invisible not only because one needs to look at individual experience to discern it, but also because many of the new forms of participation in which the women have become involved do not entail frequent open protests as vehicles for confronting or making demands upon public authorities. Many of the new organizations focus on much less visible efforts, such as citizenship training, psychological and legal counseling for women, and legal advocacy for children. This emphasis seems to reflect the experience of many grassroots groups since redemocratization. Charmain Levy (2000), for example, notes that base communities in São Paulo have in many cases continued to support social promotion activities, albeit at lower levels than previously. In addition, many are focusing on popular education and alternative community-building projects (168–69). Similarly, Goetz Ottmann (2002) describes the development of the Women's Pastoral and its work in support of women in São Paulo. These activities are less visible than protest, but they are similar to those in which many of McAdam's (1988) Freedom Summer volunteers were engaged.[2] They reflect a set of values associated with and honed in social activism. Moreover, such basic educational and community-building activities should not be dismissed as irrelevant to activism. Indeed, such processes can be crucial for building the basis of trust, mutual understanding, and confidence that undergird the formation of future social movement organizations.[3] They can be seen as part of the identity-building process that is as integral to movement formation as the creation of strategic social movement organizations themselves.

While this broad description accurately summarizes the individual impact of base community activism in the two countries, substantial differences nonetheless remain. Most important, fewer Brazilian women—though still a majority—continue to engage in community-level organizations. In addition, the majority of the women who are active organization members come from one area of São Paulo and are members of the same grassroots women's organization, AMZOL. Brazilian women were also more likely to give involvement in church-related charitable work as examples of their continued activism. In contrast, Chilean women are much more uniformly involved in organizations, and they are involved in a greater number and range of organizations and tended to reject charitable work as nonpolitical. Overall, although women in both groups remain active, Chilean women appear to be more politicized, more autonomous, and more removed from the church than Brazilians.

These differences no doubt reflect many factors, including the political and social milieu in each country and the fact that some of the Chileans were relatively highly educated and were political activists before becoming involved in the base communities.[4] Nonetheless, we believe that the differences in biographical impact also reflect differences in the way that the popular church in each county perceived and organized base communities. The Brazilian church's highly decentralized model, for example, meant that some areas—such as São Paulo's Zona Leste—emerged as hotbeds of politicized activism, while other communities, even those involved in some local

2. In fact, Levy (2000) mentions ITEBRA, a popular-theology institute created by dom Angélico Bernardino (formerly of the Zona Leste) to train base-level leaders (174). This educational effort parallels one described by McAdam (1988): the Midwest Academy, started by volunteer Heather Tobis Booth (236).

3. See Melucci 1996 and Mueller 1994 for examples of this argument.

4. The differences may support Klandermans's (1994) conclusion that activists are more likely to remain committed to a waning, religiously based movement if they have a strong connection to the religious institution and little prior political experience before becoming involved.

movements, might be less politicized. Moreover, the Brazilian church's sociopolitical model of base communities entailed a commitment by the clergy and organizers to respect popular religiosity, and their broader notion of the "political" meant that many communities continued to engage in traditional charity alongside more politicized activism. As a result, many base community members, even those who participated in movements, remained close to the church and supportive of charitable work. As Jacobs (2001) has pointed out, many of these women rather contentedly returned to primarily spiritual and charitable work when the church turned away from a liberationist path. Finally, fewer Brazilian activists were as highly critical of changes in the church as were the Chileans. Only those few who were most critical had definitively broken with the church and confined all their participation to secular arenas. Again, the Brazilian sociopolitical and decentralized models appear to have maintained more activists' allegiance to the church, with fewer leaving for exclusively secular organizations such as unions, parties, or women's groups.[5]

Overall, then, we can see demonstrable evidence of "empowerment" in women's continued participation and activism in both countries, despite the Brazilians' more mixed record. One could certainly also argue that the Chileans' nearly uniform criticisms of their church and its actions, criticisms echoed strongly by many, though not all, Brazilians, indicate that these women have a high degree of autonomy, of independent and critical thinking. They have made decisions about what is important and right, and they are not about to abandon these because the church has changed its official stance. We have no "before and after" evidence to tie their independence and outspokenness to their experience in the base communities, but many of the women themselves point to that experience as the beginning of greater awareness of critical perception.

Organizations and Alliances: Social Bases of Power

For the base communities to have empowered individuals in this way is no small feat. Nonetheless, as Doug McAdam (1988) points out, "It is not enough

---

5. Brazil did also experience a significant outflow of leaders into secular organization. Hewitt's (2000) data suggests that this may have been more likely for men than women. Ottmann's (2002) conclusions are rather different from our own, but his description of the emergence of popular feminism in northern São Paulo confirms that activists took their liberationist background in different directions, even while maintaining connections to the church.

that people be attitudinally inclined toward activism. There must also exist formal organizations or informal social networks that structure and sustain collective action" (237). Even if an earlier period of activism has produced many individually empowered activists, the outlook for future movements is bleak if they remain isolated and scattered. Thus, part of the work for a period of doldrums involves maintaining or building new organizational structures, even if these are turned to purposes other than those of earlier social movement organizations. Only by building or maintaining organizations are movements likely to survive the down phase of a movement cycle. This may be particularly true in Latin America, where social movements are continually under attack in a social and economic environment hostile to their political claims.

Suzanne Staggenborg (1998) gives us some idea of how movements may survive organizationally. She suggests that what may be most important is that movements be rooted in an institution. Institutions, she argues, may be especially important to maintaining movements during the doldrums. Further, participants in movements may typically decentralize their activities and focus on cultural rather than political activities as a means of survival (187). Many authors have suggested that alliance building is particularly important work to engage in at a time when movement survival is threatened during a period of decline. Hellman (1995) argues that this may be especially vital, and likely, in Latin America right now. "In a period like the present, when progressive forces—both social and political—are under attack from the Right," she argues, "it seems reasonable to predict that alliance strategies may well gain momentum" (180).

It is difficult to say that Brazil or Chile seems to have fared better in the battle for social movement survival. In both cases, activists expressed a sense of dismay and of battling against the odds. In both as well, base communities themselves are faring poorly. The picture is not uniformly bleak, however. Despite the discouragement voiced by many of the activists, the fact of the matter is that many also gave substantial evidence that they and their movements are struggling and strategizing to survive the doldrums. What makes it difficult to assess which country is faring "better" is the reality that activists in each nation are adopting different mixes of the strategies suggested above.

Neither the Brazilian nor the Chilean Catholic Church has proved to be a reliable institutional home for movements associated with the base communities. Both have withdrawn support from the activist model of base communities and have dismantled offices and networks that coordinated and supported the communities' activities (Levy 2000, 171). Thus, the prospects for movement survival through gaining an institutional foothold seem to be bleak. Nonetheless, the Brazilian women indicated that their communities are surviving in some important ways, through, for example, continuing to have ties to other local organizations and even political parties. They also noted that they have a persistent, if much weakened, presence within the institutional church. In Chile, individual parishes and prelates maintain a liberationist position, but they seem much more isolated within the institution.

A second strategy for movement survival, decentralization, is arguably more typical of Chile. In this case, decentralization means separation from the church. Women activists in Chile have formed and joined a plethora of locally based movements, particularly women's movements, and these autonomous movements can be seen as a decentralization of women's participation in the church. Brazilian decentralization has taken a different form. Our interviewees from Rio de Janeiro and São Paulo have formed their own new, autonomous organization (AMZOL) only in one region of São Paulo. Other groups certainly exist elsewhere, but the contrast with the Chileans, who offered a lengthy list of organizations in which they participate, is striking. In Brazil, decentralization seems to have taken place through the process of the church's "cutting free" its organizations that were designed to support popular movements, such as FASE. Activists themselves seem to have taken less initiative to create new grassroots organizations.

We have less evidence about the extent to which groups have turned to less directly political activities to survive. This is arguably true of the Brazilian activists, particularly those who remain in the church and have adopted more charitable and educational activities. In addition, many of the women's groups in both countries run consciousness-raising or other educational activities. Some run clinics or self-help programs as well. Although the direct evidence is limited, it does seem to be the case that many activists and their groups, both in and out of the church, are involved in such activities in both countries. Such work is different from previous liberationist practice, but nonetheless is part of public response to problems.[6] Moreover, it may play a role in building the "internal solidarity" that Melucci (1996) believes is so important to movement groups during a phase of "invisibility" (112–13).

6. For examples of similar responses to changing times by Peruvian Catholic activists, see Williams and Fuentes 2000.

Finally, alliance building seems to be making somewhat greater headway in Brazil than in Chile. Although Hellman (1995) suggests that movements can link with political parties and—"with relative ease"—with other movements, alliance building has been difficult and relatively limited in both countries. Nonetheless, Brazilians did comment on connections that their base communities had with other groups. They also named groups that they felt they could count on for support, often including organizations that had previously been under the church's umbrella. Moreover, although the obstacles are significant, Brazilians expressed great openness to the idea of alliances with other organized entities in their neighborhoods, such as Protestant churches, as well as cross-class women's organizations. Finally, although the connection to political parties is unofficial, many Brazilian activists do link their groups to the PT by their own membership and, in some cases, militance in it. Brazilian networking should not be overstated, but it does seem that the placement of individuals within a variety of church and secular groups and their awareness of other activists may indicate the presence of "circuits of solidarity" and information exchange that are like the loose networks Melucci (1996) describes as forming a latent basis for activism (115). In contrast, Chilean activists, with their greater variety of groups, appear to be more isolated. They seem less aware of potential allies and express great reservations about alliances with religious or feminist organizations. They appear much more concerned than Brazilians about guarding their autonomy in general, and they are particularly skeptical about political parties.

Activists, then, are trying to maintain their movements in a variety of ways in each country. One can argue that in both, much of the building work looked for in a period of movement decline is occurring, but the combination of strategies seems to be different in each. Brazilians appear to be relying more on the church and on alliance formation, as well as continuing to make personal connections with the PT. In contrast, Chileans have been more active in creating their own organizations, thus effectively decentralizing the movements. They mistrust the church and political parties to a much greater extent and are more hesitant about forming alliances.

Once again, these differences certainly have many sources. History and political culture no doubt play a role in Brazilians' lesser emphasis on autonomy. Chileans' less clientelistic culture and their political experience of the impact of a rigidly partisan society no doubt influence their rather fierce attachment to movement autonomy. Nonetheless, different base community experiences surely also play a role in these outcomes. Brazil's decentralized base communities and more gradual withdrawal of support do make it more feasible for activists to continue to maintain a foothold—albeit a tenuous one—within the institutional church. As Ivone Gebara ("Interview" 1998) suggests, national base community meetings may now be more an expression of hope than of power, but they continue to give activists a point of contact and an ability to connect with networks and resources, however limited. Similarly, the Brazilian church's strategy of relinquishing control of organizations that supported the base communities means that activists can point to organizations with which they have previous experience and that can continue to act as a base of support for them when the church does not. Finally, it is certainly possible that the Brazilians' greater eagerness to form alliances is more an expression of their need for resources (and perhaps patrons) than an openness to strategic collaboration. It may, however, also reflect their background in a liberationist church that openly and eagerly— if selectively—sought collaboration with the secular Left. In contrast, the Chilean model seems to have produced more independent and more skeptical activists. The history that they experienced as "abandonment" by both the church and, in some cases, feminist organizations seems to have left them wary of alliances and connections. They are, however, building new organizations that may carry social movements through the doldrums. Moreover, as we described in the preceding chapter, they are eager to network once again among their own grassroots women's organizations.

Implications for the Future

As Marco Giugni (1999) compellingly observes, making any causal inferences about the long-term effects of social movements is fraught with difficulty. We have tried to avoid some of the pitfalls of doing so by comparing similar cases in order to tease out potential factors affecting outcomes. We have also tried to respect the observation of Giugni, Tilly, and others that rather than "invariant" patterns, we should be looking for "historically contingent combinations of factors that shape the possibilities for movements to contribute to social change" (Giungi 1999, xxv). Our conclusions are therefore tentative and more suggestive than definitive. We hope that they will form a basis for future research. Wider surveys, and particularly those that include both activists and a random sample of the population, would enhance our understanding of the influence of activism on individual life histories. Similarly, while we have sketched some of the potential networks and alliances, more specific work on the dynamics of network building and the role of institutions—both religious and secular—remains to be done.[7]

Our interviews with women activists leave us hopeful about the impact that their activism has had on their societies. This is a difficult period for the women and their organizations. Nonetheless, we see evidence of an enduring legacy from the movements in which they have participated. In both countries, women from the base communities continue to be politically motivated. They continue to believe in the importance of organized social action. Most important, they continue to take steps to make that action possible, by creating new organizations, engaging in community-building activities, and maintaining space where they can operate within old organizations and the institutional Church.

These are admittedly small things. They are not the stuff of headlines. They are visible in the lives and activities of the women today only if we look closely. They do, however, contribute in small ways to building a civil society that is capable of organizing and mobilizing again in the future. For the moment, activists and their networks remain "latent," to use Melucci's (1966) term; only the next "transient period[s] of collective mobilization" will "bring the latent network to the surface" (115). At that time, however, we would be well advised to look toward the old base communities and the legacies of their activists both within the church and outside it in order to understand the sources of the next wave of activism.

The base communities themselves are unlikely to reemerge as foci of organizing, but, especially in Brazil, remnants of them within the church could provide a basis for new kinds of organizations in the future. Similarly, the women's groups, educational groups, and advocacy groups that women are creating and maintaining today may help give birth to new organizations in the future. The younger activists themselves may become patrons and guiding spirits of future mobilizations, even though these may take forms and make demands that we cannot foresee at present. In the future, when movements rooted in poor urban communities or run by poor women mobilize again, we will be extremely likely to find that they owe a debt to the generation of women activists who first organized in the base communities.

7. Here we should again mention Ottmann's (2002) work, which focuses more on the symbolic basis for the emergence of broader alliances, particularly feminist alliances, from the older liberationist groups. Although he is primarily interested in the symbolic nature of this work, Ottmann also highlights the importance of network building (and its at least temporary success) per se.

BIBLIOGRAPHY

Abers, Rebecca. 2000. *Inventing Local Democracy: Grassroots Politics in Brazil.* Boulder: Lynne Rienner.

Adriance, Madeleine. 1995. *Promised Land: Base Christian Communities and the Struggle for the Amazon.* Albany: State University of New York Press.

Aldunate, Trinidad, and Pedro Morandé. 1991. *Los empresarios y su visión de la Iglesia en matérias económicas.* Santiago: CISOC-Bellarmino.

Alvarez, Sonia. 1990. *Engendering Democracy in Brazil: Women's Movements in Transition Politics.* Princeton: Princeton University Press.

———. 1998. "Latin American Feminisms 'Go Global': Trends of the 1990s and Challenges for the New Millennium." In *Cultures of Politics, Politics of Cultures: Re-Visioning Latin American Social Movements,* ed. Sonia E. Alvarez, Evelina Dagnino, and Arturo Escobar, 293–324. Boulder: Westview Press.

Ames, Barry. 1999. "Institutions and Democracy in Brazil." In *Democracy and Its Limits: Lessons from Asia, Latin America, and the Middle East,* ed. Howard Handelman and Mark Tessler, 130–75. Notre Dame: University of Notre Dame Press.

Archdiocese of Santiago. N.d. "La Vicaría de Solidaridad." Photocopy.

Azevedo, Marcelo. 1987. *Basic Ecclesial Communities in Brazil.* Washington, D.C.: Georgetown University Press.

Baeza Donoso, P. Alfonso. 1985. "Evangelización y pastoral obrera en la ciudad." In Vicaría de Pastoral Obrera, *Jornada Nacional de Pastoral Obrera: Pastoral Obrera y Gran Ciudad.* Santiago: Arzobispado de Santiago, Documento de Trabajo, no. 59:113–30.

Bano Ahumada, Rodrigo. 1997. *Apatia y sociedad de masa en la democracia chilena actual.* Santiago: Nueva Serie Flacso.

Bickford, Louis, and Marcela Noe. 1997. *Public Participation, Political Institutions, and Democracy in Chile, 1990–1997.* Santiago: Nueva Serie Flacso.

Brooks, Sarah. 1999. "Catholic Activism in the 1990s: New Strategies for the Neoliberal Age." In *Latin American Religion in Motion,* ed. Christian Smith and Joshua Prokopy, 67–89. New York: Routledge.

Burdick, John. 1992. "Rethinking the Study of Social Movements: The Case of Christian Base Communities in Brazil." In *The Making of Social Movements in Latin America: Identity, Strategy, and Democracy,* ed. Arturo Escobar and Sonia E. Alvarez, 171–84. Boulder: Westview Press.

———. 1993. *Looking for God in Brazil: The Progressive Catholic Church in Urban Brazil's Religious Arena.* Berkeley and Los Angeles: University of California Press.

Calderón, Fernando, et al. 1992. "Social Movements: Actors, Theories, Expectations." In *The Making of Social Movements in Latin America: Identity, Strategy, and Democracy,* ed. Arturo Escobar and Sonia E. Alvarez, 19–36. Boulder: Westview Press.

"Cardoso Criticized over Drought in NE." *Latin American Weekly Report,* May 5, 1998, 50.

Castillo, Fernando. 1987. *Iglesia liberador y política.* Santiago: CISOC-Bellarmino.

"Catholic Church Remains Outspoken Despite Shifts." *Latinamerica Press,* August 20, 1998, 1, 8.

Chesnut, Andrew R. 1998. "The Spirit of Brazil: The Pentecostalization of Christianity in the Largest Catholic Nation." Paper presented at the Latin American Studies Association meeting, Chicago.

Cleary, Edward. 1997. "The Brazilian Catholic Church and Church-State Relations: Nation-Building." *Journal of Church and State* 39, no. 2:253–73.

Cleary, Edward L., and Stewart-Gambino, Hannah. 1997. *Power, Politics, and Pentecostals in Latin America.* Boulder: Westview Press.

Cleary, Edward L., and Juan Sepúlveda. 1997. "Chilean Pentecostalism: Coming of Age." In *Power, Politics, and Pentecostals in Latin America,* ed. Edward L. Cleary and Hannah W. Stewart-Gambino, 97–122. Boulder: Westview Press.

Cline, Sarah. 2000. "Competition and Fluidity in Latin American Christianity." *Latin American Research Review.* 35, no. 2:244–51.

Conferencia Episcopal de Chile. 1989. *Certeza, Coherencia, y Confianza: Mensaje a los Católicos Chilenos en una Hora de Transición.* Santiago: Area de Comunicaciones de la Conferencia Episcopal de Chile.

———. 1990. *Orientaciones Pastorales: 1991–1994.* Santiago: Area de Comunicaciones de la Conferencia Episcopal de Chile.

Cook, Guillermo. 1997. "Interchurch Relations: Exclusion, Ecumenism, and the Poor." In *Power, Politics, and Pentecostals in Latin America,* ed. Edward L. Cleary and Hannah Stewart-Gambino, 77–96. Boulder: Westview Press.

Coutinho, Leonardo. 2001. "Sou 100% Vaticano." *Veja,* January 31, 46–47.

Cox, Robert W. 1999. "Civil Society at the Turn of the Millenium: Prospects for an Alternative World Order." *Review of International Studies* 25:3–28.

Craske, Nikki. 1999. *Women and Politics in Latin America.* New Brunswick: Rutgers University Press.

Doimo, Ana Maria. 1995. *A Vez e a Voz do popular: Movimentos sociais e participação política no Brasil pós-70.* Rio de Janeiro: Relume-Dumara/ANPOCS.

Dooner, Patricio, ed. 1988. *La Iglesia Católica y el futuro político de Chile.* Santiago: CISOC-Bellarmino.

Drogus, Carol Ann. 1992. "Popular Movements and the Limits of Political Mobilization at the Grassroots in Brazil." In *Conflict and Competition: The Latin American Church in a Changing Environment,* ed. Edward Cleary and Hannah Stewart-Gambino, 63–86. Boulder: Lynne Rienner.

———. 1997. *Women, Religion, and Social Change in Brazil's Popular Church.* Notre Dame: University of Notre Dame Press.

———. 1999. "No Land of Milk and Honey: Women CEB Activists in Posttransition Brazil." *Journal of Interamerican Studies and World Affairs* 41, no. 4:35–52.

"Emotions Run High over Abortion Bill." 1997. *Latin America Regional Reports: Brazil Report,* September 9, (RB-97-08), p. 3.

Escobar, Arturo, and Sonia E. Alvarez. 1992. "Theory and Protest in Latin America Today." Introduction to *The Making of Social Movements in Latin America: Identity, Strategy, and Democracy,* ed. Arturo Escobar and Sonia E. Alvarez, 1–15. Boulder: Westview Press.

Fitzsimmons, Tracy. 2000a. *Beyond the Barricades: Women, Civil Society, and Participation After Democratization in Latin America.* New York: Garland.

—————. 2000b. "A Monstrous Regiment of Women? State, Regime, and Women's Political Organizing In Latin America." *Latin American Research Review* 35, no. 2:216–29.

FLACSO. 1998. *Chile '97: Analisis y Opiniones.* Santiago: Nueva Serie Flacso.

Fontaine, Arturo T. 2002 "Trends Toward Globalization in Chile." In *Many Globalizations: Cultural Diversity in the Contemporary World,* ed. Peter Berger and Samuel Huntington. Oxford: Oxford University Press.

Fontaine Talavera, Arturo, and Harold Beyer. 1991. "Retrato del movimiento evangélico a la luz de las encuestas de opinión pública." *Estudios Públicos* 44 (Spring).

Franco, Jean. 1998. "Defrocking the Vatican: Feminism's Secular Project." In *Cultures of Politics, Politics of Cultures: Re-visioning Latin American Social Movements,* ed. Sonia E. Alvarez, Evelina Dagnino, and Arturo Escobar, 278–89. Boulder: Westview Press.

Gaviola, Edda, Eliana Largo, and Sandra Palestry. 1994. *Una história necesaria: Mujeres en Chile, 1973–1990.* Santiago: Taller de Comunicación Visual.

Gay, Robert. 1994. *Popular Organization and Democracy in Rio de Janeiro: A Tale of Two Favelas.* Philadelphia: Temple University Press.

Gilfeather O'Brien, Katherine. 1992. *El rol de ecumenismo protestante como possible solución al impasse en las relaciones entre la iglesia católica y la comunidad Pentecostal.* Santiago: Centro Bellarmino-Centro de Investigaciones Sociales.

Gill, Anthony. 1999. "The Struggle to Be Soul Provider: Catholic Responses to Protestant Growth in Latin America." In *Latin American Religion in Motion,* ed. Christian Smith and Joshua Prokopy, 17–42. New York: Routledge.

Giugni, Marco. 1999. "How Social Movements Matter: Past Research, Present Problems, Future Developments." Introduction to *How Social Movements Matter,* ed. Marco Giugni, Doug McAdam, and Charles Tilly, xiii–xxxiii. Minneapolis: University of Minnesota Press.

Gonzalez P., Alejandro. 1990. "La Experiencia de la Vicaría de la Solidaridad del Arzobispado de Santiago de Chile." *Persona y Sociedad* 6, nos. 2–3:153–65.

Guider, Margaret Eletta. 1995. *Daughters of Rahab: Prostitution and the Church of Liberation in Brazil.* Minneapolis: Fortress Press.

Haas, Liesl. 1999. "The Catholic Church in Chile: New Political Alliances." In *Latin American Religion in Motion,* ed. Christian Smith and Joshua Prokopy, 43–66. New York: Routledge.

—————. 2001. "Changing the System from Within? Feminist Participation in the Brazilian Workers' Party." In *Radical Women in Latin America: Left and Right,* ed. Victoria Gonzalez and Karen Kampwirth, 249–71. University Park: Pennsylvania State University Press.

Hardy, Clarisa. 1987. *Organizarse Para Vivir: Pobreza Urbana y Organización Popular.* Santiago: Programa de Economia del Trabajo.

Hellman, Judith Adler. 1995. "The Riddle of New Social Movements: Who They Are and What They Do." In *Capital, Power, and Inequality in Latin America,* ed. Sandor Halebsky and Richard L. Harris, 165–84. Boulder: Westview Press.

—————. 1997. "Social Movements: Revolution, Reform and Reaction." *NACLA Reports on the Americas* 30/6:13–18.

Hershberg, Eric. 1999. "Democracy and Its Discontents: Constraints on Political Citizenship in Latin America." In *Democracy and Its Limits: Lessons from Asia, Latin America, and the Middle East*, Howard Handelman and Mark Tessler, 290–320. Notre Dame: University of Notre Dame Press.

Hewitt, W. E. 1991. *Base Christian Communities and Social Change in Brazil*. Lincoln: University of Nebraska Press.

———. 2000. "The Political Dimensions of Women's Participation in Brazil's Base Christian Communities (CEBs): A Longitudinal Case Study from São Paulo." *Women and Politics* 21, no. 3:1–25.

Hipsher, Patricia L. 1998. "Democratic Transitions as Protest Cycles: Social Movement Dynamics in Democratizing Latin America." In *The Social Movement Society: Contentious Politics for a New Century*, ed. David Meyer and Sidney Tarrow, 153–72. Lanham, Md.: Rowman and Littlefield.

Hola, Eugenia, and Gabriela Pischedda. 1994. *Mujeres, poder y política: Nuevas tensiones para viejas estructuras*. Santiago: Ediciones Centro de Estudios de la Mujer.

"Interview: Feminist Theologian Sr. Ivone Gebara: 'A Church with Different Faces.'" 1998. *Latinamerica Press*, November 12, 5.

Ireland, Rowan. 1999. "Popular Religion and the Building of Democracy in Latin America: Saving the Tocquevillian Parallel." *Journal of Interamerican Studies and World Affairs* 41, no. 4:111–36.

Jacobs, Els J.J. 2001. "The Feminine Way/'O Jeito Feminino:' Religion, Power, and Identity in South-Brazilian Base Communities." Ph.D. diss., Vrije Universiteit, Amsterdam.

Jaquette, Jane S. 1995. "Rewriting the Scripts: Gender in the Comparative Study of Latin American Politics." In *Latin America In Comparative Perspective*, ed. Peter Smith, 111–33. Boulder: Westview Press.

Johnston, Hank, et al. 1994. "Identities, Grievances, and New Social Movements." In *New Social Movements: From Ideology to Identity*, ed. Enrique Laraña, Hank Johnston, and Joseph R. Gusfield, 3–35. Philadelphia: Temple University Press.

Jorge, Chateau, et al. 1987. *Espácio y poder: Los pobladores*. Santiago: FLACSO.

Junqueira, Eduardo. 1997. "E Deus ganhou." *Veja*, July 30, 62–63.

Kamsteeg, Frans. 1999. "Pentecostalism and Political Awakening in Pinochet's Chile and Beyond." In *Latin American Religion in Motion*, Christian Smith and Joshua Prokopy, 187–204. London: Routledge.

Klandermans, Bert. 1994. "Transient Identities? Membership Patterns in the Dutch Peace Movement." In *New Social Movements: From Ideology to Identity*, ed. Enrique Laraña, Hank Johnston, and Joseph R. Gusfield, 168–84. Philadelphia: Temple University Press.

Lago, Humberto, and Arturo Chacón Herrera. 1987. *Los evangélicos en Chile: Una lectura sociológica*. Concepción: Ediciones Literatura.

Lagos, Humberto. 1982. *La función de las minorías religiosas: Las transacciones del protestantismo chileno en el período 1973–1981 del gobierno militar*. Louvain: La Nueve.

———. 1985. *Sectas en Chile*. Santiago: PRESOR.

Laraña, Enrique, Hank Johnston, and Joseph R. Gusfield, eds. 1994. *New Social Movements: From Ideology to Identity*. Philadelphia: Temple University Press.

Lebon, Nathalie. 1998. "The Labor of Love and Bread: Professionalized and Volunteer Activism in the São Paulo Women's Health Movement." Ph.D. diss., University of Florida, Gainesville.

Lesbaupin, Ivo, org. 1996. *Igreja: Comunidade e Massa*. São Paulo: Paulinas.

"Letter to the People of God from Members of the non-Catholic Churches Participating in the Tenth Interecclesial." http://www.cnbb.org.br/setores/sei/SEI10IEcartaPovo.rt

Levine, Daniel. 1986. "Religion, the Poor, and Politics in Latin America Today." In *Religion and Political Conflict in Latin America*, ed. Daniel Levine, 3–23. Chapel Hill: University of North Carolina Press.

———. 1992. *Popular Voices in Latin American Catholicism*. Princeton: Princeton Unversity Press.

———. 1995. "On Premature Reports of the Death of Liberation Theology." *Review of Politics* 57, no. 1:105–31.

Levine, Daniel H., and David Stoll. 1997. "Bridging the Gap Between Empowerment and Power in Latin America." In *Transnational Religion and Fading States*, ed. Susanne Hoeber Rudolph and James Piscatori, 63–103. Boulder: Westview.

Levy, Charmaine. 2000. "CEBs in Crisis: Leadership Structures in the São Paulo Area." In *The Church at the Grassroots in Latin America: Perspectives on Thirty Years of Activism*, ed. John Burdick and W. E. Hewitt, 167–82. Westport, Conn.: Praeger.

Lievesley, Geraldine. 1999. *Democracy in Latin America: Mobilization, Power, and the Search for a New Politics*. Manchester: Manchester University Press.

Lladser, Maria Teresa. 1989. "La Investigación en ciencias sociales en Chile: Sus desarrollo en los centros privados, 1973–1988." In *Una puerta que se abre*, ed. José Antonio Abalos K., 213–89. Santiago: Taller de Cooperación al Desarrollo.

Llona, Cristian. 1988. "Iglesia y partidos políticos: Situación actual y proyecciones hacia una futura democracia II." In *La Iglesia Católica y el futuro político de Chile*, ed. Patricio Dooner, 193–202. Santiago: CISOC-Bellarmino.

McAdam, Doug. 1988. *Freedom Summer*. New York: Oxford University Press.

———. 1995. "'Initiator' and 'Spin-off' Movements: Diffusion Processes in Protest Cycles." In *Repertoires and Cycles of Collective Action*, ed. Mark Traugott, 217–39. Durham: Duke University Press.

———. 1999. "The Biographical Impact of Activism." In *How Social Movements Matter*, Marco Giugni et al., 119–46. Minneapolis: University of Minnesota Press.

McAdam, Doug, and David A. Snow. 1997. "Social Movements: Conceptual and Theoretical Issues." In *Social Movements: Readings on Their Emergence, Mobilization, and Dynamics*, ed. Doug McAdam and David A. Snow, xviii–xxvi. Los Angeles: Roxbury.

Machado, Leda. 1993. "'We Learned to Think Politically': The Influence of the Catholic Church and the Feminist Movement on the Emergence of the Health Movement of the Jardim Nordeste Area in São Paulo, Brazil." In *"Viva": Women and Popular Protest in Latin America*, ed. Sarah A. Radcliffe and Sallie Westwood, 88–111. London: Routledge.

Mainwaring, Scott. 1986. *The Catholic Church and Politics in Brazil, 1916–1985*. Stanford: Stanford University Press.

Mariz, Cecilia. 1995. *Coping with Poverty: Pentecostals and Christian Base Communities in Brazil*. Philadelphia: Temple University Press.

Marques-Pereira, Berengere. 1998. "Linking Social and Political Citizenship: Women's Action in the Southern Cone." *Social Politics* 5, no. 2:214–31.

Martins, José Pedro. 1991. "Protestants Work for Social Change in Brazil," *Latinamerica Press*, November 21, 6.

———. 2000. "New Millenium Without Exclusion." *Latinamerica Press*, April 17, 4–5.

Matear, Ann. 1997. "Desde la protesta a la propuesta: The Institutionalization of the Women's Movement in Chile." In *Gender Politics in Latin America: Debates in Theory and Practice,* Elizabeth Dore, 84–100. New York: Monthly Review Press.

Melucci, Alberto. 1994. "A Strange Kind of Newness: What's 'New' in New Social Movements?" In *New Social Movements: From Ideology to Identity,* ed. Enrique Laraña, Hank Johnston, and Joseph R. Gusfield, 101–32. Philadelphia: Temple University Press.

———. 1996. *Challenging Codes: Collective Action in the Information Age.* Cambridge: Cambridge University Press.

Meyer, David S., and Sidney Tarrow, eds. 1998. *The Social Movement Society: Contentious Politics for a New Century.* New York: Rowman and Littlefield.

Minkoff, Debra C. 1997. "Producing Social Capital: National Social Movements and Civil Society." *American Behavioral Science* 40, no. 5:606–20.

Morris, Aldon. 1984. *The Origins of the Civil Rights Movement: Black Communities Organizing for Change.* New York: Free Press.

Moyer, Bill. 2001. *Doing Democracy: The MAP Model for Organizing Social Movements.* Gabriola Island, Canada: New Society.

Mueller, Carol. 1994. "Conflict Networks and the Origins of Women's Liberation." *New Social Movements: From Ideology to Identity.* ed. Enrique Laraña, Hank Johnston, and Joseph R. Gusfield, 234–63. Philadelphia: Temple University Press.

Nagle, Robin. 1997. *Claiming the Virgin: The Broken Promise of Liberation Theology in Brazil.* New York: Routledge.

Navarro, Marysa, and Susan C. Bourque. 1998. "Fault Lines of Democratic Governance: A Gender Perspective." In *Fault Lines of Democracy in Post-Transition Latin America,* Felipe Aguero and Jeffrey Stark, 175–202. Miami, Fla.: North-South Center Press.

Navia, Patricio. 1998. "Tendencias de participación electoral en Chile en 1997." In *Chile '97: Análisis y Opiniones,* by FLACSO, 61–86. Santiago: Nueva Serie Flacso.

Noe, Marcela, Patricia Correa, Soledad Jana, and Luis Vial. 1998. "Aproximaciones a la participación ciudadana," In *Chile '97: Análisis y Opiniones,* by FLACSO, 87–102. Santiago: Nueva Série Flacso.

Oro, Ari Pedro. 1996. *Avanço Pentecostal e Reação Católica.* Petrópolis: Vozes.

Ottman, Goetz Frank. 2002. *Lost for Words? Brazilian Liberationism in the 1990s.* Pittsburgh: University of Pittsburgh Press.

Oxhorn, Philip. 1995. *Organizing Civil Society: Popular Sectors and the Struggle for Democracy in Chile.* University Park: Pennsylvania State University Press.

———. 1999. "The Ambiguous Link: Social Movements and Democracy in Latin America." *Journal of Interamerican Studies and World Affairs* 41, no. 3:129–46.

Paley, Julia. 2001. *Marketing Democracy: Power and Social Movements in Post-Dictatorship Chile.* Berkeley and Los Angeles: University of California Press.

Parker, Cristian. 1996. *Popular Religion and Modernization in Latin America.* Maryknoll, N.Y.: Orbis Books.

Pierucci, Antonio Flavio, and Reginaldo Prandi. 1995. "Religiões e voto: A eleição presidencial de 1994," *Opinião Pública* 3, no. 1:20–44.

Posner, Paul W. 1999. "Popular Representation and Political Dissatisfaction in Chile's New Democracy." *Journal of Interamerican Studies and World Affairs* 41, no. 1:59–85.

Prado, Juan Guillermo. 1992. *Seminários e institutos teológicos evangélicos.* Santiago: Centro Bellarmino-Centro de Investigaciones Sociales.

Puga, Mariano. 2000. "Los Vía Crúcis de las Comunidades Cristianos." In *Crónicas de una Iglesia Liberadora,* by José Aldunate et al., 131–35 Santiago: LOM Ediciones.

Razeto, Luis, Arno Klenner, Apolonia Ramirez, and Roberto Urmeneta. 1990. *Las Organizaciones Económicas Populares, 1973–1990.* Santiago: PET.

"Return of the Progressive Catholic Church." *Latinamerica Press,* May 3, 1999, 6.

Rosado Nunes, Maria José. 1994. "De mulheres, sexo e Igreja: Uma pesquisa e muitas interrogações." In *Alternativas escassas: Saúde, sexualidade e reprodução na America Latina,* org. Albertina de Oliveira Costa and Tina Amado, 177–203. São Paulo: PRODIR/Fundação Carlos Chagas.

Rupp, Leila J., and Verta Taylor. 1987. *Survival in the Doldrums: The American Women's Rights Movement, 1945 to the 1960s.* New York: Oxford University Press.

Sandoval, Jose Miguel, Juan Allende, and Hugo Castillo. 1998. "Los Evangélicos en Chile hacia el ano 2000." In *Chile '97: Análisis y Opiniones,* by FLACSO, 61–86. Santiago: Nueva Série Flacso.

Sandoval, Salvador A. M. 1998. "Social Movements and Democratization: The Case of Brazil and the Latin Countries." In *From Contention to Democracy,* ed. Marco G. Giugni, Doug McAdam, and Charles Tilly, 169–201. New York: Rowman and Littlefield.

Schneider, Ronald M. 1996. *Brazil: Culture and Politics in a New Industrial Powerhouse.* Boulder: Westview Press.

Serbin, Kenneth P. 1992. "Latin America's Catholic Church: Postliberationism?" *Christianity and Crisis* 52, no. 18:403–7.

———. 1999. "Brazil: Religious Tolerance, Church-State Relations, and the Challenge of Pluralism." In *Religious Freedom and Evangelization in Latin America: The Challenge of Religious Pluralism,* ed. Paul E. Sigmund, 204–19. Maryknoll, N.Y.: Orbis Books.

———. 2000. *Secret Dialogues: Church-State Relations, Torture, and Social Justice in Authoritarian Brazil.* Pittsburgh: University of Pittsburgh Press.

Skidmore, Thomas E., and Peter Smith. 2001. *Modern Latin America.* 5th ed. Oxford: Oxford University Press.

Smith, Brian. 1982. *The Church and Politics in Chile: Challenges to Modern Catholicism.* Princeton: Princeton University Press.

Smith, Christian. 1991. *The Emergence of Liberation Theology: Radical Religion and Social Movement Theory.* Chicago: University of Chicago Press.

———. 1996a. "Correcting a Curious Neglect, or Bringing Religion Back In." In *Disruptive Religion: The Force of Faith in Social Movement Activism,* Christian Smith, 1–25. New York: Routledge.

———. 1996b. *Resisting Reagan: The U.S. Central America Peace Movement.* Chicago: University of Chicago Press.

Staggenborg, Suzanne. 1998. "Social Movement Communities and Cycles of Protest: The Emergence and Maintenance of a Local Women's Movement." *Social Problems* 45, no. 2:180–204.

Stepan, Alfred. 1988. *Rethinking Military Politics: Brazil and the Southern Cone.* Princeton: Princeton University Press.

Stephen, Lynn. 1997. *Women and Social Movements in Latin America: Power from Below.* Austin: University of Texas Press.

Sternbach, Nancy, et al. 1992. "Feminisms in Latin America: From Bogota to San Bernardo." In *The Making of Social Movements in Latin America: Identity, Strategy, and Democracy,* ed. Arturo Escobar and Sonia Alvarez, 207–39. Boulder: Westview Press.

Stewart-Gambino, Hannah. 1992. *The Catholic Church in the Chilean Countryside.* Boulder: Westview Press.

———. 1997. "Latin American Pentecostals: Old Stereotypes and New Challenges." In *Power, Politics, and Pentecostals in Latin America,* ed. Edward L. Cleary and Hannah Stewart-Gambino, 227–45. Boulder: Westview Press.

Tarrow, Sidney. 1998. *Power in Movement: Social Movements and Contentious Politics.* 2d ed. Cambridge: Cambridge University Press.

Taylor, Charles. 1990. "Modes of Civil Society," *Public Culture* 3, no. 1:95–118.

Taylor, Lucy. 1998. *Citizenship, Participation, and Democracy.* London: MacMillan Press.

Taylor, Verta. 1997. "Social Movement Continuity: The Women's Movement in Abeyance." In *Social Movements: Readings on Their Emergence, Mobilization, and Dynamics,* ed. Doug McAdam and David Snow, 409–20. Los Angeles: Roxbury.

Thieje, Marjo de. 1998. "Charismatic Renewal and Base Communities: The Religious Participation of Women in a Brazilian Parish." In *More than Opium: An Anthropological Approach to Latin American and Caribbean Pentecostal Praxis,* ed. Barbara Boudenwijnse, Andre Droogers, and Frans Kamsteeg, 225–48. Lanham, Md.: Scarecrow Press.

Tilly, Charles. 1995. "To Explain Political Process." *American Journal of Sociology* 100:1594–610.

Townsend, Janet, Emma Zapata, Jo Rowlands, Pilar Alberti, and Marta Mercado. 1999. *Women and Power: Fighting Patriarchies and Poverty.* London: Zed Books.

Valdés, Teresa. 1994. "Mujeres en acción: Instituciónes y organizaciónes sociales." In ed. *Organizaciónes sociales y medio ambiente,* ed. Marcelo Charlin and Sergio Rojas, , 41–70. Santiago: Libros Flacso.

———. 1998. "Las mujeres en 1997: Ciudadanía e invisibilidad." In *Chile '97: Análisis y Opiniones,* by FLACSO, 103–26. Santiago: Nueva Série Flacso.

Valdés, Teresa, and Marisa Weinstein. 1993. *Mujeres que sueñan: Las organizaciones de pobladoras en Chile, 1973–1989.* Santiago: Libros Flacso.

Valenzuela, J. Samuel. 1992. "Democratic Consolidation in Post-transitional settings: Notion, Process, and Facilitating Conditions." In *Issues in Democratic Consolidation: The New South American Democracies in Comparative Perspective,* ed. Scott Mainwaring, Guillermo O'Donnell, and J. Samuel Valenzuela, 57–104. Notre Dame: University of Notre Dame Press.

Varas, Augusto. 1998. "Democratization in Latin America: A Citizen Responsibility." In *Fault Lines of Democracy in Post-transition Latin America,* ed. Felipe Aguero and Jeffrey Stark, 145–74. Miami, Fla.: North-South Center Press.

Vásquez, Manuel. 1997. "Structural Obstacles to Grassroots Pastoral Practice: The Case of a Base Community in Urban Brazil." *Sociology of Religion* 58, no. 1:53–68.

———. 1998. *The Brazilian Popular Church and the Crisis of Modernity.* Cambridge: Cambridge University Press.

———. 1999. "Toward a New Agenda for the Study of Religion in the Americas," *Journal of Interamerican Studies and World Affairs* 41, no. 4:1–20.

Vega, Humberto. 1988. "Reivindicaciones: Entre la estabilidad y la justicia." In *La Iglesia Católica y el futuro de Chile,* ed. Patricio Dooner, 173–78. Santiago: CISOC-Bellarmino.

Vicaría de Solidaridad. 1991. *Vicaría de Solidaridad: Historia de su trabajo social.* Santiago: Ediciones.

Walker, Ignacio. 1988. "Iglesia y partidos políticos: Situación actual y proyecciones hacia una futura democracia III." In *La Iglesia Católica y el futuro político de Chile,* ed. Patricio Dooner, 203–12. Santiago: CISOC-Bellarmino.

Weyland, Kurt. 1996. *Democracy Without Equity: Failures of Reform in Brazil.* Pittsburgh: University of Pittsburgh Press.

Waylen, Georgina. 1994. "Women and Democratization: Conceptualizing Gender Relations in Transition Politics." *World Politics* 46 (April), pp. 327–54.

———. 1996. *Gender in Third World Politics.* Boulder, Colo.: Lynne Rienner.

Williams, Philip J., and Vilma Fuentes. 2000. "Catholic Responses to the Crisis of Everyday Life in Lima, Peru." *Journal of Church and State* 42, no. 1:89–114.

Wilson, Everett. 1997. "Guatemalan Pentecostals: Something of Their Own." In *Power, Politics, and Pentecostals in Latin America,* ed. Edward L. Cleary and Hannah Stewart-Gambino, 139–62. Boulder: Westview Press.

Zald, Mayer N., and Roberta Ash. 1966. "Social Movement Organizations: Growth, Decay, and Change," *Social Forces* 44, no. 3: 327–41.

Zald, Mayer N., and John D. McCarthy. 1987. "Religious Groups as Crucibles of Social Movements." In *Social Movements in an Organizational Society: Collected Essays,* ed. Mayer N. Zald and John D. McCarthy, 67–95. New York: Transaction Books.

INDEX

abeyance structures, 33
Academy for Christian Humanism (ACH) (Chile),
    63 n. 25, 78
activism, 5–6. *See also* Brazilian women activists;
    Chilean women activists; women activists
    of Catholic women, 8–12
    church, 29
    empowerment and, 4–5, 188–90
    forces that undermine, 25
    impact of: long-term, 187–95; personal, 2–5,
    36
    political, 3–4
    rebuilding, in Brazil, 106–9
    social impact of, 5–8
    social movement, 12–15
    times of passivity and, 104–6
    union, 28
activists. *See* Brazilian women activists; Chilean
    women activists; women activists
alliances
    building, 194–95
    interdenominational, 130–31
    during periods of decline for social movements,
    192
AMZOL. *See* Association of Women of the Zona
    Leste (AMZOL) (Brazil)
Arns, Paulo Evaristo (archbishop of São Paulo), 55
    n. 17, 80
Assembly of God, 135, 136–37
Association of the Families of the Disappeared, 77,
    77 n. 7
Association of Women of the Zona Leste (AMZOL)
    (Brazil), 107, 109, 156–57, 158, 165–66
associations. *See* civic associations

Balduino, dom Tomas, 84
Baptists, in Brazil, 135–36
base communities, 41. *See also* Brazilian base
    communities; Chilean base communities
    adaptation and, 33

advantages of movement cycle model of,
    24–31
    long-term impact of, 1–2, 25–26
    as networks, 58–59
    redemocratization, 23; cycles of, and, 27–31
    social movements and, 21–24
    as sources of activists for movements and
    organizations, 110–11
    types of, 39–40
    uniqueness of, as social movements, 23
base ecclesial communities (CEBs), 4, 37. *See also*
    base communities
    as catalyst for social and political change, 5
    in context of social movement theory, 20
    defined, 39
    types of, 39–40
Boff, Leonardo, 42, 80
Brazil
    Catholic-Protestant alliances in, 132–35
    cost-of-living movement (1973) in, 59
    democratic process in, 21
    feminists in, 156–59
    neighborhood movements in, 46–47
    pastoral organizations in, 108–9
    Pentecostals in, 81, 98, 129
    Protestant denominations in, 130 n. 2, 132–35
    rebuilding activism in, 106–9
    redemocratization in, 28, 30–31; role of
    Catholic Church in, 28–29, 37
    social change in 1950s in, 39
Brazilian base communities, 42–48, 95 n. 35. *See
    also* base communities; Chilean base
    communities
    composition of, 95 n. 35
    cost-of-living movement and (1973), 59
    decentralization of, by Brazilian Catholic
    Church, 54–60
    decline of, 90–101
    networks and, 58–59
    pastoral organizations and, 108–9

social change in 1950s in, 39

social class and feminism in, 173–79

Chilean base communities, 48–53. *See also* base
communities; Brazilian base communities

activities of women activists in, 51–53

Chilean Catholic Church and, 48–53

local organization of, 51

Chilean Catholic Church: role of, and, 66–67;
support of, and, 61–68; types of, and, 40–42

Chilean Catholic Church. *See also* Brazilian
Catholic Church; Catholic Church

base communities and, 40–42, 48–53, 61–68

commitment to democracy by, 65–66

cooperation with Protestants and, 144–48

grassroots activities and, 64

human rights and, 65–66

during military regime, 48–49

opposition to: collaboration with feminist
organizations, 170–72; dictatorship, 60–68;

participation in, Chilean women activists and,
119–22

partisan activities and, 66–68

redefinition of poverty by, 76

resurgence of conservative control of, 71–79

social movements and, 192–93

withdrawal from civil society by, 71–79;
experiences of Chilean women activists,
85–90

Chilean National Bishops' Conference, 74–75, 76

Chilean women activists, 8–9, 11–12. *See also*
activism; Brazilian women activists; women
activists

activities of, in base communities, 51–53

average age of, versus Brazilian women activists,
101

biographies of personal change for, 119–22

Catholic-Protestant cooperation and, 142–48

consumerism and, 176–77

cooperation with Pentecostals and, 150–51

empowerment and, 188–91

experiences of, and Chilean Catholic Church's
withdrawal from civil society, 85–90

feminism and, 168–70, 173–79

gender identity and, 179

human rights movement and, 123

individualism and, 176–77

methodological issues in studying, 13–15

new paths for participation by, 123–27

new paths taken by, 123–27

participation in Catholic Church and, 119–22

party affiliation and, 118–19

today's local organizing context for, 117–19

working with Pentecostals and, 149

church activism, 29

citizenship schools, 33

civic associations, poor women and, 21. *See also*
networks

civil society, 2, 2 n. 3

class, social, feminism and, 163–64

in Chile, 173–79

CNBB. *See* Brazilian National Bishops Conference
(CNBB)

collective action, efficacy of, 10–11

community organizations. *See* base communities

Confraternidad Critiana de Iglesias (Chile), 147

consciousness-raising, 45–46

Con-spirando (Chile), 78

consumerism, Chilean women activists and,
176–77

Coordinadora Nacional de Comunidades de Base
(Chile), 77

cost-living movement (1973) (Brazil), 59

decentralization, as survival strategy for social
movements, 193

democratization. *See* redemocratization

drug addiction, as social problem, 10

ecumenism, Brazilian Catholic Church and,
140–42

empowerment, 21

activism and, 4–5

Brazilian and Chilean women activists and,
188–91

poor women and, 2–3

evangelicals, 135. *See also* neo-Pentecostals;
Pentecostals; Protestant denominations

Facultad Latinoamericana de Ciencias Sociales
(FLACSO) (Chile), 63 n. 25

Federation of Organs for Social and Educational
Assistance (FASE) (Brazil), 59

feminism, 155–56

Brazilian Catholic Church and, 159–61

Brazilian women activists and, 162–66

Chilean Catholic Church and, 170–72

Chilean women activists and, 168–70, 173–79